Educating for the Knowledge Economy?

The promise, embraced by governments around the world, is that the knowledge economy will provide knowledge workers with a degree of autonomy and permission to think which enables them to be creative and to attract high incomes. What credence should we give to this promise?

The current economic crisis is provoking a reappraisal of both economic and educational policy. Policy makers and educationists across the world see education as central to economic competitiveness. However, this book asks fundamental questions about the relationship between the economy and education since, in contrast to policy makers' rhetoric, the relationship between the two sectors is not straightforward. An unorthodox account of the knowledge economy and economic globalisation suggests that autonomy in the workplace and permission to think will be only given to the elite. In this view many aspirant well-educated middle-class young workers are doomed to disappointment.

In this book leading scholars from the USA, the UK, Australia and New Zealand discuss these issues and interrogate the assumptions and links between the different elements of education and how they might relate to the economy. Even if we assume that the official view of the knowledge economy is correct, are we educating young people to be autonomous, creative thinkers? Are current policies relating to knowledge, learning and assessment consistent with the kinds of workers and skills required for the knowledge economy?

Educating for the Knowledge Economy? will appeal to academics, policy makers, teachers and students interested in the central role of education in the knowledge economy.

Hugh Lauder is Professor of Education and Political Economy at the University of Bath.

Michael Young is Professor of Education at the Institute of Education and Visiting Professor at the University of Bath.

Harry Daniels is Professor and Head of the Centre for Sociocultural and Activity Theory at the University of Bath.

Maria Balarin is Lecturer in Education at the University of Bath.

John Lowe is Lecturer in Education at the University of Bath.

Educating for the Knowledge Economy?

Critical Perspectives

Edited by
**Hugh Lauder, Michael Young,
Harry Daniels, Maria Balarin
and John Lowe**

Routledge
Taylor & Francis Group

LONDON AND NEW YORK

First published 2012
by Routledge
2 Park Square, Milton Park, Abingdon, Oxon OX14 4RN

Simultaneously published in the USA and Canada
by Routledge
711 Third Avenue, New York, NY 10017

Routledge is an imprint of the Taylor & Francis Group, an informa business

British Library Cataloguing in Publication Data
A catalogue record for this book is available from the British Library

Library of Congress Cataloging in Publication Data

Educating for the knowledge economy? : critical perspectives / [edited by] Hugh Lauder ... [et al.].
p. cm.
Includes bibliographical references and index.
1. Education—Economic aspects. 2. Globalization and education.
3. Knowledge workers—Training of. I. Lauder, Hugh.
LC65.E313 2012
338.4'337—dc23
2011027056

ISBN: 978-0-415-61506-8 (hbk)
ISBN: 978-0-415-61507-5 (pbk)
ISBN: 978-0-203-81769-8 (ebk)

Typeset in Galliard
by Book Now Ltd, London

MIX
Paper from
responsible sources
FSC
www.fsc.org   FSC® C004839

Printed and bound in Great Britain by
CPI Antony Rowe, Chippenham, Wiltshire

Contents

List of illustrations

Figures

Tables

Contributors

David P. Baker is Professor of Education and Sociology at Pennsylvania State University.

Maria Balarin, Grade Research Institute, Lima, Peru.

Phillip Brown is Distinguished Research Professor, School of Social Sciences, Cardiff University.

Bernard Charlot is Professor at the Faculty of Education and the Federal University of Sergipe, at Aracujo, Brazil.

Harry Daniels is Professor and Head of the Centre for Sociocultural and Activity Theory at the University of Bath.

Ankie Hoogvelt was formerly at the Department of Sociological Studies, University of Sheffield.

Hugh Lauder is Professor of Education and Political Economy at the University of Bath.

John Lowe is Lecturer in Education at the University of Bath.

Johan Muller is Professor of Education at the University of Cape Town.

Michael A. Peters is Professor of Education at the University of Illinois at Urbana-Champaign and Professor elect at the University of Waikato.

Thomas S. Popkewitz, is Professor at the University of Wisconsin-Madison.

Gerbrand Tholen, SKOPE, Education Department, University of Oxford.

Harry Torrance, is Professor of Education, Director of the Education and Social Research Institute (ESRI) at Manchester Metropolitan University.

Leesa Wheelahan is Associate Professor at the L.H. Martin Institute for Higher Education Leadership and Management at the University of Melbourne.

Geoff Whitty was formerly the Director of the Institute of Education, London University and Visiting Professor at the University of Bath.

Michael Young is Professor of Education at the Institute of Education and Visiting Professor at the University of Bath.

Acknowledgements

The chapters in this book were originally papers presented as part of an ESRC Sponsored Series, 'The Knowledge Economy and Education' at the University of Bath between March 2008 and May 2009. Our thanks go to the ESRC for supporting these seminars and to Sarah Cox for her work in organising the seminars for the ESRC.

A version of the paper by Ankie Hoogvelt was published in *Globalisations* 7(2), 2010 and those by David Baker, Johan Muller, Leese Wheelahan and Michael Young in a special issue of the *Journal of Education and Work* 22(3), 2009. Our thanks to Taylor and Francis for permission to reproduce these papers; and to *Sísifo Educational Sciences Journal* (2009, vol. 10, pp.87–94) for permission to use Bernard Charlot's paper.

Our thanks to Madeleine Arnot, Andrew Dobson and Kris Gutierrez who contributed papers to the Seminars and Harriet Marshall, Yolande Muschamp and Andy Stables who commented on the papers.

Our thanks also to Geraldine Jones who created miracles with her technological expertise; and finally to Anna Clarkson for her sagacity and great patience.

1 Introduction

Educating for the knowledge economy? Critical perspectives

Hugh Lauder, Michael Young, Harry Daniels, Maria Balarin and John Lowe

In the city of Bath (UK) there is a famous Abbey dating from the ninth century. Beside the main doors are two ladders carved into the stone and on the ladders angels are ascending towards heaven. Some angels, who have sinned, are falling down the ladder, but not many. The contemporary secular version of this story is that of education and the knowledge economy.

Until the financial crisis of 2008 and the ensuing economic recession in the American and British and some European economies, policy makers, many economists and management gurus bought into the idea that we were on the sunny uplands of a new stage of capitalism driven by knowledge.[1] If individuals invested in their education and ascended the credential ladder they could secure well paid, high status jobs, in which creativity was at a premium. The most articulate disciple of this vision was Peter Drucker (1993), the management guru, who suggested that in this new stage of capitalism power would transfer from capitalists to knowledge workers because the new 'capital' would be knowledge.

Founded on this belief, a new informal social contract was struck between citizens and the state: the state would provide the educational opportunities for citizens to ascend the credential ladder and in return they had to study and achieve to the best of their abilities (Brown *et al.*, 2011). Through this contract it was thought the state could achieve both economic competitiveness and social justice. Knowledge was assumed to be at the heart of economic competitiveness and hence better educated nations would have an edge in the global economy. Underlying this assumption was the view that the knowledge economy would usher in an increasing proportion of well paid, 'knowledge' jobs. This would then allow for upward social mobility and social justice since well educated students from all social backgrounds could then aspire to high status knowledge economy jobs.

This is the story that has been told by policy makers, economists and management gurus. In effect they have bought into, and spread, an ideology about how the economic world is structured and how individuals can play their part in its success. It is a social imaginary that has education at its centre.[2]

The notion of a social imaginary is important in understanding the hold of the idea of education and its centrality to the knowledge economy. Rizvi and Lingard (2010) describe it as follows:

a way of thinking shared in a society by ordinary people, the common understandings that make every day practice possible, giving them sense and legitimacy. It is largely implicit, embedded in ideas and practices carrying within
deeper normative notions and images, constitutive of society.

(Rizvi and Lingard, 2010, p.34)

We can see the work of both the descriptive and the prescriptive in this imaginary. The claims made for education in relation to the knowledge economy can
be summarised as 'learning = earning' and the prescription that follows is that all
those interested in gaining well paid jobs should invest in their education (Brown
et al., 2011).

The point about the notion of a social imaginary, in relation to the knowledge
economy, is that it is buttressed not only by the rhetoric of policy makers but also
of policy-driven research by, for example, the OECD and the International
Association for the Evaluation of Educational Achievement (IEA), resulting in
comparative league tables on national educational performance. Since this research
is the subject of editorial comment and debate in the world's major newspapers it
shows how compelling this imaginary has become. Arne Duncan, US Secretary of
Education, defines the improvements needed in US education by reference to the
global league tables constructed by the OECD while using a quote from President
Obama, 'The nation that out-educates us today is going to out-compete us tomorrow' as a warning.[3] Michael Gove, the Minister of Education in Britain, has said of
the Head of Indicators and Analysis (Education Directorate) for the OECD, that
he is the 'most important man in English education'.[4] This research throws out a
fundamental challenge concerning this book. If indeed a sound explanation(s)
could be reasonably inferred from these league tables to economic competitiveness
then questioning what this relationship involves would be redundant.

Flat world, flat education systems?[5]

In his best seller, *The World is Flat* (2005), Thomas Friedman articulates two of
the key neo-liberal assumptions concerning the idea of a global knowledge economy: that labour markets are now global and it is within them that all nations
must compete. Those who compete successfully will do so on the basis of knowledge and innovation:

America, as a whole, will do fine in a flat world with free trade – provided it
continues to churn out knowledge workers who are able to produce idea-
based goods that can be sold globally and who are able to fill the knowledge
jobs that will be created as we not only expand the global economy but connect all the knowledge pools in the world. There may be a limit to the number of good factory jobs in the world, but there is no limit to the number of
idea-generating jobs in the world.

(Friedman, 2005, p.230)

This peon to a neo-liberal view of economic globalisation stands little scrutiny (Brown *et al.*, 2011), yet the idea that nations must compete in a flat world is reproduced in the interpretation placed on the comparative studies of educational performance undertaken by the OECD and the IEA in the studies conducted by these organisations (e.g. PISA, PIRLS, TIMMMS). What these international comparative studies do is to 'iron out' fundamental differences in the culture, knowledge, pedagogy and assessment of educational systems by reducing them to the technical problems raised by comparing student achievement across the globe (see Popkewitz, Chapter 10). As such, they can construct a hierarchy of 'performance' in league tables by which policy makers can judge national achievements against those of 'competitors'.

Torrance (2006) has described this as a form of globalising empiricism where fundamental differences in education systems can be reduced to what is 'observable' and measurable. However, Dale (2009) has noted that there is at least one powerful theory that could support the construction of these league tables, World Polity Theory (Meyer *et al.*, 1992).

This theory explicitly argues for the convergence of national education systems on the basis of the dominant Western ideology of modernity, which explains why curricula in many countries appear the same and which has led to the rise of standardised models of society (Benavot *et al.*, 1992, p.41) and in particular in education. As Schofer and Meyer put it: 'The same subjects are taught with the same perspectives leading to very similar degrees and to credentials that take on worldwide meaning' (Schofer and Meyer, 2005, p.917).

The consequence is that at the core of educational systems is:

> a 'rational' discourse on how the socialization of children in various subjects areas are linked to the self-realization of the individual and, ultimately, to the construction of the ideal society. This discourse is highly standardized and universalistic in character.
>
> (Cha, 1992, p.65)

In this way, the theory asserts a convergence in the structuring of education and in its outcomes; hence the kind of international league tables that dominate so much of political debate may be seen as justified on theoretical grounds.

However, there are at least three problems with this account. The first concerns the claim that schools teach the same kind of knowledge globally. Whether there is a global convergence in curricula turns on the kind of knowledge taught in schools and here, as contributors to this volume make clear, the claims made by World Polity Theorists are open to doubt. Young (Chapter 8) argues that in Britain and America, despite the rhetoric about the importance of knowledge, it is conspicuous by its absence in many curricula. Schools may have many aims but as Young (2009) has noted what is distinctive about them is their claim to impart abstract or universal knowledge represented by academic disciplines and theories.

Moreover, even when it is a key curriculum element, the conditions under which knowledge is learned is crucial to both economic competitiveness and social justice, and it is this that is ignored when it is assumed that there is a direct translation from positions in global league tables to economic success.[6] We know from Alexander's (2001) magisterial comparative study of primary schooling that pedagogies, forms of assessment and the way the curriculum is structured vary from nation to nation. And these differences will in turn affect students' conceptions of learning and indeed this ideal of the learner to which they should be aspiring (Hempel-Jorgensen, 2009). These varying approaches to curricula, pedagogy and assessment are germane to the question of *economic* competitiveness precisely because these different approaches to the intellectual, social and emotional lives of students are likely to have a profound effect on the knowledge, skills, dispositions and practices that enable an economy to develop. For example, the best performing countries in science and maths in the league tables constructed by the OECD and IEA are often those from East Asia, Taiwan, Singapore and South Korea, and yet these are countries with long held concerns over whether their students are sufficiently creative to compete in the 'knowledge economy'.[7]

The third problem concerns the idea that the knowledge economy will increase social mobility and hence social justice by enabling all those who wish to take the opportunity to invest in their education to do so on the understanding that knowledge-based jobs will be available when they graduate. However, the process of selection and stratification in education always produces inequalities that cannot be justified on the basis of merit. Inequalities not only ration access to knowledge and skills but also structure student horizons and identities. Education is about the construction of character, broadly construed, as well as knowledge and its application. If we see the imparting of abstract knowledge as central to a school's aims then the question of inequality is one about how the working class and the dispossessed can gain this knowledge, rather than suffer what Sennett and Cobb (1972) describe as the hidden injuries of class inflicted by the experience of education.

The chapters in this book focus on social class because it intersects with the other central inequalities of gender and ethnicity. This is not, however, to deny or seek to obscure the significance of these inequalities. While the social imaginary of the knowledge economy trains attention on well paid, interesting jobs, knowledge capitalism is about cutting costs wherever possible and employing women is one of the principle means by which this is achieved. It is not only in terms of average salaries that women earn less than men in every country but also when education levels are taken into account. This is true for highly educated men and women in advanced economies, such as the United States, the Netherlands and Sweden (Evertsson *et al.*, 2009) where we might expect knowledge to be a dominant economic principle. As Lauder, Brown and Tholen (Chapter 3) make clear, the starting wages for graduate women in the United States has been consistently below that of men for nearly 30 years.

What makes these data so shocking is that in the past decade women have outperformed men in most areas of education in the advanced economies, yet this has not been translated into equality in the labour market. Initially it might be thought that it is in the reproduction of families and workers that these inequalities lie (Folbre, 2009). However, this insight does not take account of the many women who are now the major breadwinners as well as having responsibility for the processes and work of reproduction. It might be expected that if the power of patriarchy lay in the labour market, we would be witnessing changes in women's compensation by now.[8] Debates about capitalism and patriarchy that were prominent in the early 1980s should perhaps be prominent again.

A similar point can be made with respect to ethnicity. While ethnicity and class are interrelated in terms of educational achievement (Rothon, 2008), many ethnic groups suffer an ethnic penalty in the labour market. In a globalised economy, class is also related to skilled migrants (Kamat *et al.*, 2006) and as with women, employment of these migrants from developing countries is also a means of reducing labour costs.

These inequalities raise fundamental questions about the principles by which some groups remain dominant over others which are barely touched upon by flat world comparisons in either education or the labour market, as well as challenging the promise of social justice that accompanies the rhetoric of the knowledge economy.

If the claims of a flat global economy and flat education systems throw up one challenge to the themes in this book, then another comes from an altogether different direction: quite simply, that the social imaginary of education and the knowledge economy has evaporated in the light of the Great Recession.

Will the knowledge economy imaginary survive the recession?

Clearly, this question is primary because if the economic recession had dealt a death blow to the ideology of education and the knowledge economy, or what Grubb and Lazerson (2006) call the educational gospel, then a critical examination of its presuppositions would be of no more than historical interest. However, there are good reasons for thinking that this ideology will persist, despite significant fraying at the edges, because there is no viable political alternative on the horizon.

In different ways the policies and practices relating to tests and examinations and gaining qualifications, what passes in the rhetoric for learning, have suffered, partly through the development of trends prior to the recession and partly as a result of the recession. In Britain, it was the previous Labour government's intention to have 50 per cent of each age cohort attend university (currently some 44 per cent attend). But in 2010 the new coalition government has refused to fund places at university for some 210,000 eligible students. At the very time when it might be thought that investment in the future was paramount, the concern is increasingly of a 'lost generation' of those without education or employment opportunities. Youth unemployment is double that of the overall level of unemployment.

In the United States, there has been a 6 per cent increase in enrolments in tertiary institutions, a response in part to the very high levels of teenage unemployment (21 per cent), with an 11 per cent increase in two-year community colleges in contrast to a 4 per cent increase at universities. However, while American tertiary education enrolments have expanded, the demand for skilled workers, especially graduates is in doubt. Unemployment for graduates, although at 50 per cent of total unemployment is higher than at any time since 1979. However, it is estimated that only 20 per cent of college graduates can find jobs relevant to their education and training (Rothstein, 2010). More recent research shows that graduate incomes have declined since the recession and as in the United Kingdom about 20 per cent of recent graduates are unemployed (Godofsky *et al.*, 2011).

These data certainly raise questions about the viability of the informal contract between the state and students. However, despite the problems graduates have encountered in the labour market, students clearly feel that further education is the most rational response to the current problems in that market. At the same time, we should note that a majority of Americans no longer believe that a good education and hard work is enough to find good jobs and financial security (Kusnet *et al.*, 2006).

Yet this apparent paradox can be explained by Brown's (2006) notion of an 'opportunity trap'. In his view, many young people have to commit to education because it provides the only possibility for a job with some interest and rewards above the minimum wage, even though the costs of tertiary education are rising and the labour market rewards are likely to be diminished. So individuals willingly enter a trap because there are few or no alternatives. Here again we should note that it is not a trap for everyone. For those attending elite universities, it is not so much a trap as a palatial antechamber to their future careers.

Even if for the majority the promise of the opportunity bargain is empty and the evidence is mounting (see Chapter 3 by Lauder, Brown and Tholen), there may be 'rational' economic arguments as to why politicians will continue to beat the drum for the 'learning = earning' contract.

Here there are at least two possible broad and seemingly opposing arguments. The first turns on the observation that countries like South Korea and the Republic of Ireland significantly 'over produced' graduates before their respective economic take-offs. In both cases it could be argued that drawing on this pool of talent was central to their subsequent periods of economic success (Kim, 2000; Fields, 2002). Although, of course, the recent fate of the two countries have now significantly diverged with economic growth continuing in Korea,[9] based on innovative industrial production and Internet related services, while Ireland, having adopted the Anglo-American financial model, is crippled. This suggests that it may be the nature of the graduates produced and the kind of industrial model that is developed which is crucial to economic success. So the question then is what kind of graduates and what kind of economic model might be developed in countries like the USA and Britain that could utilise graduates productively? At the time of writing, apart from some rather vague and tendentious references to the green economy and expanding so-called STEM subjects (science, technology, engineering and maths), no such model is emerging.

Of course, in more extreme neo-liberal economic theories such as that expounded by Friedman (2005), the global market economy and optimism are inextricably linked. The problem with Friedman's view of limitless possibilities for creativity in the global marketplace is that many will argue that it turns its face away from the realities of economic history. There are times when in the early periods of an industrial revolution ideas played precisely the role Friedman describes. However, the key historical point about industrial revolutions is that once cost and competition come into the picture, the drive to reduce costs leads to the standardisation of new social technologies. Indeed Jay Tate, has argued, 'industrial revolutions are revolutions in standardization' (Tate, 2001). Once standardisation comes to dominate the economic model, the space for innovation of the kind assumed by Freidman narrows dramatically.

What the debates about the nature and future possibilities of the knowledge economy raise is the inherently political nature of the education–economy link, both in the tacit sense reflected in the notion of the social imaginary and more explicitly.

The politics of the 'knowledge economy'

Seeking to understand the linkages between policies and practices is important. But an ill-defined notion of a 'knowledge economy' may do valuable political work. Here we should note that it is not just that it obscures the darker effects of capitalism by referring to a knowledge economy rather than knowledge capitalism (Brown *et al.*, 2011) but it has been cast in the context of a global competition for competitive advantage, represented by the constant comparisons between national education systems. This is a version of the 'we are all in it together' mantra which obscures the educational and life chance inequalities within nations (Brown and Lauder, 1996). Politically, the notion of the 'knowledge economy' has also been useful in rationalising the contract between the state and the citizen in which the imaginary of learning = earning has been translated into a range of policies and practices which start at the school gates. So significant has been the idea of a link between education and the 'knowledge economy' that in the United States and Britain the state has taken extraordinary powers to 'lever up' educational standards. But the very image of a lever suggests an over-mechanistic view of how education can 'deliver' the knowledge economy worker.

This is not the first time politicians have tried to reduce complex elements of social practice, like education, to a simple set of governing principles. In his classic description of the way business principles and especially the utilisation of scientific management techniques were applied to education in 1920s America, Raymond Callahan's (1962) *Education and the Cult of Efficiency* prefigures the current policies of what may be called the state theory of learning (STofL) (Lauder *et al.*, 2006). Callahan describes how in the 1920s in the United States efficient business practices were seen as a paradigm for state sectors such as education. Now, under the state theory of learning it is assumed that 'standards' can be raised by assessment-led strategies based on repeated testing and the rating of schools on test outcomes, just as companies in America and Britain are judged on their outcomes, profits.

Precisely because the United States and Britain represent the most extreme examples of a mechanistic model of policy making, the chapters in this book focus on them. The hope is that readers in other countries will have a lot to learn from our contributors' analyses of this experiment and that policy makers who are tempted to increase their power over education by introducing such mechanistic policies will pause to reflect on their likely consequences

The chapters in this book are framed by the question of linkages between the various aspects of education and the knowledge economy, and in subjecting these to critical scrutiny it is hoped that the limits and possibilities of aligning the social practices of education with those of the economy may be explored.

The book is structured by the following questions:

- How can we best understand the 'knowledge economy' and what are the implications of the idea for education?
- How are the various elements of current educational policies related to the knowledge economy? In particular, how are we to understand knowledge in relationship to economic utility?
- How do different forms of pedagogy and assessment relate to the demands of the knowledge economy and social justice? Is the way they construct learners conducive to the knowledge economy? Do they exacerbate the tensions between knowledge acquisition and inequalities or are there ways in which these tensions can be overcome?

How can we best understand the 'knowledge economy' and what are the implications for education?

Once we peer behind the rhetoric of education for the knowledge economy, there are several vital questions that we might ask of policy makers. For a start we have to understand what is meant by the 'knowledge economy', and here there is considerable debate. Peters *et al.* (2010) have chartered the different accounts given of what in public discussion is called the knowledge economy, ranging from Castells' notion of Informational Capitalism through to the often used term of Cognitive Capitalism. What these different views of the 'knowledge economy' have in common is that they insist that the knowledge economy should be understood in its proper context: that of capitalism. What has clearly been forgotten in the euphoria associated with the knowledge economy is that capitalism is driven by finance and that it is the cause of many, although not all, of the crises endemic to it (Harvey, 2010).

In the four chapters in Part I the question as to the nature of the knowledge economy is interrogated. In Chapter 2 Ankie Hoogvelt sets the scene with a discussion of the global financial crisis and its implications for the future of capitalism. She charts the rise of finance within capitalism and shows how it has now become dominant. The implications for education are profound: it has led to a reduction of resources in the most affected countries, a restructuring of sectors such as higher education and has raised major questions as to the employment of graduates, who once saw the finance sector as a lucrative destination.

In Chapter 3, Lauder, Brown and Tholen advance a particular account of global knowledge capitalism in which the processes of market advantage will price Western graduates out of the global market because their jobs can be transferred to equally skilled but much cheaper graduates in East Asia; coupled with the routinisation of much knowledge work, including in the financial sector. A consequence of this view is that over time graduate incomes will become much more widely dispersed as some who are recruited to transnational companies will take the fast track route to executive positions while a majority will be involved in routinised knowledge work. In developing this argument the authors critically examine the various forms of research and data analysis that have appeared to support the idea of the knowledge economy through the claim that there is a graduate premium which reflects the rise in demand for knowledge workers. The implication of this analysis for professional middle-class students is profound since it follows that many graduates will not obtain the kinds of job or income that they might expect.

If these two chapters raise fundamental questions about the knowledge economy then those by Michael Peters and Harry Daniels take a different approach. Michael Peters (Chapter 4) points to the potentially liberating and creative possibilities of digitalisation and the potential it creates for an open society. Clearly in the 'Arab Spring', the political influence of access to the Internet was crucial. However, it remains an open question as to whether the possibly liberating influence of information technology on an open society would extend to the economy. Peters calls for the development of a critical intellectual history which:

> would bring out both the differences and dangers of different conceptions of 'openness', the distinction between open society and open democracy on the one hand versus open markets on the other. It would also plot the rise of the 'information utility' and new forms of 'information imperialism' within knowledge capitalism.

Harry Daniels begins Chapter 5 with one of the key developments in knowledge capitalism: changes in the division of labour relating to knowledge work. Professionals are being asked to work in interdisciplinary teams, which means that they have to leave the certainties of their own disciplinary training and collaborate to address problems that cannot otherwise be solved. However, this is not just a matter of coming to an intellectual and practical understanding but of also dealing with power relations. The question then is how do skilled workers learn to transcend disciplinary and practical boundaries? In raising this question he maps out the literature necessary for developing an understanding of the key issues.

When taken together these chapters question aspects of the nature of the knowledge economy, or more accurately knowledge capitalism, and open the discussion about the knowledge and learning that relate to it. Here, one of the key questions raised by the idea of the knowledge economy is that of the knowledge that is relevant to such an economy.

How are we to understand knowledge in relationship to the economy?

One of the key questions raised by the learning = earning contract is what precisely the relationship is between education, the labour market, productivity and rewards. Much of the focus in addressing these questions has been concerned either with the nature and role of credentials or with the role of education as socialising individuals in preparation for paid work. Credentials can be seen as passports to the labour market reflecting individuals' skills or as positional goods, subject to inflation and competition between competing groups. Education can also be seen as a form of discipline and social control in which, as Bowles and Gintis (1976) argue, the authority structures of the school correspond to those of paid work.

What has been marginalised in these debates is the question of academic knowledge and its relationship to the labour market. This is the focus of this section of the book. As Johan Muller notes, the social structures of academic knowledge were not developed to directly service the economy, and in relation to academic qualifications, at school and university, education and the labour market can be seen to be operating in separate fields, as described by Bourdieu (1988, 2005). Arguably, therefore, the rules, norms, incentives and systems of thought are quite different in the two fields. If this is so, then the attempt to apply the 'education gospel' through a seamless connection between education and paid work is likely to be fraught with difficulties, and so it is.

The obvious point of connection is that between research, innovation and the market place, and there is no doubt that economic interests are fundamentally reshaping the nature of university research (McSherry, 2001). Moreover, as Muller notes, universities have long been in the business of developing disciplinary-based professional knowledge in fields such as engineering which represent a more direct but often contested relationship between knowledge and occupations. However, once that is acknowledged, puzzles remain which are central to the relationship between education and labour markets. We have known since Max Weber that formal education systems have been about the social production of mind and character and that this is bound up with issues of power and culture in relation to social class, gender and ethnicity. Moreover, the cultures of different countries tend to relate mind and character to jobs in different ways. In America, and to some extent in the United Kingdom, a business or liberal arts degree seems to be considered a necessary first step in the development of workers and citizens; in East Asia, an engineering degree is taken to serve the same purposes (Brown *et al.*, 2011). Moreover, political and business classes on both sides of the Atlantic seem to imbue the Harvards and Oxfords with an almost mythical ability to produce excellence of both mind and character. But the rules, norms, processes and aims by which education has sought to 'shape' both mind and character are different to those found in the labour market: how then can a conceptual bridge be built between these two fields?

One answer has already been given by the Ivy League and Oxbridge examples: that is, that recruitment into the labour market is undertaken not on the basis of merit and 'character' in any neutral sense but on the basis of social class assumptions (Collins, 1979). But while the social class bridge between education and paid work may explain in general terms the entry of ruling elites into politics and business, it does not detail the mechanisms by which a classed education system translates into privilege in the labour market (Kupfer, 2011). Nor does it explain how 'merit' enters the picture: some occupations are less class based than others (Goldthorpe and Jackson, 2008).

Broadly speaking, policy makers have adopted several poorly articulated strategies in attempting to breach the boundaries of these two fields in order to make them into a single structure. The first is to claim that, while academic knowledge is indeed different to the kinds of knowledge needed for many kinds of job, it nevertheless promotes generic skills that are essential in the workplace. Many educational institutions have bought into the rhetoric of 'generic skills', but it remains problematic because it is not at all clear that the systems of thought characteristic of an induction into academic knowledge relate to many of the practical aspects of paid work.

Related to this rationalisation is another: that of competence. Here the idea is that education provides a complex of skills and dispositions required for paid work. The skills may be technical, as in the forms of computation or scientific investigation, but the term skills has also increasingly come to mean the 'soft' skills of interpersonal communication, team work and problem solving. Competence then is defined in terms of an amalgam of technical and soft skills. But again, it is not clear why educational institutions are uniquely fitted to educate for soft skills. Certainly mathematical and written forms of communication are essential for academic success, but oral forms of communication are not, nor is team work, although it may have its place in some corners of academia, while problem solving in the labour market may take quite different forms to those relating to specific academic problems. By extending the sense of what constitutes skill from technical to 'soft', policy makers have unified the notion of skill to encompass both mind and character and lifted it from its traditional, and in Anglophone contexts, devalued associations with 'hands' in the hope of creating a convincing account of the significance of education for the labour market.

In Britain, there may be continuity between these policies and the traditional idea that students were best educated for work through a liberal education which had an implicit view of generic skills. Arguably, recruiters did not care which degree graduates from Oxford and Cambridge had studied: a similar point could be made at lower levels of academic achievement when top companies and legal and accountancy practices recruited those with university entrance qualifications. In this reading, it is making the social class assumptions embedded in the explicit notion of generic skills that is new and has raised the problems in the links between education and the labour market.

How then are we to understand the relationship between academic knowledge and the labour market?

In the opening chapter of this section David Baker gives what may be considered one of the most powerful defences of the dominant economic theory which has sought to connect education to the labour market: human capital theory. He has a theory of how education produces both minds and characters which are productive in the labour market, and furthermore he argues that education has fundamentally changed the workplace, in turn changing the nature and level of demand for educated workers. This latter claim is implicit in human capital theory in that it assumes that an increased supply of educated workers will prompt employers to change their organisations. This is because employers can then accommodate the potential for greater productivity represented by better educated workers. What Baker does is to flesh out this assumption, through the tenets of what has become known as neo-institutionalism. This theoretical movement, in which he has played a major role, has argued that in a range of ways, education creates the demand for new forms of professionalism (Meyer, 1977). Baker, citing Luo (2006, p.230), argues that the schooled society creates 'thinking and choosing actors, embodying professional expertise and capable of rational and creative behaviour'. This is part of what he calls the rise of the culture of academic intelligence which he claims has influenced the construction of formal organisations that are global and are similar 'regardless of their mission'. Educated workers of the kind described above enable intensive rationalisation in the workplace through the rise of accounting and auditing, elaborate legal contracts, corporate social responsibility, human relations and strategic planning, amongst other characteristics.

This is a powerful claim and can be seen as an extension of his work as one of the World Polity theorists (Meyer *et al.*, 1992; Baker and LeTendre, 2005) who have argued that school curricula around the world are remarkably similar because they are based on the rationality and values of Western modernity. In terms of globalisation this group of theorists have made the case for educational convergence, and in this chapter Baker also argues for organisational convergence.

However, as Dale has noted in a critique of the World Polity theorists, 'globalization may shape spaces but it does not determine practices' (Dale, 2009, p.6). This insight is a way of introducing the remaining three chapters in this section by Michael Young, Johan Muller and Leesa Wheelahan which are no less ambitious in their scope and argument in raising fundamental questions about the relationship of knowledge to education and the labour market. They argue that what is taught and the reasons for teaching it are crucial, and in this sense they offer a challenge in different ways to the idea of academic intelligence and the culture it has created.

Michael Young (Chapter 8) starts with what he argues is a contradiction between the idea that knowledge has become a key organising category in educational policy, yet it is an entirely rhetorical 'category' since these same policies never make explicit what they mean by knowledge, and deny that 'access to knowledge [in the sense of 'powerful knowledge' (Young, 2008)] ... is central to the whole purpose of education'. Like Baker, he sees 'knowledge' as a new global narrative and to illustrate how pervasive it is he identifies its use by multilateral agencies and secondary education in Norway, as well as in England. In order to articulate a strong view of knowledge which nevertheless is socially produced, he establishes a dialogue between a form of social realism as articulated by Moore (2007), Bachelard and three of the great sociologists and social psychologists, Durkheim, Vygotsky and Bernstein. From this dialogue he is able to create a synthesis which enables a strong account of knowledge but which is nevertheless subject to the shifting foundations of the social world. This position allows him to critique some of the current practices in education that pass for induction into knowledge when, he argues, they do no such thing. In particular he argues that what Moore calls, 'the voice of knowledge' brings knowledge and the knower back together when current policy and practice divorces knowledge from knowers and thinking from judgement.

In Chapter 7 Johan Muller develops the idea that the forms of the academic disciplines, including those that relate to vocational knowledge have 'their roots in historical struggles and innovations, as well as the diversifying division of labour'. In this respect his view is consistent with Young's in arguing that knowledge is socially produced, but his historical account of the emerging disciplines on which knowledge is based elaborates on this view in detail. Whereas Baker sees the emergence of an academic intelligence and culture as embedded in the rationality of Western modernity, the implications of Muller's account is that the struggles which have brought us to the disciplines we have today make them far more contingent and less the outcome of a rational zeitgeist then perhaps Baker's position suggests.

The struggles Muller identifies have been structured by the academic 'fault lines' between liberal and practically useful knowledge, and within the former between the humanities and natural sciences. In turn, these fault lines have given us different forms of knowledge which have mapped onto the changing division of labour to yield different routes between education and the labour market. These routes are a response to questions about the degree of specialisation and the conceptual demands required for particular occupations. Underlying these questions is a more profound one about the identities and hence mind and character which these routes structure.

If this is the case, and Johan Muller is persuasive in his argument, then it follows that the idea that there is a generic set of knowledge structures acquired through education, as policy makers assume, is simply false because the more specialised a discipline becomes the less transferable its understandings and skills. Against this argument may be set the recruiting practices of corporations such as banks that in Britain have sought physics graduates. However, a recruiting strategy of this kind may be based on specific universities and the more 'rounded' education they might provide.

Leesa Wheelahan in Chapter 9 provides a critique of competency-based training (CBT). This is the pervasive form of vocational education in Australia and there are elements of it to be found in many vocational education systems, including National Vocational Qualifications (NVQs) in Britain. Units of competency are related to specific workplace tasks or roles where competency, which has to be shown in behaviours, describes the set of attitudes and skills needed to complete a task to the standard specified. Wheelahan's argument is that this approach excludes access to theory-based disciplinary knowledge because 'it only provides students with access to contextually specific applications of knowledge, and not the system of meaning in which it is embedded'. She notes that there are social class divisions between those that have access to disciplinary knowledge through university and those undertaking vocational education and training (VET). However, without access to theory-based disciplinary knowledge VET students are disadvantaged because they neither have the intellectual basis to study in higher education nor access to a system of meanings by which the world can best be understood.

Underlying CBT is a marriage between constructivism and progressivism which gives the impression that CBT is a form of progressivism. But by bringing together critical realism and Bernstein's account of knowledge, in itself a daring and innovative strategy, Wheelahan is able to argue that constructivism confines understanding to specific contexts and 'by seeking meaning within the contextual, constructivism and instrumentalism deny students access to the conditions of knowledge needed to understand the contextual'. Yet being able to place the particular within the frame of the general, which is what disciplinary-based theories do, is essential both for understanding one's place in the world and for creating new and innovative forms of thinking about the particular.

The chapters by Michael Young, Johan Muller and Leesa Wheelahan point to the differentiation of education systems in ways that raise questions about the notion of academic intelligence and culture. Implicit within these critical accounts is a powerful alternative vision of the education–economy relationship. The failure of VET systems to enable students to access what elsewhere Young (2008) has called 'powerful knowledge' can be seen narrowly as a question of lack of productivity and the ability of workers to innovate, but it can also be seen as a failure to realise the German principle of equality of productive labour; a failure of equality of opportunity and a failure to produce the critically reflective worker-citizen. While Young and Wheelahan present powerful cases for the teaching of discipline-based knowledge, fundamental questions remain as to how their critiques could be translated into pedagogies, curricula and modes of assessment that would enable working-class youth to access disciplinary knowledge. It is this question that the third section addresses.

What is clear is that these chapters represent the first sustained attempt, for some time, to unpack how the education of mind and character relate to the world of work, and in this the issues are far more complex and merit far greater analysis in guiding policy than merely a reliance on comparative league tables.

How do different forms of pedagogy and assessment relate to the demands of the knowledge economy and social justice?

The question of the relation between forms of pedagogy and assessment and the knowledge economy cannot be entirely divorced from that of systematic inequalities. This is because all education systems have at their core principles of selection and stratification. It is well established that these principles will inform not only what is taught by way of knowledge but of how it is taught and assessed, and in consequence how key elements of identity are constructed for different groups within education systems.

Certainly there are some general observations that can be made about the possible effects of the state theory of learning that has been embraced in the United States and Britain. The STofL takes the view that the way for learning to be achieved is through high stakes testing. But these tests point in three directions. They are intended to aid learning, to judge the performance of teachers when test results are aggregated to the school level, and when formulated into league tables they act as a market signal to consumers (parents) as to which schools are performing best. In England this has been accompanied by a national curriculum and mandated periods spent in primary schools for the teaching of numeracy and literacy for which there are prescribed methods for teaching. In the United States, the No Child Left Behind legislation requires every state to administer standardised tests and accountability systems, with penalties for those schools that do not meet their targets.

The theory of learning implicit in the STofL is that repeated testing will enable students to acquire the necessary forms of knowledge and skill, largely, as Torrance points out, through training for the test. It is assumed that once learnt, students will not forget what they have learned and that as such constitutes the building blocks for later learning. Underlying the STofL is a set of assumptions about human motivation and how young people learn, in which the former are consistent with the view that human beings are fundamentally driven by external stimuli. These are represented by the spurs and sanctions of competition in education coupled with and reinforced by state judgements about school performance. For management teams and teachers this means that their prospects for reward and future promotion are intimately tied to largely quantitative judgements about school performance. If there is additional motivation it is in terms of hitting or exceeding targets for test results. For students the aim is also to meet or exceed test results. In both cases the principle of competition between schools and pupils is a key principle of motivation.

The problem with the STofL is that memorising techniques for answering a particular set of questions may be quite different from developing the kind of understanding that can enable further learning. And, as Broadfoot and Pollard (2006) have noted, if students think education is about meeting test targets, rather than about developing curiosity and intrinsic interest, then once test targets have been achieved, the job, so to speak, has been done, the certificate gained. Torrance makes a similar point with respect to training for the test: 'Coaching for tests is producing learners who are too dependent on support to operate effectively in other more challenging environments.'

It is hard to imagine how such a strategy for learning can be consistent with the demands for creativity in the knowledge economy, if indeed such demands exist (Araya and Peters 2010; Brown *et al.*, 2011).

Undoubtedly, testing is in the interests of politicians because the results can be easily placed in the public domain. But it is worth noting that the detailed pedagogy prescribed by the state in Britain and teachers' self-disciplining in training for the test are not that far away from the digital-Taylorism described above. Both have standardisation at their root and both kinds of work are likely to be demotivating.

This then brings us to the central problem, which is that, despite the long period in which the STofL has been embedded within the education system, it is strongly resisted by teachers, as evidenced by their recent refusal to administer tests. In part, this is because it is in tension with a strongly held professional view that teaching should be about developing curiosity and intrinsic interest. In professional middle-class schools, teachers seem to meet the testing demands while also fostering curiosity but this proves much more difficult in working-class schools (Hempel-Jorgensen, 2009).

It should be emphasised that teachers' practice often seeks to yoke together these two competing forms of pedagogy. As well as teaching to the test teachers have a commitment to individualised learning and often theories of learning styles. As Maguire *et al.* (2012) show in the way schools translate policy into practice, teachers can shift from one mode of pedagogy to another, which for students must, at best, be confusing.

It is also clear that the strategy of repeated testing has not raised the educational and labour market prospects of working-class students. Given the length of time that the STofL has existed in Britain, it is arguable as to whether it will make a difference. Early indications from mobility studies suggest it will not: the advantage of the wealthy and the professional middle class persists. It is this point that the five chapters in this section address. They are concerned with two broad questions. The first is a critical discussion of the way sociologists have come to understand working-class underperformance in modern education systems: what in official circles is described as 'educability' but may from the perspective of the working class and dispossessed be seen as a form of symbolic violence (Bourdieu, 1977). The second is that given these understandings how best can pedagogy and assessment be put in the service of greater equality in processes and outcomes.

Chapter 10 by Thomas Popkewitz places the current obsession with testing and the statistics of success and failure in historical context. The chapter makes several fundamental points about the role of numbers in education. The first is that the way numbers are used to classify students 'enters into the ways people structure experience and think about what is practical and useful as people come to think of themselves and their choices with an apparatus created with the fictions [of league tables and test constructions]'.

But these standards of assessment 'embody cultural theses about who the child is and should be, and who is *not* that child. The production of human kinds in schools entails a simultaneous process of exclusion and abjection…'.

However, students' identities are not only framed by the system of testing and classification but also by the way knowledge is translated into the curriculum:

> The procedures of classification and ordering are an alchemy through which academic practices (performed in labs, university science buildings, historical societies, etc.) are translated and transformed into the school curriculum … The translation tools of curriculum are cultural theses about who the child is and should be. Learning more 'content' knowledge is never just that. It embodies learning how to see, think, act and feel.

Popkewitz's analysis takes us to the core point that these mechanisms of classification and control permeate the way in which students' identities are framed. Given the way statistics and the underlying assumptions about human nature that they represent have permeated our culture, the question is raised as to how fairer and more open systems of classification can be created.

In Chapter 11 Harry Torrance probes the role of assessment further by critically examining the policies related to assessment in Britain under the STofL. Even in terms of the STofL's stated aims the results have at best been mixed. Results flatlined in tests for 7- and 11-year-old students from the turn of this century, while the same is true of the exams taken at 16 for those that have gained what is often seen as the minimum grades that employers will accept. While those who come from working-class backgrounds continue to underperform.

Given these equivocal results Torrance levels a series of criticisms against the testing culture. As we have noted, coaching for tests seems to provide the best explanation for the initial gains that were made when the tests were introduced and continue to play a key role in the lives of school children. But he also argues that the use of a narrow range of tests 'impacts negatively on the educational experience of even successful students, let alone unsuccessful ones'. And he points to 40 years of research that shows that it is the quality of interaction between teacher and student that is the key to sustained learning.

There is a further criticism to be made: the way school performance on tests is measured is at best misleading. This is especially the case in the use of indicators of disadvantage. The consequence is that many schools may not be judged fairly with all that entails for the reputations of schools and teachers and the resources accruing to them (Lauder *et al.*, 2010).

Why then do governments insist on the STofL? Accountability, the insistence that educational standards must keep rising in the cause of global competitiveness and as Torrance observes: 'System control outweighs the nebulous benefits of trying to improve quality by other means. Tests and testing allows governments to exert direct pressure on schools and classrooms and they are unlikely to relinquish them lightly.'

Given the failure of the STofL, especially for those children from working-class backgrounds, we need to return to the perennial issue of working-class underperformance.

Bernard Charlot in Chapter 12 sets the stage for a debate about working-class underperformance at school. He notes that some of the key theorists, on the reproduction of inequality in education (e.g. Bowles and Gintis, 1976), do not enter the classroom. While others such as Bourdieu and his co-writers do so in respect of the habitus and the related dispositions of students. But none of these theorists ask the key questions by which cycles of reproduction might be broken. To do this Charlot takes three steps. First he notes that the practices and activities of a school and classroom may be different from what may be 'read off' from a pupils' social background or gender; this has the effect of opening a space for the interruption of cycles of reproduction. Second, the pupils and the meanings they generate about their activities in school, and especially the question of why they are studying, is central to understanding an activity. However, for working-class students pedagogic activities face the problem of how to make sense of abstract concepts and theories when they often seem to have little relation to their every-day experience. As Charlot notes:

> Very often an attempt is made to solve school failure by linking everything to the pupil's daily life. This connection can, however, constitute both a support and an obstacle at the same time. It is a support because it gives meaning to what the school teaches. It is an obstacle when it hides the specific meaning of the school activity.

Here he sees the central purpose of school activity as the teaching of principles similar to those advocated by Young: 'distancing, objectivation, systemisation' by which he means developing, in pupils, the ability to reflect on the world and oneself in it. And as with Nash (2009), while he agrees that these principles have been developed by the middle classes, he insists that they constitute the basis of 'powerful knowledge' for all.

Charlot's chapter is followed by Geoff Whitty's revisiting of the sociology and politics of the school curriculum in the twenty-first century (Chapter 13). He begins with the fundamental problem of how to address the concerns that Charlot has outlined. His argument is 'that some of the key challenges in giving disadvantaged pupils access to powerful knowledge – and giving it meaningful and critical purchase on their everyday lives – are pedagogic ones'.

In order to develop this argument, he provides a rich discussion of various attempts, particularly in Northern Ireland, to address this problem. A consideration of these examples brings him to the work of Basil Bernstein in a search for pedagogical principles that might guide working-class students into the study of powerful knowledge. Here he returns to two key sets of theoretical tools developed by Bernstein: 'classification' and 'framing' and recognition and realisation rules.

Classification is understood as the 'distribution of power and principles by which boundaries are established between categories'. Strong classification is underpinned by the rule that 'things must be kept apart, weak classification embraces the opposite. Framing reflects the distribution of control over communication. Strong framing in this case would include where a teacher has a didactic form of pedagogy in which students are initiated into disciplinary knowledge. Weak framing would be where students have an element of control in how they learn and what they learn.

He argues that in Britain the curriculum, which has so advantaged the middle class, has been characterised by strong classification and framing. And he notes that 'it seems unlikely that just giving working-class pupils more of the very kinds of activities at which they are failing is likely to work'.

For Whitty an answer may lie in retaining the strong classification of the curriculum combined with weak framing. Here he introduces the concepts of recognition and realisation. The key here is for pupils to be able to recognise what counts as the specialised discourse involved in subjects, and pedagogy should be aimed at doing so, while giving pupils a degree of control over their learning within this context. Realisation here refers to the activities pupils engage in which are appropriate to their recognition of disciplinary knowledge.

Intuitively this seems an attractive proposal because it enables pupils some control in their learning in an area which may be foreign to them and hence under strong classification and framing they may feel alienated. It may also address one of the key points made by Popkewitz, that there is a translation process from academic knowledge to the curriculum, which presupposes a particular view of how the child is and should be. What giving pupils some control over their learning does is to weaken this presupposition which may also contribute to their alienation.

Giving pupils some control over their learning may loosen the assumptions made about them and give them the confidence to step into a territory that may have seemed alien.

Conclusion

There are five broad points to be made from this discussion. The first is that claims about the importance of education to the knowledge economy run into trouble the moment attempts are made to link arguable notions of the knowledge economy with claims about knowledge, pedagogy and assessment. These are all contested areas. It is only if we buy into the notion of a flat world and flat education systems that any plausibility can be given to the idea that the links between these areas are relatively straightforward. Even in areas such as professional higher education, which appear to be straightforwardly vocational, Muller has shown the contested nature of the linkages between knowledge and vocational practice.

This brings us to the second point. Rather than inferring a 'top down' set of claims about knowledge, pedagogy and assessment from some concept of the knowledge economy, as policy makers do, perhaps we should be approaching the issue from the 'bottom up', inferring a view of the knowledge economy from policies concerning knowledge, the curriculum, pedagogy and assessment. When we look at the STofL, then this suggests a view of the knowledge economy which in some ways is consistent with Brown *et al.* (2011), where permission to think is given to an elite, while for the many, teaching to the test, and emphasising everyday experience over powerful knowledge, may socialise students into a world of work dominated by digital routinised work. Viewed from this perspective the rhetoric of education and the knowledge economy takes on a different and unduly limiting role for education. In this case, the STofL is not only about the socialisation of students into a particular form of work but also social control: it is about controlling thought and behaviour through the interminable rhythms of training and testing.

In turn, the experience for school students must be confusing when the repeated mantra of performing in tests through constant practice is coupled with a professional understanding of learning which emphasises the idea that individuals have different approaches to learning.

The third point, which follows from the above, is that there are two key fissures in the discourse about education and the knowledge economy that threaten to become wider, stretching its credulity further. The idea that if only individuals will see that learning = earning so they will be rewarded with good jobs in the knowledge economy is likely to be false: the aspirations and expectations of the middle classes will not be met. If the jobs that provide a comfortable middle-class existence are either now being offshored to East Asia, where the same skills can be exercised for a fraction of the cost, or substituted by computer algorithms that encapsulate and codify knowledge that was previously embodied in individuals, then education cannot deliver on middle-class aspirations.

At the same time, the fourth point is that, despite the introduction of a powerful architecture of control and micro management, exemplified by the STofL, the problem of working-class underperformance in education remains. These fissures represent an historic turning point in which the connections between education, the labour market and upward mobility are being broken.

Finally, it should be emphasised that our focus has been on the British and American cases. There are other countries, for example Germany and Singapore, that have achieved a much clearer and more effective articulation between education and work (Hansen, 2011). In the German case this has been achieved by an industrial structure in which manufacturing remains crucial to German export success, a vocational education system, which although under stress continues to attract students, and a much smaller university system. There has been a cost in terms of class and gender inequality, and this is true of vocational and higher education (Kupfer, 2010). As is often the case with German exceptionalism, the idea of mass higher education being central to the knowledge economy was rejected. It is the case that there are now shortages in high skill areas (Jacoby, 2011) but it seems easier to expand a higher education system than have to live with high levels of graduate unemployment. In Singapore, the education system has been tightly integrated to the demands of multinational companies and changes in technology, coupled with a social imaginary about a small island state having to survive the caprices of the global economy (Ashton and Green, 1996).

In Britain and the United States, it is likely that policy makers will continue to rely on testing to legitimise their policies by reference to international league tables because, as we have seen, it is in their interests to do so. And, as we have argued, there seems to be no plan B. However, there is another possibility: it may be that now, with the confounding of middle-class expectations and the failed education imaginaries of the dispossessed and the working class there is the possibility of a new educational project which is driven by optimism in the powers of education, rather than with an exclusively economic narrative in the interests of a minority.

Notes

1 The roll call of politicians that have signed up to this ideology includes Bill Clinton, the two Bush presidents, Tony Blair, Gordon Brown and amongst economists Gary Becker and Paul Krugman, as well as management theorists like Peter Drucker.
2 How it is possible for opinion leaders from so many different fields to develop a consensus which, in its effects on the everyday thinking and practices of citizens, has so coloured our view of education and the economy would constitute an important study in its own right: a study of the relationship between dominant social classes, ideas and resulting practices.
3 Duncan, A. (2010) 'Back to school: Enhancing US education and competitiveness', *Foreign Affairs*, (Nov/Dec): 65–74. See, however, Diane Ravitch, 'School "reform": A failing grade,' *The New York Review of Books*, 20 September 2011.
4 Cited in the *Education Guardian*, 29 March 2011, p.2.
5 This idea came out of a discussion with Phillip Brown.
6 See also Chapter 10 by Popkewitz in this volume.
7 This raises the question of how transnational corporations can integrate different nationalities into their skill webs (Ashton *et al.*, 2010). There are at least two possible answers: their incentives, sanctions and cultures re-socialise their workers, including their understanding of learning. A further answer may lie in the type of international education that many senior managers will have experienced, either through school or elite universities, that is rapidly developing, which may be crucial to creating a transnational class (Brown and Lauder, 2009).
8 This point was raised by Antonia Kupfer.
9 Although it too now has high graduate unemployment.

References

Alexander, R.J. (2001) *Culture and Pedagogy: International Comparisons in Primary Education*, Oxford: Blackwell.

Araya, D. and Peters, M. (eds) (2010) *Education in the Creative Economy*, New York: Peter Lang.

Ashton, D. and Green, F. (1996) *Education, Training and the Global Economy*, Aldershot: Edward Elgar.

Ashton, D., Brown, P. and Lauder, H. (2010) 'Skill webs and international human resource management: Lessons from a study of the global skill strategies of transnational companies', *International Journal of Human Resource Management*, 6(21): 836–850.

Baker, D. and LeTendre, G. (2005) *National Differences, Global Similarities: World Culture and the Future of Schooling*, Stanford, CA: Stanford University Press.

Benavot., A., Cha, Y.-K., Kamens, D., Meyer, J. and Wong, S.-Y. (1992) 'Knowledge for the masses: World models and national curricula, 1920–1986', in Meyer, J., Kamens, D. and Benavot, A. (eds) *School Knowledge for the Masses*, Brighton: Falmer Press.

Bourdieu, P. (1977) 'Symbolic power', in Gleeson, D. (ed.) *Identity and Structure*, Driffield: Nafferto Books, pp. 112–119.

Bourdieu, P. (1988) *Homo Academicus*, Cambridge: Polity Press.

Bourdieu, P. (2005) *The Social Structures of the Economy*, Cambridge: Polity Press.

Bowles, S. and Gintis, H. (1976) *Schooling in Capitalist America*, London: Routledge and Kegan Paul.

Broadfoot, P. and Pollard, A. (2006) 'The changing discourse of assessment policy: The case study of English primary education', in Lauder, H., Brown, P., Dillabough, J.-A. and Halsey, A. (eds) *Education, Globalization and Societies*, Oxford: Oxford University Press.

Brown, P. (2006) 'The opportunity trap', in Lauder, H., Brown, P., Dillabough, J.-A. and Halsey, A.H. (eds) *Education, Globalization and Social Change*, Oxford: Oxford University Press.

Brown, P. and Lauder, H. (1996) 'Education, globalization and economic development', *Journal of Education Policy*, 11: 1–26.

Brown, P and Lauder, H. (2009) 'Globalization, the nation state and international education', in Rvzi, F. and Popkewitz, T. (eds) *Globalization and Education*, Chicago, IL: NSSE (National Society for the Study of Education).

Brown, P., Lauder, H. and Ashton, D. (2011) *The Global Auction: The Broken Promises of Opportunities, Jobs and Rewards*, New York: Oxford University Press.

Callahan, R. (1962) *Education and the Cult of Efficiency*, Chicago, IL: University of Chicago Press.

Cha, Y.-K. (1992) 'The origins and expansion of primary school curricula', in Meyer, J., Kamens, D. and Benavot, A. (eds) *School Knowledge for the Masses*, Brighton: Falmer Press.

Collins, R. (1979) *The Credential Society: An Historical Sociology of Education and Stratification*, New York: Academic Press.

Dale, R. (2009) 'Pedagogy and cultural convergence', in Daniels, H., Lauder, H. and Porter, J. (eds) *Educational Theories, Cultures and Learning: A Critical Perspective*, London: Routledge.

Drucker, P. (1993) *Post-Capitalist Society*, London: Butterworth-Heinemann.

Duncan, A. (2010) 'Back to school: Enhancing US education and competitiveness', *Foreign Affairs*, (Nov/Dec): 65–74.

Evertsson, M., England, P., Mooi-Reci, I. and Hermsen, J. (2009) 'Is gender inequality greater at lower or higher educational levels? Common patterns in the Netherlands, Sweden, and the United States', *Social Politics: International Studies in Gender, State and Society*, 16(2): 210–241.

Fields, B. (2002) *The Accidental Tiger: An Exploration of the Irish Economic Disposition during the Belated Golden Age of Development*, PhD Thesis, University of Leicester.

Flobre, N. (2009) 'Varieties of patriarchal capitalism', *Social Politics: International Studies in Gender, State and Society*, 16(2): 204–209.

Friedman, T. (2005) *The World is Flat*, New York: Penguin.

Godofsky, J., Zukin, C. and Van Horn, C. (2011) *Unfulfilled Expectations: Recent College Graduates Struggle in a Troubled Economy*, New Brunswick, NJ: Rutgers University, John J. Heldrich Centre for Workforce Development.

Goldthorpe, J. and Jackson, M. (2008) 'Education-based meritocracy: The barriers to its realisation', in Lareau, A. and Conley, D. (eds) *Social Class: How Does It Work?*, New York: Russell Sage Foundation.

Grubb, N. and Lazerson, N. (2006) 'The globalization of rhetoric and practice: The education gospel and vocationalism', in Lauder, H., Brown, P., and Dillabough, J.-A. and Halsey, A.H. (eds) *Education, Globalization and Social Change*, Oxford: Oxford University Press.

Hansen, H. (2011) 'Rethinking certification theory and the educational development of the United States and Germany', *Research in Social Stratification*, Special Issue, Bills, D. and Brown, D. (eds), forthcoming.

Harvey, D. (2010) *The Enigma of Capital and the Crises of Capitalism*, London: Profile Books.

Hempel-Jorgensen, A. (2009) 'The construction of the "ideal pupil" and pupils' perception of "misbehaviour" and discipline: Contrasting experiences in a low and high socio-economic primary school', *British Journal of Sociology of Education*, 30(4): 435–448.

Jacoby, T. (2011) 'Germany's immigration dilemma: How can Germany attract workers it needs?', *Foreign Affairs*, 90(2): 8–14.

Kamat, S., Mir, A. and Mathew, B. (2006) 'Producing hi-tech: Globalization, the state and migrant subjects', in Lauder, H., Brown, P., and Dillabough, J.-A. and Halsey, A.H. (eds) *Education, Globalization and Social Change*, Oxford: Oxford University Press.

Kim, L. (2000) 'Korea's national innovation system in transition', in Kim, L. and Nelson, R. (eds) *Technology Learning and Innovation: Experiences of Newly Industrialised Economies*, Cambridge: Cambridge University Press.

Kupfer, A. (2010) 'The socio-political significance of changes to the vocational education system in Germany', *British Journal of Sociology of Education*, 31(1): 85–97.

Kupfer, A. (2011) 'Towards a theoretical framework for the comparative understanding of globalisation, higher education, the labour market and inequality', *Journal of Education and Work*, 24 (1–20): 185–208.

Kusnet, D., Mishel, L. and Teixeira, R. (2006) *Talking Past Each Other: What Everyday Americans Really Think (and Elites Don't Get) About the Economy*, Washington, DC: Economic Policy Institute.

Lauder, H., Brown, P., Dillabough, J.-A. and Halsey, A.H. (2006) 'Introduction: The prospects for education: Individualization, globalization and social change', in Lauder, H., Brown, P., Dillabough, J.-A. and Halsey, A.H. (eds.) *Education, Globalization and Social Change*, Oxford: Oxford University Press.

Lauder, H., Kounali, D., Robinson, T. and Goldstein, H. (2010) 'Pupil composition, and accountability: An analysis in English primary schools', *International Journal of Educational Research*, 49: 49–68.

McSherry, C. (2001) *Who Owns Academic Work? Battling for Control of Intellectual Property*, Cambridge, MA: Harvard University Press.

Maguire, M., Ball, S. and Braun, A. with Hoskins, K. and Perryman, J. (2012) *How Schools Do Policy: Policy Enactments in Secondary Schools*, London: Routledge.

Meyer, J. (1977) 'The effects of education as an institution', *American Journal of Sociology*, 83: 55–77.

Meyer, J., Kamens, D. and Benavot, A. (1992) *School Knowledge for the Masses: World Models and National Primary Curricular Categories for the Twentieth Century*, Brighton: Falmer Press.

Moore, R. (2007) *The Sociology of Knowledge and Education*, London: Continuum Press.

Nash, R. (2009) 'The school curriculum, theories of reproduction and necessary knowledge', in Daniels, H., Lauder, H. and Porter, J. (eds) *Knowledge, Values and Educational Policy: A Critical Perspective*, London: Routledge.

Peters, M., Britez, R. and Bulut, E. (2010) *Cybernetic Capitalism, Informationalism and Cognitive Labour*, Urbana-Champaign, IL: School of Education, University of Illinois.

Rizvi, F. and Lingard, B. (2010) *Globalizing Education Policy*, London: Routledge.

Rothon, C. (2008) 'Women, men and social class revisited: An assessment of the utility of a "combined" scheme in the context of minority ethnic educational achievement in Britain', *Sociology*, 42(4): 691–708.

Rothstein, R. (2010) *Is Education on the Wrong Track?* Washington: Economic Policy Institute, 24 March.

Sennet, R. and Cobb, J. (1972) *The Hidden Injuries of Class*, New York: Norton.

Schofer, E. and Meyer, J. (2005) 'The worldwide expansion of higher education in the twentieth century', *American Sociological Review*, 70 (Dec): 898–920.

Tate, J. (2001) 'National varieties of standardization', in Hall, P. and Soskice, D. (eds) *Varieties of Capitalism: The Institutional Foundations of Comparative Advantage*, New York: Oxford University Press.

Torrance, H. (2006) 'Globalizing empiricism: What if anything can be learned from international comparisons of educational achievement?', in Lauder, H., Brown, P., Dillabough, J.-A. and Halsey, A.H. (eds) *Education, Globalization and Social Change*, Oxford: Oxford University Press.

Young, M. (2008) *Bringing Knowledge Back In*, London: Routledge.

Young, M. (2009) 'What are schools for?', in Daniels, H., Lauder, H. and Porter, J. (eds) *Knowledge, Values and Educational Policy: A Critical Perspective*, London: Routledge.

Part I

The 'knowledge economy' and education

2 Globalisation, risk and regulation

The financial crisis and the prospects for sustainability

Ankie Hoogvelt

A note on methodology

The title of this chapter suggests a rather wide ambit. Therefore, I would like to start with a note on methodology. After all it is the task of any scientist, including social scientists, to apply a certain *discipline* to the organisation of data and information.

I have always held the view that the Marxist method of historical materialism is the most appropriate conceptual tool for analysing, tracking, and indeed even predicting, the likely course of capitalist development both national and global. But along with neo-Gramscians like Robert Cox (1981) and other post-structuralist Marxists, for example Regulation theorists (e.g. Lipietz, 1987, cf. Hoogvelt, 2001a, *passim* p.115), I suggest that we break with the 'determinism' of historical materialism, and hold that, contrary to what Marx said, the future of capitalism is *not* a foregone conclusion, that there is no inevitability about the historical process, and that alternative scenarios *are* possible. Nor are we humans helplessly, if teleologically, caught up in the maelstrom of history. We do have free will and in specific local and historical struggles choices can be made.

Even so, the two great merits of the method of historical materialism is that, first, it identifies the principle of the dialectic as a source of transformative changes between sequential world orders. By 'dialectic' I simply mean 'contradictions'. We must search for contradictions in social life as the main spring of social change. And second, because it is a method that says that of all the millions of contradictions in social life, the most important ones in moving history are those related to *the social forces shaped by production relations*. This is a mouthful that tends to stump the uninitiated but simply put it means that we have to look at the way production is organised, time and again – in each epoch or phase of the development of capitalism, around new material or social inventions and technologies. It is these *forces* of production that not only shape the *relations* between capital and labour, between producers and consumers, and between different segments of capital, but through these *relations* that in turn generate a whole architecture of laws and norms, institutions, and values, and even ideologies or worldviews.

It has been the merit of the Regulation School that they have added to this historical method the twin concepts of 'regime of accumulation' and 'mode of regulation', along with the understanding that a relatively stable regime of accumulation has to do with balancing both production and consumption *at the level of the international economy as a whole*, and that in turn such stability can only materialize if it becomes embedded in an appropriate 'mode of regulation'. 'Regulation' in the original French meaning of the term describes a much broader canvas of norms and institutions and social practices than the narrow English preoccupation with government regulation. However, for the purposes of this chapter, and since I am focused on the financial crisis, I too will use the term regulation in the restricted sense of government regulation, although this includes the various forms of legislation that have deregulated markets and transferred responsibility for conduct in these markets to voluntary and 'self-regulatory' bodies.

The classic example that the reader will be familiar with is the crisis-ridden transition from the post-war Fordist mode of production to the neo-liberal post-Fordist or flexible regimes of accumulation that occurred in the 1970s. While the former had necessitated domestic mass consumerism in the developed world and hence had become embedded in a 'mode of regulation' characterised by Keynesian welfare institutions, progressive union legislation and social market sentiments wrapped up in a worldview of universalism and collective social responsibility, the latter, as Bob Jessop (1994) has succinctly summarised, engendered a supply-side orientated Schumpetarian workfare state, that displaced welfarism and promoted inter-nation competition, and used social policy instruments *not* to generalize norms of mass consumption but rather to encourage flexibility and niche marketing for elite consumption on a global scale. Furthermore, in the higher realm of worldviews, the post-Fordist mode of regulation emphasised individual responsibility and self-interest as essential paragons in an economic model that offered up General Equilibrium Theory as the foundation of self-correcting markets, including financial markets. In this narrative even the speculative excesses of individual agents were thought to cause merely 'random' deviations of actual prices from the general equilibrium. In a final confirmation of the hegemonic credo of this 'market fundamentalism', Nobel prizes were awarded to leading lights of the Efficient Market Hypothesis School, such as Milton Friedman, and others who had devised spuriously precise mathematical models of risk calculations and trading techniques (cf. Chancellor, 2000 p.243; Soros, 2008, p.73). All of this comes under the heading of a 'mode of regulation'.

A final methodological point to make regarding the historical method is that it has heuristic value in so far as it allows one to understand the dialectic and diachronic unfolding of world orders as a sequence of crises and solutions in which the solutions to one crisis always harbour the seeds of the next. Thus my main thesis in this chapter is that globalisation was part and parcel of the post-Fordist regime of accumulation that came out of the crisis of the Fordist regime that preceded it and which collapsed in the early 1970s, and that this current financial crisis, in its turn, is the outcome of what was effectively part of the solution to that preceding crisis.

Globalisation

Thus, the current financial crisis is happening, quintessentially because of globalisation, and not because of the US sub-prime mortgage market which was only a 'minor hitch that triggered it off', as Samir Amin once put it in an interview (Amin, 2008). Now it is pretty much commonplace to observe that this crisis is a global crisis because of the 'global village' character of the world economy; that is to say everybody knows that financial markets are integrated, that banks and corporations are interlinked all over the world, and therefore a fire raging in one part of the world immediately affects another and a stock market crash on Wall Street is echoed within hours in Hong Kong or Tokyo. But that is not the point I am making.

What I am saying is that the financial crisis was born out of the fundamental character of globalisation itself. Run-of-the-mill definitions of globalisation typically refer to an increase of international trade in goods and services, the internationalisation of production and real investments, the increased integration of financial markets and a high degree of policy convergence among countries (WTO, 1998, p.35; Sakbani, 2008, p.3) but such definitions do not distinguish between the accumulation and the regulatory aspects of globalisation, and at best only describe symptoms or aspects of it. But what is it fundamentally? What is at its core?

Following Manuel Castells (1996) and other sociologists (Harvey, 1989; Giddens, 1990) I would argue that globalisation is fundamentally connected to the ascendancy of real time over clock time, or *time/space compression*. The technological innovation which spurred this time/space compression was the fusion of telecommunications and information technology, usually referred to as ICT. This fusion can be timed precisely to the beginning of the 1980s. This information revolution broke down barriers between geographically dispersed markets, thereby giving rise to virtually instantaneous, electronic trading in financial markets. As we shall see below, the information revolution also proved to be an important spur to the *securitisation* of markets (where debts are pooled together and sold on to third parties) because it reduced the need for a direct relationship between borrower and lender, and the systematic treatment of large amounts of data on the creditworthiness of individual firms made it possible for more borrowers to enter the market (UNCTC, 1988, p.106).

The ascendancy of real time over clock time meant that the core dichotomy between capital and labour was fundamentally altered, with capital operating in real time and labour continuing in clock time. Capital hence could escape into the hyperspace of pure circulation, while labour dissolved its collective entity into infinite variations of individual existences. In other words, it disappeared as a social force. Under conditions of the globalised informational economy capital became globally coordinated while labour became individualised, as Castells put it (Castells 1996, p.476).

Within capital, furthermore, it is the financial sector in its pure monetary form that has moved along furthest in respect of 'real-time' (or, if you like, electronic) transactions, and this means in turn that this sector has come to dominate and direct all other sectors, literally sucking the life blood out of them as profits made in the lower sectors of clock-time commerce and investments are siphoned off into the hyperspace of pure circulation. I remember being very awed when it was first reported sometime in the late 1980s that first the automaker Porsche, and subsequently nearly every other industrial corporation, was making more money in the money markets than from producing cars or widgets or whatever. When we first heard of it we were quite astounded to hear that companies and local authorities and even NGOs would park real monies that would pay for wages and workers overnight in the Tokyo money markets to come back in time the next day to serve as working capital. These days, of course, all that is commonplace. Thus, as Castells concludes, the annihilation and manipulation of time by electronically managed global capital markets are the source of new forms of devastating economic crises (Castells, 1996, pp.436–437).

Let us have a few statistical data to exemplify what I mean.

In a very rough sketch, imagine one of those sight-seeing balloons, with a basket carrying real people underneath. Imagine this basket represents the 'real' world economy including the total of international trade. In 2007 this basket was worth some US$55 trillion (IMF, 2008, p.185). The World Bank reckons that in that year international trade, including merchandise and commercial services trade, amounted to about 54 per cent of world GDP (World Bank, 2006). We put that inside the basket. Total capital flows, direct and portfolio investments, came to roughly US$18 trillion (IMF, 2008, p.182). Let us imagine these to be the ropes that connect the basket to the balloon.

Now, look at the balloon itself. The bottom part of the balloon is still, however tenuously, attached to the basket of the real world economy, consisting of the global sum total of bonds, equities and bank assets, which in 2007 came to some US$230 trillion or just over four times the size of world GDP (ibid., p.185). Now go even further up into the stratosphere of pure money circulation in the top five-sevenths of the balloon where we encounter first the global financial derivatives market with a (notional value) of about US$600 trillion in 2007 (ibid. p.186), or about 11 times the total value of the world economy, and finally the foreign exchange markets where daily turnover averages out on an annual basis of over US$1000 trillion or 20 times the world GDP (BIS, 2007, p.1). These are not precise figures, even though I have taken them from the International Monetary Fund and the Bank for International Settlements. They will include some double counting and overlap. But at least it will give a flavour of the relative magnitudes involved.

Financial markets, boom and bust

How did we get to this point where money careens around the world in a frenzy of credit creation?

In a most entertaining book on the history of financial speculation, *Devil Takes the Hindmost*, Edward Chancellor describes how almost every transaction, however speculative, or even corrupt and outright fraudulent, that we witness today in the financial markets was known from the days that stock markets first emerged in seventeenth-century Amsterdam. When the stock market first arrived in the coffee houses of 'Exchange Alley' in London in the 1690s it was referred to as Dutch finance, and gambling was its essence (Chancellor, 2000, p.44).

Futures (or as they were called in those days 'time-bargains'), options and margin calls (where loans were made against the collateral of stock) and short selling were used right from the word go. In those days speculating on stocks was simply seen as an extension of the favourite pastime of betting. It was a popular, indeed plebeian, pursuit, frequently led by a breed of unprincipled and self-seeking characters – the so-called moneyed men – who turned the financial innovations of the day to their personal advantage; not unlike what happens today. What started out as pure gambling in the adrenaline-fuelled pursuit of risk and excitement swiftly morphed into a rational analysis of risk and probability in which the assumption of risk and the reward for offsetting risk became a rational undertaking. Soon it became legitimated in a liberal ideology in which 'self interest replaced the noblesse oblige and former vices of avarice and consumption were seen as having beneficial economic effects' (ibid., p.33). All this as early as the turn of the eighteenth century.

By the nineteenth century the prevailing liberal consensus had hit on the concept of 'efficient markets' in which speculation was benignly viewed in the words of one contemporary testifying to a legislative committee as a 'method for adjusting differences of opinion as to future values, whether of products or of stocks. It regulates production by instantly advancing prices when there is scarcity, thereby stimulating production and by depressing prices when there is over production' (Henry Clews quoted in Chancellor, 2000, p.187). In the twentieth century this liberal ideology attained the still more elevated status of Economic Science in the work of the 'Efficient Market Hypothesis' school (led by Milton Friedman), which held that financial prices tend towards equilibrium and when actual prices do deviate from a theoretical equilibrium it is only ever in a ' random' manner. The key postulate of the theory namely 'perfect knowledge' was thought to be satisfied in the age of electronic information. Several adherents to this faith received Nobel prizes. In such a beautiful world the activities of speculators are seen as neither irrational in motivation nor destabilising in effect. Hardly surprising that by the late twentieth century the EMH had become the working ideology of financial capitalism. It had become 'holy writ' in the words of the world's topmost financer, Warren Buffett, who, however, himself was not convinced (Chancellor, 2000, *passim* pp.242–243).

Chancellor also takes us through the history of all the booms and busts that have blotted the landscape of capitalist progress through the centuries. From the Tulip Fever in Amsterdam in the mid-1630s, and the South Sea Bubble in London in 1720s, through the first Latin American debt crisis (1820s), through all the manias of the nineteenth century (the canal mania, the railway mania, the mining mania), to the depression of 1929, and beyond, to the stock market crashes of the late twentieth century. What is striking, as Chancellor never tires of pointing out, are the obvious similarities in these boom and bust cycles despite the minor differences which are historically specific. And he quotes Kindleberger: 'details proliferate, structure abides'. A boom always commences with some innovation or new product or technology that promises increased profitability; it is followed by positive feedback when more and more inexperienced investors join the fray; it results in euphoria, mania even, when the enthusiasm spreads to other classes of assets; next, investors leverage their gains by piling in more and more debt against collateral, credit becomes overextended, swindling and fraud proliferate; and then there is sudden panic when the tide turns and assets have to be sold in a hurry to meet margin calls, followed by a crash and economic contraction. Periods of speculative mania are forever followed by anti-speculative regulation when governments wake up and rein in whichever financial fad or gimmick is seen to have caused the excesses.

And so, if history just repeats itself, the question arises, how dare I think that this crisis is different? Different, not merely as in a different order of magnitude because now it is global, but different as in *systemic*? Systemic in a way that cannot be put right by government regulation, even if – and it is a big if – intergovernment cooperation, such as is earnestly being attempted in present-day world economic summits, succeeds in the limited objectives of oversight and coordination that are formulated?

The political geography of risk

One hardy perennial in mainstream narratives of capitalist crises is a stubborn refusal to take account of the political arena in which these crises occur. The economic sphere is forever depicted as some independent realm in which individuals go about their rational self-seeking business without much interference from political authorities or collective concern for political goals. For sure there is often plenty of critique and condemnation of individual instances of corruption, and of manipulation and venality by members of the political class, but rarely does one find a conception of the way the economic arena is importantly structured by political interests of classes or groups of people, and in the international arena by *power relations between states*.

Even if one were to argue that, in the past at least, most financial and commercial transactions occurred within the national territorial context (although this too is arguable, see below), it is still surprising that in the contemporary era when clearly by far the fastest growing markets are the international currency markets (with a turnover of US$3.1 trillion *per day!*) the political terrain of currency competition between states is largely ignored. And yet, the right to print currency, and set interest rates, is probably the last remaining seigniorial right of the sovereign state. Amending Manuel Castells' important dictum that in the era of globalisation, the power of flows overtakes the flows of power, my second thesis is that today, the international currency markets are the terrain where the power of flows do not overtake but *collide* with the flows of power.

Let us look a bit closer at the origin of the international credit and currency markets.

International credit flows, in the form of international direct investments and portfolio lending (bank lending – and bond issuance) have existed for a long time. The period of formal colonialism, especially between 1875 and 1914, witnessed an extraordinary and globe-girding internationalisation of capital when a handful of countries in Europe together with the USA were responsible for 85 per cent of all international lending, totalling, by 1913, US$44 billion. As the distinguished economic historian Alex Cairncross observed:

> It was symptomatic of the period, that western Europe had invested abroad almost as much as the entire national wealth of Great Britain, the leading industrial country, and a good deal more than the value of the capital physically located in Great Britain.
>
> (Cairncross, 1975, p.3)

Now credit of course, as the root of the word reminds us, means credo, or faith. Where did the faith and confidence for these far flung international transactions come from? In no small measure it came from the political power and force that accompanied it. That was what the gunboat diplomacy of the early pre-colonial period (the Dutch East India trading company, VOC, had a private army of 10,000 men) and then the territorial annexations of the colonial period was all about. It was about establishing worldwide economic and financial relations by force. Moreover, during the colonial period, the mother countries established 'monetary zones' (the sterling area, the franco zone) in their dependencies where the value of the currency was linked to the mother currency and colonial reserves were kept in the mother country's central bank. There was not much need, therefore, for hedging against either commercial or currency risk!

After the end of World War II, when the USA and her allies emerged victorious, the colonial system was dismantled, while on the eve of the end of the war, the international conference at Bretton Woods in 1944 had established a monetary order to fix exchange rates. It is a well known story. The two intellectuals who drafted the settlement, the Brit, John Maynard Keynes, and the American, Harry Dexter White, agreed on many things but diverged on some crucial issues: where Keynes wanted a world currency, the Bancor, against which all national currencies would be exchangeable at fixed rates, and an International Clearing Union, a kind of world central bank, White proposed the use of the dollar – at fixed parity against gold – and the International Monetary Fund as a stabilisation fund. The American view held sway. For a while, under the aegis of this American imperial system, international trade and investments proceeded, indeed expanded, relatively smoothly. But over time this historical settlement was brought down by its own contradictions. The de facto 'dollar standard' led over time to an overvaluation of the dollar, and a massive outflow of American capital. The consequent prolonged US balance of payments deficit thus became a principal source of international liquidity and gave rise to 'offshore' or 'eurodollar' markets. The practical impossibility of reverting these offshore dollars into 'native' dollars, due to the restrictions of the Bretton Woods agreement, which precluded a reassessment of the value of the dollar, and political/diplomatic pressures by the US governments on the central banks of Europe, led to speculative movements against the dollar in these markets. By 1971 these speculative movements had reached such crisis proportions that in August of that year the US Government under Nixon, declared the dollar no longer convertible into gold, thereby effectively ending the Bretton Woods exchange regime. A 10 per cent devaluation of the dollar soon followed.

The consequences of this were twofold: on the one hand a tremendous increase in volatility in the international currency markets and on the other, more generally, a huge increase in international credit risk. Companies or banks investing abroad would have to run the whole gauntlet of volatile currencies as well as the commercial risk of dealing with counter parties who could go bust or default in countries where effective legal redress might not be possible. This increase of risk, *over time*, led to the invention of a whole class of new financial instruments, to spread risk, to reduce exposure and to insure against risk, the most important of these being, besides futures and options, currency swaps, interest rate swaps, credit default swaps (CDSs), and collateral debt obligations (CDOs). What began as earnest 'hedging' against risk soon developed into a source of endless speculation and gambling.

First came the currency swaps and currency futures (the first currency futures market was opened in 1972, in Chicago) and later on, from the 1980s when liberalisation and deregulation of financial markets had become established as the new *mode of regulation* worldwide, there developed a huge wizardry of new financial derivatives. A financial derivative at bottom is a security created by *contract*, which derives its value from some underlying asset. For example you take out a futures contract on a commodity, like oil, and the contract says you promise to take delivery of this oil at a certain date for a certain price. If the price is higher than what you bid for you lose, if it is lower you win. Since you only have to make a down payment of say about 5 per cent at the time of the contract, you just gamble on being lucky (and in the process become part of the credit creating process). In the past there was a legal distinction between pure gambling (in which there is always settlement in cash) and derivatives where you were supposed to always take delivery in the specified commodity, but part of the 'deregulation' of financial markets was that this legal distinction was abandoned. So you can now take out a contract on an interest rate (which in any event is physically impossible to deliver), or on the future price of a Renoir painting, and you do not take delivery of the interest rate or the Renoir painting. There is a cash settlement at the end of it rather than the transfer of the asset. In consequence there is no longer a difference between gambling and derivative trading.

A subsequent development was *securitisation*. Securitisation simply means loan selling. It is really about turning debts into assets and selling the fixed income (interest payments flowing from them) on to third parties. The elegant idea behind it is that by pooling debts, such as mortgages or car loans and credit card loans and company start up loans, into bonds and parcelling them out in little chunks you can de-link borrowers from lenders and spread the risk of all these debts over a wide political geography. And you can hide the poor risks underneath the better performing loans. This is the origin of the much decried CDOs. They became really big in the 1990s; at the height of the sub-prime mortgage disaster, the size of the CDO global market was estimated anywhere between US$500 billion and US$2 trillion.

The political economy of the currency markets

Now let us bring the power of states into this soup of global credit flows. Hard on the heels of the end of the Bretton Woods era came the oil shock of 1973, when the OPEC countries formed a successful cartel of oil-producing countries and increased the price of oil fourfold. Now why did they do this at exactly that time? Mainstream economic discourse, which habitually underplays the political context, cannot offer a satisfactory explanation. But documentary evidence uncovered by writers standing in the critical Marxist tradition who are more attuned to the interplay between politics and economics have come up with an altogether plausible version of events that places the blame not at OPEC's door but on the Nixon administration which was desperate to regain control over the global money markets and safeguard the interests of American capital (cf. Fitt *et al.*, 1979; Engdahl, 1992; Gowan, 1999).

By the time of the Bretton Woods collapse, there were about three times as many dollars circulating outside the USA than in. To prevent these dollars coming back in and causing intolerable inflation inside the USA something had to be done about this 'dollar overhang' as it was called. The solution was to give these foreign dollars something to do that would create demand for them and force all states to keep the dollar as a reserve currency even in the absence of the now defunct Bretton Woods monetary system. The Nixon administration was planning to get OPEC to greatly increase its oil prices a full two years before OPEC did so and for the US private banks to recycle the petrodollars when OPEC finally did take US advice and jack up oil prices (Gowan, 1999, p.21). The scheme was ingeniously devised by Henry Kissinger, then Secretary of State and a good friend of the Shah of Iran (the Chairman of OPEC at the time). Kissinger's scheme would kill not one or two but three or even four birds with one stone. First it would solve the dollar overhang because oil transactions had always been settled in dollars and a deal signed in 1974, when Kissinger established the US–Saudi Joint Commission on European Cooperation, ensured that not only they would do so in the future, but that any surplus of oil price increases would be invested in US treasury bonds, stocks and mutual/hedge funds (Fouskas and Gokay, 2005). Next it would deal a hopefully fatal blow to the challenges posed to US imperialism by the European states and Japan who were a serious competitive challenge, but who were much more dependent on imported oil than the USA was at the time. Third it would give the OPEC countries the necessary surplus dollars to endlessly buy US military equipment (which they duly did – the Yom Kippur war in 1973 providing a convenient excuse) and finally it would help the – at that time – dominant US oil companies who needed an instant increase in revenues. So this was a brilliantly clever scheme and there is enough evidence today to suggest that this is exactly what happened. William Engdahl reports that corroboration for this thesis was provided a few years ago in an interview with no one less than Sheikh Yamani, oil minister of Saudi Arabia at that time: 'King Faisal sent me to the Shah of Iran who said: "Why are you against the increase in the price of oil? That is what they want? Ask Henri Kissinger – he is the one who wants a higher price"' (Engdahl, 2008a).

So out of the demise of the Bretton Woods system came a US strategy for regaining reserve status for the dollar and US hegemony in the world monetary order. The US administration understood the way in which the US state could use expanding private financial markets (post Bretton Woods) 'as a political multiplier of the impact of US Treasury moves with the dollar'. In this way, what Peter Gowan has referred to as the 'Dollar-Wall Street Regime' was born (Gowan, 1999, p.21). Globalisation and the freeing of international financial markets from 'financial repression', as the Nixon administration referred to it, became key to preserving the privileged global position of the USA. The change was summed up by Helleiner as a shift from direct power over other states to a more market-based or 'structural' form of power (Helleiner, 1995 in Gowan, 1999, *passim* p.23).

While globalisation, with the attendant policies of deregulation and liberalisation of financial markets, not only put the international financial markets at the apex of global capitalism, it also vastly increased international trade and foreign investments in hitherto inaccessible areas of the world, including China. Here is not the place to go into the emergence of the Washington Consensus (late 1970s) and the role played by international financial institutions like the World Bank, the IMF and the WTO in the imposition of open-door policies on indebted developing countries; that is for another occasion. All I want to say here is that, as before, what was a solution to one crisis in turn sowed the seeds for the next. There is no doubt that, at the level of economic fundamentals, globalisation was successful in spurring the growth of East Asia and China, thereby giving a new lease of life to a moribund world capitalism, but – in so doing – also created the foundation of a counter hegemonic pole, a rivalling centre that will ultimately challenge the dominance of the USA.

At the level of economic fundamentals, the success of China's export-led development eventually created the same problems of overproduction that has plagued the world capitalist economy since its inception. Which new markets can be found now?

At the same time, the continuing reserve status of the US dollar in international markets allowed the US to run a balance of payment deficit that was time and again plugged by its more successful competitors, particularly in Asia, for whose exports the American consumer provided by far the largest market. The USA is their biggest customer, and until recently Americans were spending the equivalent of 6 per cent of their annual output on imports. And the money for this was being furnished by the same people who sold them the goods. First Japan and then China came to hold vast dollar reserves and effectively became the USA's bankers. At the time of the 2008 crash Japan held US\$1.197 billion in US bonds and treasury bills and China US\$922 billion (Bulard, 2008). But this presented an unprecedented and unsustainable contradiction in the present world order because, as Engdahl (2006) points out, there is nothing now to back up this US reserve status except naked military power. The neo-conservative cabal that ran the Bush administration understood this perfectly and opted for a strategy of massive expansion of US military bases worldwide, including military encirclement of China. The Pentagon's New Strategic Defense Document of 2005 explicitly fingered China as a potential enemy. It says: '... The US military ... is seeking to dissuade rising powers, such as China, from challenging US military dominance' (Chossudovsky, 2005, p.4).

It is rumoured that when the Bush administration did the unthinkable and bailed out the mortgage giants Fannie Mac and Freddie May, it was after a phone call from the Chinese president, Hin Juntao, in which he threatened Bush that if they were not rescued, China would stop buying US treasury bills (Bulard, 2008, p.1). And so, China and the USA are well and truly like prisoners in a chain gang shackled to each other – but it is a most dangerous chain gang in which one prisoner holds, for the moment, the military trump card.

Hedge funds: instruments of financial warfare?

Hedge funds are private wealth funds that invest not in stocks or bonds directly but mainly in financial derivatives of all kinds, like currency futures and interest rate swaps and credit default swaps.

Even if one generously and innocently surmises that when hedge funds first appeared on the scene during the volatile currency heydays of the 1970s they provided a useful function in arbitraging risks in the currency markets, their subsequent exponential growth soon transformed them into becoming betting syndicates for the super rich.

The amounts of money they handle are mind bogglingly large because with the monies at their disposal they can leverage ever more monies in from banks and other financial institutions for their speculative activities. Already in the mid-1990s a study by the IMF (Vrolijk, 1997) estimated that hedge funds in the foreign exchange derivatives market could mobilise up to US\$1 trillion to bet against currencies in speculative attacks. That is sufficient to wreck the currencies, the financial markets and the economies of most countries, as was the case during the Asian crisis of 1997/8. In the mid-2000s there were about 10,000 hedge funds around the world with assets under management (AUM) amounting to US\$2.5 trillion (Chan, 2007). Hedge funds trade in risk and they are completely unregulated, partly because regulators like the Financial Services Authority and the US Securities & Exchange Commission (SEC) by their own admission do not understand them and partly because the regulators have for political reasons decided to collude with the wild frontiers of modern-day finance (Bush, 2006). Engdahl has turned up an interesting fact laid bare at a Congressional hearing that points to a political stratagem:

> In recent testimony under oath, Mr Lynn Turner, Chief Accountant of the Securities & Exchange Commission (SEC) testified that the SEC Office of Risk Management which had oversight responsibility for the Credit Default Swap market, an exotic market worth nominally $62 trillion, was cut in Administration 'budget cuts' from a staff of one hundred people down to one person. Yes that was not a typo. One as in 'uno.'
>
> Vermont Democratic Congressman Peter Welsh queried Turner, '... was there a systematic depopulating of the regulatory force so that it was impossible actually for regulation to occur if you have one person in that office? ... and then I understand that 146 people were cut from the enforcement division of the SEC, is that what you also testified to?' Mr. Turner, in Congressional testimony replied, 'Yes ... I think there has been a systematic gutting, or whatever you want to call it, of the agency and it's capability through cutting back of staff.'
>
> (Engdah, 2008b)

To argue that hedge funds may be used and have been in the recent past (for example during the Asia crisis of 1998) as instruments of statecraft begs three important questions: collusion, political coordination and intentionality.

The official neo-liberal consensus has always been that no one speculator can engineer structural shifts in prices on financial markets because there are so many players and they all act rationally in their own interest, playing against each other in a zero-sum game. This for a start ignores the contagion effect, or 'momentum' trading as it is now called, as when one large speculator may, for example, off load the yen, which prompts other smaller participants to follow suit driving the price of the yen even further down, allowing the first to withdraw from his position, taking a profit. But more importantly it ignores the concentration of financial firepower within the hedge fund community. According to an IMF study in 1997 just ten hedge funds at that time handled 75 per cent of the business in the financial centres of the USA, London and Canada (where nearly all worldwide hedge fund activity takes place anyway). And these ten worked very closely together and were dominated by the US funds (Vrolijk, 1997). Given the evident cross-staffing and the shared social milieu of the top political and economic elites (the outgoing US Treasury secretary Hank Paulson was one time Chief Executive of Goldman Sachs) it beggars belief that the highest and mightiest would not discuss common political/economic interests. At a charitable minimum, and to avoid the charge of conspiracy theory, one might say that they would have what is sometimes called 'group think' or 'pensée unique' as the French call it.

But what exactly are these common interests? In the aftermath of the Asian crisis of 1997 one could surmise (Gowan, 1999, ch. 6; Hoogvelt, 2001a, pp.232 ff) that the Clinton administration had felt threatened by the competitive challenge of the East Asian emerging economies and was sufficiently irked by the financial regulations in place in those countries to want to unleash the destructive power of the hedge funds, and next engineer a rescue package duly implemented by the IMF that attached a structural reform agenda opening previously closed financial and economic sectors to international capital. And so it came to pass. Whether there was strategic planning on the part of the Clinton administration *prior* to the crisis, or merely a strategic handling of the crisis in the interest of deepening and furthering American dominated globalisation is not really what matters. What matters is that the fall of East Asia was both opportunistically and strategically seized upon by the USA to reoccupy the economic high ground, and that an alternative scenario involving a proposed Japanese led Asian Monetary Fund was scuppered, because the USA relied on Japan's and other East Asian dollar hold-ings which might have been sold to finance such a fund. Scuppered, too, was the consolidation of regional integration that such a fund would have implied (cf. Hoogvelt 2001a, pp.236/7).

The question for the immediate future is whether the US authorities can or will play the same financial strategic game in relation to China whose currency – and financial markets – are still relatively shielded from the fall out of the global financial collapse because of its independent and restrictive national regulatory framework. It is certainly interesting to note that the two architects of the Asian crisis 'rescue' package, namely Larry Summers and R. Rubin, were appointed to Obama's inner circle, and that one of the President-elect's early utterings on for-eign policy was a promise to tackle China on its currency policy.

Regulation and sustainability

The term 'sustainability' has two quite diverse meanings. The first refers to the ability of the world capitalist system to overcome its recurrent crises and renew itself. The other refers to environmental sustainability for the planet as a whole. It has been clear for some time that capitalist progress and environmental sustain-ability are at loggerheads. On all fronts – climate change, depletion of the earth's resources, and systemic exclusion of the mass of the world's population – capital-ism in its present stage of globalisation is unsustainable (Woodin and Lucas, 2004; Hoogvelt, 2007).

At the time of this article appearing in print, the combined intervention by the world's leading economies has – on the surface – rescued world capitalism from immediate collapse by shifting the burden of debt from the financial superstruc-ture to the base. By bailing out the banks, governments have shifted private debt to sovereign debt. Austerity programmes and public budget cuts bear down on taxpayers, consumers, house owners, wage earners, the jobless and welfare clai-mants. The price for financial wizardry and irresponsibility is being paid by ordi-nary people in the real economies throughout the Western world. With sovereign defaults imminent and relentless inflation about to play havoc with the world's currencies, it is clear that there is so far no plan B, other than a pious hope that the still resilient emerging economies of the East will pull world capitalism away from the abyss.

A prolonged collapse and depression, while bringing wrenching adjustment problems in the immediate and medium term, would nevertheless also open up real spaces for the emergence of alternative forms of social and economic organisation that meet the demands of both social justice and ecological balance. It is at the very moment, or historical juncture, when these spaces are opened up that collective social and political struggles have their best chance of success. So which are these real spaces that are opening up? Here I sketch out just a few.

Localisation

The first and most important one is *localisation*. The next worldwide credit crunch and recession will put paid, hopefully, to the more extreme forms of international trade – as when goods and services that are perfectly capable of being produced locally travel great distances to reach our supermarkets. I am thinking of German cow's milk going first to Greece to be turned into yoghurt before travelling back to our supermarkets, or pigs from Taiwan being processed as pork in Holland to end up via Italy as 'Parma ham' on our shelves. Green beans from Ethiopia or onions from America. Flowers from Kenya, and so on. Elsewhere I have formulated an economic principle of subsidiarity as a basis for a hierarchical ordering of international trade and a transaction cost principle to replace market-based competitive pricing (Hoogvelt, 2001b). In *Green Alternatives to Globalisation: A Manifesto*, Michael Woodin and Caroline Lucas (Woodin and Lucas, 2004, p.111) describe numerous examples of already existing local alternatives and they point out that the beauty of such schemes is that they can be introduced from the grassroots and piecemeal rather than requiring some massive bureaucratic, internationally agreed, top-down reform programme.

Investing in alternative energy and infrastructure

A second space lies in the interstices between on the one hand the instinctive readiness of national governments to return to Keynesian spending programmes and, on the other, the choice as to where such investment should be directed. There is an urgent need to target investment on green energy and infrastructure. At the present time governments dither and differ in their approach to Keynesian stimulus packages, opting either for putting money directly into consumers' pockets through tax cutting measures (United Kingdom) or creating jobs by investing in massive infrastructural projects (France, Germany). On the campaign trail, President-elect Obama proposed creating jobs in green infrastructure and energy. Here is a space where real choices can be made and collective political pressure can be applied to good effect.

Inward looking development strategies

The bigger developing countries with a potential of mass domestic demand have every reason to re-examine the merits of inward-looking development strategies that were in many cases – and certainly for a time – broadly successful in the 1950s and 60s. These strategies lost favour owing to the combined onslaught of the forces of globalisation and political arm-twisting through the Washington Consensus. While the neo-liberal dominated press has generally uncritically accepted spurious statistics of growth associated with export-led development strategies and so-called open door policies, in my view the case of growth with distribution has yet to be proven (Hoogvelt, 2007, pp.21–28). On the contrary, generally such policies have turned out to be systemically exclusionary. In a sign that the loss of export markets may herald a new more inclusive era, the Chinese authorities have already announced far-reaching agrarian reforms to stimulate domestic-led demand and growth.

Other positives include the release of the better brains and smart thinking from the clutches of greed-fuelled private financial markets to the more humble domain of public servitude – as when the financial contraction brings about the shedding of clever staff with nowhere else to go.

These are just a few of the positive changes that may come out of this crisis. The list could be longer but it all depends on political will and imagination, and popular anger; a popular anger that feeds from the realisation that for thirty years we have allowed ourselves to be conned by a false ideology masquerading as economic science and an abuse of power that went with it.

References

Amin, S. (2008) 'The new challenge of the peoples internationalism', interview with *L'Humanite* (cf. mikeely.wordpress.com/2008/11/07).

Bank for International Settlements (September 2007) *Triennial Central Bank Survey of Foreign Exchange and Derivatives Market Activity in April 2007 – Preliminary Global Results*. www.bis.org/pub/rpfx07.htm (accessed 21 November 2008).

Bulard, M. (2008) 'Financial realities after the dollar', *Le Monde Diplomatique*, November.

Bush, J. (2006) 'Sell-Out: Why Hedge Funds will Destroy the World', *New Statesman*, 31 July, pp.26–29.

Cairncross, A.K. (1975) *Home and Foreign Investment*, New York: Harvester Press.

Castells, M. (1996) *The Rise of the Network Society*, Oxford: Blackwell.

Chan, K.C. (2007) 'Hong Kong: Hedge fund hub of Asia', *speech by the Secretary for Financial Services and the Treasury at the 5th Annual Hedge Funds Conference*, 11 December, Hong Kong.

Chancellor, E. (2000) *Devil Take the Hindmost: A History of Financial Speculation*, New York: Penguin.

Chossudovski, M. (2005) 'New undeclared arms race: America's agenda for global military domination', www.global research.ca/articles/CHO503A.html.

Cox, R. (1981) 'Social forces, states and world orders: Beyond international relations theory', *Millennium: Journal of International Studies*, 10(2): 126–155.

Engdahl, W. (1992) *A Century of War – Anglo American Oil Politics and the New World Order*, London: Pluto Press.

Engdahl, W. (2006) 'No, the Iranian oil bourse is not a casus belli', www.globalrese arch.ca/articleid=2076 (accessed 15 March 2006).

Engdahl, W. (2008a) 'The fake oil crisis of 1973', www.engdahl.oilgeopolitics.net/1973_Oil_shock/1973 (accessed 1 December 2008).

Engdahl, W (2008b) 'Behind the panic: Financial warfare over future of global bank power', www.engdahl.oilgeop0oltics.net/2008.

Fitt, Y., Faire, A. and Vigier, P. (1979) *The World Economic Crisis*, London: Zed Press.

Fouskas, V.K. and Gokay, B. (2005) *The New American Imperialism: Bush's War on Terror and Blood for Oil*, Westport, CT: Praeger.

Giddens, A. (1990) *The Consequences of Modernity*, Cambridge: Polity Press.

Gowan, P. (1999) *The Global Gamble: Washington's Faustian Bid for World Dominance*, London: Verso.

Harvey, D. (1989) *The Condition of Postmodernity*, Oxford: Basil Blackwell.

Helleiner, E. (1995) 'Explaining globalization of financial markets: Bringing states back in', *Review of International Political Economy*, 2: 2.

Hoogvelt, A. (2001a) *Globalization and the Post Colonial World*, London: Palgrave.

Hoogvelt, A. (2001b) 'Globalisation and localisation: Applying the subsidiarity principle', *Conference Proceedings of the International Forum on Globalization and Contemporary Capitalism*, Wuhan, China, 2001.

Hoogvelt, A. (2007) 'Globalisation and imperialism: Wars and humanitarian intervention', in Dominelli, L. (ed.) *Revitalising Communities in a Globalising World*, Aldershot: Ashgate, pp.17–42.

International Monetary Fund (IMF) (October 2008) *Global Financial Stability Report*, Statistical Appendix.

Jessop, R. (1994) 'Post-Fordism and the state', in Amin, A. (ed.) *Post-Fordism: A Reader*, Oxford: Basil Blackwell, pp.280–315.

Lipietz, A. (1987) *Mirages and Miracles*, London: Verso.

Sakbahni, M. (2005) 'A re-examination of the architecture of the international economic system in a global setting: Issues and proposals', Research Publication No. 181, Geneva: UNCTAD.

Soros, G. (2008) *The New Paradigm for Financial Markets: The Credit Crisis of 2008 and What it Means*, London: Perseus.

United Nations Conference on Transnational Corporations (UNCTC) (1988) Transnational Corporations in World Development, Trends and Prospects, New York: United Nations.

Vrolijk, C. (1997) 'Derivative effects on monetary transmission', Working Paper WP/ 97/121, Washington: IMF (cited in Gowan, 1999, p.98).

Woodin, M. and Lucas, C. (2004) *Green Alternatives to Globalisation: A Manifesto*, London: Pluto Press.

World Bank (2006) 'World development indicators', wb.worldbank.org/WBSITE/ EXTERNAL/DATASTATISTICS (accessed 12 November 2008).

World Trade Organization, (WTO) (1998) *Annual Report*, Geneva: WTO.

3 The Global Auction Model, Skill Bias Theory and graduate incomes

Reflections on methodology

Hugh Lauder, Phillip Brown and Gerbrand Tholen

A fundamental intellectual task is theory appraisal. Currently, there are two theories on offer that seek to understand the nature of the knowledge economy and to derive empirical consequences in relation to graduate incomes: the Global Auction Model and Skill Bias Theory. The former is a model influenced by political economy while the latter can be seen as squarely within orthodox economics. The radical differences in understanding of the knowledge economy that they offer makes the appraisal crucial to policy makers and potential university students, because they depict quite different fates not only for individuals but for the informal bargain that has been struck between the state and individuals. This is the opportunity bargain by which if the state provides the basis for a good education and individuals commit to education, then they will be rewarded in the knowledge economy. In effect learning = earning.

We begin by sketching the background to the claims made about the knowledge economy, followed by a characterisation of the two theories. In the case of Skill Bias Theory a brief discussion of Human Capital Theory precedes the exposition because it can be seen as a predecessor to Skill Bias Theory. At the same time it has been firmly lodged in the popular imagination in a way in which the potentially more powerful Skill Bias Theory has not. Drawing the connections between these two theories, therefore, is apposite.

It may seem unusual that the authors of one of these models should then write a chapter based in part of an appraisal of their model. We do so for two reasons. To clarify the methodology that we employed: this is important since viewed from orthodox economics the model developed would not just be seen as flawed, it would not be considered at all precisely because it steps outside the methodological strictures of orthodox economics. However, given the significance of the issues raised by these theories, it also seems important to outline the differences in methodology they adopt and the implications these have for theory appraisal. In these respects the chapter is an invitation to a debate.

Background

A central claim made by most governments in developed and developing economies is that education is crucial to global economic competitiveness. This is because they assert that we live in a global knowledge economy in which the key to competitiveness lies in education and in particular higher education. Higher education, it is assumed, can provide the research for innovation and the skills necessary for a knowledge economy. It is further assumed that the demand for knowledge workers will far exceed the numbers now graduating, hence the need for mass higher education systems. For the West, the key to succeeding in the global knowledge economy lies in what was assumed to be the superior systems of innovation and the quality of graduates. These systems would ensure that Western knowledge workers would earn a premium over others because of their superior knowledge and skills. In essence the West would 'win' the global knowledge wars because it had the advantage in knowledge production and application.

One consequence of these assumptions is that the state has struck an informal contract or bargain – the opportunity bargain – with individuals. This bargain turns on the educational resources and support the state will provide in order for individuals to take advantage of the opportunities that the global knowledge economy affords: those that learn, from whatever social background, have the opportunity for upward social mobility. In this respect, education is the key to the promotion of economic development and social justice.

However, in *The Global Auction: The Broken Promises of Education, Jobs and Rewards* (Brown *et al.*, 2011) we identified four trends in education and the labour market which raise fundamental questions about the learning = earning thesis, with profound implications for the politics of the opportunity bargain and the future development of some Western economies, in particular the United States and Britain. These trends are contrary to the predictions made by Skill Bias Theory and hence generate quite different expectations as to the future direction of the knowledge economy or more precisely, in terms of our model, knowledge capitalism.

In what follows we outline the model as the basis for reflections on the methodology underlying it. In turn, this enables us to clarify the conditions for further testing the model and the status of the knowledge claims that would arise from such testing.

The model

The four trends which comprise the model are: the rise of mass higher education systems in developed and developing economies; the revolution in quality *and* price; the introduction of *digital Taylorism*; and the creation of a 'war for talent' (Michaels *et al.*, 2001). When brought together, these trends form a particular account of the global knowledge economy which is capable of generating a set of effects which can contribute to an explanation of the changing relationship between education, jobs and incomes. In what follows we outline the model and discuss how key aspects of this model could be put to the test, drawing on various sources of quantitative data that could be used to assess the strength of support for our thesis. Our model does not depict a 'race to the bottom' but one of increasing polarisation, as many of those at the 'top of their game' continue to operate in a 'forward' auction, typified by a Sotheby's art auction, while many others with graduate qualifications find themselves in a 'reverse' auction in which employers are seeking to reduce their labour costs (Brown *et al.*, 2011: 7) through various strategies including the offshoring of high-skilled employment. Putting the model to the test also permits comparison with competing explanations such as Human Capital and Skill Bias Theories.[1]

The rise in mass higher education

The rapid expansion of higher education in China, along with other emerging economies, has led to a significant increase in the global supply of high-skilled workers. By 2020 China expects to have close to 195 million graduates. The expansion of higher education in India has been less spectacular but it is following an expansionary path. As Manmohan Singh, India's Prime Minster exhorted, 'each one of us must set our sights higher and aim to be the best in what we do. Our schools and colleges must aim to be the best in the world. So too our businesses and laboratories.'

While the available data on participation rates should be treated as indicative, enrolment figures do not tell us how many actually enter the global job market on an annual basis due to high levels of dropouts in some countries. Nevertheless, based on our analysis of enrolment figures for 113 emerging and developed countries, we found that undergraduate and postgraduate enrolments virtually doubled within a decade, from 72.5 million in 1996 to 136.1 million in 2007.

There is, therefore, a good supply of highly qualified Indian, Chinese and Russian workers entering the global labour market in unprecedented numbers, which makes it crucial to understand the fundamental changes occurring in the global economy. Transnational companies (TNCs) now have the capacity to utilise far cheaper skills, challenging the comfortable assumption that graduates in the West will earn a premium because of the quality of their certified knowledge.

Quality and price revolution

Companies have consistently tried to improve quality while reducing their costs. But these attempts have not only been limited by the supply of skilled labour, which has now been resolved, but also because of the problem of delivering high quality goods and services in lower-cost emerging economies. While these issues remain, companies report a rapid narrowing of this quality and productivity gap, which in turn is transforming the way they think about the global supply of talent. The new competition is based on quality and cost, challenging Western assumptions about the inherent competitive advantage of the developed economies for high-skilled, high-value economic activity.

Our research shows how the quality revolution is gathering pace. It highlights the rapidity with which quality standards are improving around the world, making it more difficult for highly qualified workers in developed economies to shelter from the global competition for jobs. But as the performance gap narrows rapidly, differences in labour costs between developed and developing economies are narrowing far more slowly, except in a few hot spots in China and India. Even here there is still a long way to go before the price advantage is seriously eroded. Consequently, companies have greater scope to extract value from international webs of people, processes and suppliers, based on a Dutch or reverse auction where quality is maintained while labour costs go down.

However, there is another potential threat to graduate jobs in the West and this comes from changes in the labour process.

Digital Taylorism

Historically, productivity has not come from allowing people to apply their knowledge and skill but from imposing barriers to individual initiative and control through a detailed division of labour. While the management of knowledge workers poses problems for HR professionals, there is also a major shift to what we called digital Taylorism (Brown *et al.*, 2011). If the era of Fordism, characterised by mechanical Taylorism, involved the transformation of craft work through 'scientific management' (Taylor, 1911; Braverman, 1974), today we are witnessing the translation of knowledge work into working knowledge.

Digital Taylorism enables innovation to be translated into routines that might require some degree of education but not the kind of creativity and independence of judgement that is often associated with the knowledge economy. In order to reduce costs, companies have to move from knowledge work to working knowledge; that is, from the idiosyncratic knowledge that a worker has and applies, to working knowledge, where that knowledge is codified and routinised, thereby making it generally available to the company rather than being the 'property' of an individual worker.

There are many ways in which digital Taylorism can be applied; for example, a leading company producing and selling software handling credit card transactions and credit rating expanded very rapidly over the last decade both within the United Kingdom and abroad, mainly through acquisitions. In an interview in 2006 the CEO defined the company's major problem as one of how to encourage his staff (mostly university graduates) to be innovative. He thought this was essential for the continued success of the business as they developed products for new markets and customers. Today the problem has changed dramatically. The company has achieved an annual growth rate of 25 per cent and opened offices across the developed and developing world, including China, India and Bulgaria. There has been a change in CEO, and the major issue in no longer defined as innovation, but of how to align business process and roll out software products to a global market. The creative work in producing new platforms, programs and templates has been separated from what they call routine 'analytics'. 'Permission to think' is restricted to a relatively small group of knowledge workers in the

United Kingdom, while the more routine work (i.e. customising products to different markets and customers), also referred to as the 'grunt work', is offshored to their offices in Bulgaria (where graduates can be hired at a third the cost of the United Kingdom) and India.

Moreover, the increased sophistication of software has meant the application of digital Taylorist techniques further up the skills ladder; it could be argued that now many highly skilled jobs are having their 'knowledge' content hollowed out by computer algorithms. Four years ago we interviewed senior personnel in a multinational law firm. Much of the work of 'discovery' sorting through and analysing documents relevant to law suits that at the turn of the century was done by lawyers was at that time being offshored. Now there is software that can do the same job. Indeed, a recent study of this activity appeared to show that the software was more efficient than *Homo sapiens* (Markoff, 2011).

The war for talent

Transnational companies seek to identify outstanding talent because it is claimed global corporations now need a range of skills in leadership positions that were not in demand when corporations were embedded in national economies (Brown and Hesketh, 2004). These new skill sets that only the small minority of 'talented' are deemed to have are therefore highly rewarded in contrast to those considered 'worthy' or subject to the routines of digital Taylorism. These TNCs gravitate towards the global elite of universities because they are believed to have the best and brightest students. This view is actively promoted by leading universities as higher education has become a global business. The branding of universities and faculty members is integral to the organisation of academic enquiry. Claims to world-class standards depend on attracting 'the best' academics and forming alliances with elite universities elsewhere in the world, while recruiting the 'right' kinds of students. Universities play the same reputational games as companies, because it is a logical consequence of global market competition between universities.

The consequence of the war for talent is that we might anticipate that while many who aspire to professional middle-class jobs will have their expectations confounded a few will command very high salaries indeed.

These trends were identified as a result of 125 interviews with senior managers in 30 TNCs in three sectors: electronics and IT, automobiles, and finance. Where possible, interviews within companies were triangulated between head office (in America, Britain, Germany and South Korea) and their subsidiaries in China, India and Singapore. In addition we interviewed 65 senior policy makers in the seven countries within which these multinationals operated. The timing of the interviews is important because it enabled us to gauge what has turned out to be very rapid change within TNCs over the period between 2004 and 2007. This qualitative study enabled the identification of key trends in terms of the skill strategies of TNCs, while the policy maker interviews enabled us to gauge how the respective nation states were responding to these trends. However, the trends that we identified are in their infancy, although they appear to be developing rapidly, and there is a need to test this model further through the analysis of quantitative data.

The model is complex, as befits an attempt to understand developments in the global economy, and it gives rise to a range of possible effects. These include: changes in where knowledge jobs are located, what is known as offshoring, which has given rise to estimates about the potential loss of jobs in the West (Blinder, 2009); consequent changes in the occupational structure of jobs in the West, particularly with respect to professional middle-class jobs, and hence changes in the demand for skill and graduate incomes; and changes in our understanding of who wins and loses from international trade. As such, the model challenges the dominant neo-classical economic theories such as Human Capital Theory (e.g. Becker, 2006) and Skill Bias Theory (e.g. Goldin and Katz, 2008a) that have assumed that the better educated workers are, the higher will be their income; along with a challenge to the proponents of international trade and assumptions about who wins and loses from it, both in terms of countries and workers (Gomory and Baumol, 2000)

The methodology behind the model

The methodology that we have adopted is related to critical realism (Bhaskar, 1978) and the work of Haig (1996, 2005) in that we have attempted to create an underlying model of key aspects of the global economy that can be expected to generate effects or what Bhaskar (1978) describes as tendencies. Critical realism has adherents across the social sciences, including in economics (see e.g. Lawson, 1997, 2003, 2006; Fleetwood, 1999, 2010). Critical realists fundamentally differ in their approach to methodology from orthodox economists.[2] Lawson (2006) has identified mathematisation, that is, the employment of calculus and other mathematical techniques, as central to orthodox economics. In contrast because critical realists are fundamentally concerned to construct models of generative mechanisms, these models may be described in a range of ways and they may, as in this study, rely on qualitative rather than quantitative methods. Methodologically, Haig (1996) has argued that, from a realist perspective, qualitative and quantitative methods can both be considered as part of scientific method.

Typically, orthodox economists construct their calculations within empiricism, admitting into their ontology only that which can be observed, whereas critical realists emphasise several levels of 'reality', including what a theory deems to be real. For them ontology can be understood at three levels, in contrast to the one observable level in empiricism. These comprise structures and the generative mechanisms to which they give rise which may not be observable, the actual level of events or states of affairs which is a manifestation of that reality, and the empirical level of observed phenomena and perceptions, which are the observations that, for example, orthodox economists may identify. Here the empirical is a subset of the actual which is generated by the underlying generative mechanisms or structures. There are, therefore, a number of crucial differences in approach between critical realists and orthodox economists. The most prominent relates to the question of causality, touched on in the description above. In economics, critical realists posit underlying causal generative mechanisms that can produce effects or as Bhaskar (1978) terms them, tendencies. In contrast, neo-classical economists infer causality from forms of inductive and deductive reasoning, and posit predictions on the basis of 'law like regularities' according to a Humean account of causality, while critical realists will infer causality by abductive reasoning from data patterns to an underlying causal model or mechanism.

Bhaskar (1978) emphasises the significance of tendencies over predictions because while predictions may be possible under, for example, closed laboratory conditions they are much more difficult to identify in open systems such as the global economy, as orthodox economists have discovered. Tendencies can be formed as conditional statements of what may happen. However, unlike the classic *ceteris paribus* clauses of orthodox economics which presupposes some form of a closed system, these conditional statements arise because the actual and the empirical may reflect the effects of a range of generative mechanisms which can often only be understood and indeed explained in retrospect.

This brings us to another key difference between the approach we have taken and that of orthodox economics: our fundamental concern is to explain rather than to predict. In this case, looking at the effects we might expect as regards graduate incomes, to see where the data are consistent and where they challenge the model, is a way of developing the explanatory power of the model, while at the same time acknowledging that where there are anomalies if they are sufficiently intractable then no amount of change within the model may deal with them. In this case our model would have to be abandoned. It will be clear, however, that this is a long and complex process that is not amenable to any form of naïve falsification, simply because, as suggested above there are a range of effects or tendencies that can be inferred from the model. When looking at changes in graduate professional job opportunities or incomes, there may be a range of effects, caused by different policy and economic contexts. And, they may produce countervailing tendencies.

The global labour market: models and theories

In looking at the global labour market, which forms the core of our model, we need to distinguish between 'theory' and 'model' and in doing so further elaborate on the difference between orthodox economics and the form of heterodox political economy presupposed by the arguments in our book (Brown *et al.*, 2011). Fleetwood (2010) draws attention to a key difference between orthodox economists and heterodox realists. While the former are methodological individualists the latter can entertain the possibility of structures, which he terms socioeconomic phenomena and agents with respect to the labour market. The key point is that workers enter a pre-formed set of labour market structures which go far beyond the focus of orthodox economists on contracts between employers and workers and the laws of supply and demand. These pre-formed structures are necessary to any fully developed explanation for their changing employment conditions. Such explanations with respect to structures entail power relations, which orthodox economists only comprehend within market structures, e.g. monopoly power. Power in the social world, including that related to the economy, may or may not be observed (Lukes, 2005), and the most 'hidden' form of power is when structures or agents get others to act in ways that they are unaware of – as with some forms of oppression. However, agents can also act against such forms of power. As Archer (2003) notes, agents, although born into a pre-existing world, can either reproduce or transform it, so the same can be said of workers. For example, the recent strikes and protests in South East China led to an increase in the minimum wage. These considerations lead Fleetwood (2010) to the following definition of labour markets:

> Labour markets, as social mechanisms that coordinate the labouring activity of society, are sets of socio-economic phenomena [structures] that are reproduced or transformed by labour market agents who draw upon these phenomena in order to engage in actions they think (consciously or unconsciously) will meet their employment-related needs.
>
> (Fleetwood, 2010, p.19)

This account enables questions of supply and demand and related contractual relations to be placed within the wider political and social contexts within which labour markets are constructed. In seeking to understand the nature of the global economy and labour market, this is crucial, as we shall see.

Turning to our model, it may be argued that it is consistent with, or could be translated into, the theories of orthodox economics. What it describes is four empirical trends where a key motivation for the trends identified is a competition between TNCs based on quality and price which has profound effects on national economic systems. Indeed, even our emphasis on changes to labour processes brought about by digital technology (digital Taylorism) could be translated, although not without loss, into orthodox economics, in that the trends we identify are, in principle, observable. However, the model is also explanatory in that these four trends comprise a generative mechanism which produces, amongst other tendencies, a growing disparity in professional jobs between job title, job quality and incomes.

Underlying this model are elements of an explanatory theory. These include the conditions or structures underlying labour markets in the West, particularly Britain and the United States, and in China and India and the role of TNCs as institutions that are the ringmasters in the changes we document. All these factors would be part of a developed explanation of the events and related data we document.[3]

However, at the core of all these structural factors must be an account of knowledge capitalism that explains what is different about this kind of capitalism to previous forms by showing how it relates to the Global Auction and how it plays out in different national contexts.[4]

It will be clear from this discussion that when it comes to the specific question of graduate incomes our understanding of tendencies is particular important because, while the effects we identify may be global, national labour markets will be distinctive in a range of ways which may have an impact on these effects or tendencies (Fleetwood, 2010). In these cases the question is why and in what ways the general generative mechanisms and tendencies we describe may vary in different national contexts. To take an example, graduate premiums over non-graduate incomes in the United States and Britain appear to be far higher than in countries such as Germany (Boarini and Strauss, 2007). But Germany has a range of well paid intermediately skilled jobs that do not exist in neo-liberal countries, and it may well be for this reason that graduate premiums are higher in the latter countries than in Germany. In other words, the explanation for these differences in premia may not be because the English speaking economies are more advanced knowledge economies but may be much more about the differences in industrial and occupational structures.

However, even within countries, changes to policies relating to the funding of higher education may have intended and/or unintended consequences that may impact on the tendencies we describe. So, for example, in England the tripling of university fees may have the effect of reducing the numbers going to university, while at the same time the offshoring of graduate jobs may reduce the number of such jobs. In this scenario trends in the disparity in graduate incomes may decline, although the number of available graduate jobs might also decline.

Graduate incomes: analysing the competing hypotheses

The idea that the knowledge economy would give rise to a large rise in the demand for graduates has led to mass higher education systems in many countries with the interesting exception of Germany (Hansen, 2011). Alongside policies of mass higher education have been a range of studies over a long period of time that purport to show that indeed there is a graduate or college premium and that this provides an incentive for students to attend university.

These studies have been buttressed by the orthodox economic theories of human capital (Becker, 2006) and Skill Bias Theory (Goldin and Katz, 2008a). Indeed, it could be argued that so powerful is the grip of these theories on the imaginations of orthodox economists that it has coloured their methods of investigation and the conclusions they have drawn.

Human capital theory

At its core, Human Capital Theory offers a simple model:

Educational investment → Productive contribution → Differential incomes

The theory predicts that the better educated a person is the more productive they are likely to be, for which they will earn a higher income. The theory has three significant assumptions: that it is in the self-interest of individuals to pursue education because it will lead to higher economic returns, which forms the basis for aspiration and a sense of personal progress in society; that education is fundamentally meritocratic because employers will not hire people who will prove to be incompetent; and that employers will respond to a better educated workforce by investing in technology that they can harness to capitalise on the productive potential of educated workers. These assumptions are highly debatable (Brown *et al.*, 2011) on theoretical and empirical grounds (see, e.g. Brown *et al.*, 2001).

From this theory the prediction is deduced that the higher the education level of the workforce the higher will be personal and national income: effectively, increased education ratchets up the levels at which demand and supply are in equilibrium. Underlying this theory is the assumption of material progress through education: a 'win win' story for individuals and nations.

Skill Bias Theory

Skill Bias Theory adopts many of the assumptions of Human Capital Theory but sees technology as the major driving force for economic competitiveness. Its central insight, that as technology becomes more sophisticated so the demand for higher skilled workers rises, has assumed the status of common sense as this quote from the Nobel prize winner Paul Krugman demonstrates:[5] 'It seems undeniable that the increase in the skill premium in the advanced world is primarily the result of skill-biased technological change' (Krugman, 1994).

Its significance lies in the support that it has provided and continues to provide for the rapid expansion of university education, while assuming that technology will drive the corresponding organisational and economic changes to utilise the skills that graduates acquire.

There are at least two accounts of the Skill Bias Thesis (Acemoglu, 2002). The first takes the view that as an exogenous variable new technologies influence the demand for skills and that this demand is skill biased rather than skill replacing. That is to say that technology does not replace skills but rather increases the demand for skills. Here various forms of technology and skill are seen as complementary. The second, articulated by Acemoglu (2002) is endogenous. More specifically new technologies are endogenous in that their adoption is a response to incentives; in particular, the increase in the supply of skills will lead to acceleration in the demand for skills. As he puts it:

> This reasoning implies that machines complementary to skilled workers will be more profitable to develop when there are more skilled workers to use them. New technologies have become more skill-biased throughout most of the twentieth century because the supply of skilled workers has grown steadily. This perspective also suggests that a faster increase in the supply of skills

can lead to an acceleration in the demand for skills ... so the timing of the increases in supply and demand is not a coincidence – instead it reflects technology responding to the supply of skills.

(Acemoglu, 2002, p.12)

Such as view is consistent with Human Capital Theory in that it also assumes that demand will respond to supply for similar reasons to those quoted. Clearly the endogenous theory is preferable to the exogenous precisely because it specifies a mechanism by which the supply and demand for skilled labour is linked to new technology. Acemoglu's (2002) theory also builds in the possible influence of organisational and labour market institutional changes and the influence of international trade, especially to explain the decline in wages of those with lower skills over the past thirty years in the United States:

Organizational change, labour market institutions and international trade have interacted with technical change in a fundamental way, amplifying the direct effect of technical change on inequality and likely causing the decline in the wages of less skilled workers.

(Acemoglu, 2002, p.13)

The reference to organisational change, labour market institutions and international trade are an advance on Human Capital Theory precisely because the latter does not have a theory of economic development. Rather, it is assumed that as the supply of increasingly skilled labour comes onto the market, equilibria will rise to accommodate the productive potential of higher skills.

Skill Bias Theory also provides an account of the polarisation of incomes by explaining that where there is an under-supply of skilled labour the premia for skilled labour (e.g. graduates) will rise (Goldin and Katz, 2008a). The solution in this case is to enable more students to obtain university or college qualifications. Again, this is an advance on Human Capital Theory, which, given the assumption that individuals will pursue their self-interest by gaining high level qualifications, finds it difficult to explain systematic inequalities with respect to social class, gender and ethnicity.

There are three anomalies or puzzles that can be put to skill bias theorists within the framework of their theory, which we will discuss in the following sections of this chapter. The first concerns the question of why there is an insufficient supply of graduates to meet demand; the second, why is technology understood as skill biased rather than skill replacing; and the third, why international trade is only likely to threaten the jobs and wages of the low skilled.

The first puzzle is addressed in the United States in terms of the poor quality of education (Heckman, 2008). Heckman argues that if education from pre-school through to college could be improved so would the life chances of the poor in terms of achieving a college education. In one way this explanation makes good one of the fundamental flaws in both Human Capital and Skill Bias Theories, which has been to see education as a 'black box' or production function without paying attention to how the content and forms of socialisation in education relate to the labour market. More recently, the breakdown of graduate incomes by subjects studied has helped to address one part of the content of education–labour market relationship but it says little about the question of socialisation. Indeed, skill bias theorists parse this problem into one of unobserved skills. This rather mystical and surprising *ad hoc* hypothesis has been posited to explain a further feature of graduate incomes: that there is increasing polarisation within occupations as well as between occupations. This constitutes an anomaly for skill bias theorists because if graduates enter the labour market with roughly equivalent skills then why do some earn so much more than others? For them the possession of these unobserved skills constitutes an explanation. Acemoglu is not the only economist to posit such unobserved skills as an explanation but there are others who argue that high earners within occupations are distinguished by their superior intelligence (Pryor and Schaffer, 2000). What has been less considered has been the structure of labour markets. Frank and Cook (1996) have addressed the question of labour markets with orthodox economics by arguing that the polarisation of income within occupations can be explained by winner-take-all markets. A heterodox explanation is given by Newfield (2010), who argues that employers hiring engineering graduates have changed their global strategies to minimise costs.

What human capital and skill bias theorists do not consider are the links between social class, gender, ethnicity and education and its relationship to the labour market. Skill Bias Theory is quite simply silent on these key questions affecting education. The focus is on credentials attained rather than on the content and processes of education or occupational recruitment. The emphasis on the formal outcomes is not only because they have no substantive view of education but also an attenuated view of the economy. The kinds of questions that sociologists have asked since Weber (1948), and most starkly raised in recent times by Bowles and Gintis (1976), as to the relationship between educational structures and processes, character formation, knowledge acquisition and the division of labour have simply not been part of their theoretical universe. This is because, as we have seen from Human Capital Theory, it is assumed that merit will always drive recruitment because it is more efficient. Indeed one of the major legacies of these economic theories is that educational policies have been driven by an outcomes model in terms of test results and credentials, rather than with a concern with the fundamental questions relating to knowledge and pedagogy, as Michael Young shows in Chapter 8.

Comparing Human Capital and Skill Bias Theories with the Global Auction Model

From the theoretical discussion above, a major issue concerns the explanatory and predictive power, in the case of Human Capital and Skill Bias Theories, and tendencies in the case of the Global Auction Model. The differences between predictions and tendencies also points up the crucial point about explanatory power, since these theories have radically different frameworks. There are also differences between Human Capital and Skill Bias Theories. Arguably the latter is more powerful in explaining income polarisation. Whereas Human Capital Theory can only point to the assumption that those earning less are less productive, because of some inherent quality such as IQ, Skill Bias Theory adds to the explanatory power of these theories by positing that the education system is not producing sufficient graduates to operate the new technologies.[6] In effect the technology-driven demand for graduates has outstripped supply. This brings us to a comparison of the empirical differences between the theories.

The explanations and predictions arising out of Skill Bias Theory

Skill Bias Theory recognises that new technology can be skill replacing but that the general thrust is to replace low-skilled operations with those requiring higher levels of skill. This view has occasioned a major debate within orthodox economics turning on the question of how new technology increases the demand for educated workers (Lauder *et al.*, 2005).

It should be said immediately that the majority of empirical studies, until recently, have shown a premium accruing to graduates over non-graduates, to the point where it seemed that the persistence of this correlation over time points to something akin to a Humean law-like regularity (OECD, 2010).

The clearest statement of Skill Bias Theory, consistent with studies of the relationship between graduate and non-graduate incomes, has been written by Goldin and Katz (2008a). They argue that the polarisation of incomes in the United States can be explained by difference in the supply and demand for graduates. The policy consequence of this view is that a better education system would enable more students to attain high-skilled employment.

However, as we have seen, skill bias theorists also acknowledge that there is a polarisation of incomes within occupations as well as between them. Here, it is argued that there are unobserved skills which account for these differences.

While the policy prescription is clear in terms of reducing the polarisation of income, this prescription can take us only so far, for two reasons. In a fascinating but separate study of gender differences in the income of Harvard graduates, Goldin and Katz (2008b) show that, after a range of controls, women did not earn as much as men by a significant sum, but that all Harvard graduates earned substantially more than the general graduate population. This is particularly so for those who studied economics. Now this might be explained by the grade point average for those who entered Harvard but it is most unlikely that these scores could explain the massive advantage in income that Harvard graduates enjoy, especially since there are gender differences in income pointing to a social account relating to inequality. So we might infer that as well as gender, reputation is a key factor in differences in graduate income. Given the social class composition of the student body at elite universities such as Harvard, the bare bones of an account that explains income differences in terms of a gender and socially classed educational and labour market institutions is clearly worth exploring.

The second point follows from the first: far from resorting to individualistic accounts of mysterious 'unobserved' skills, it is through the kinds of explanation that are prohibited by orthodox methodologies, including the operation of gender and class power relations that need exploring.

In turn this raises the spectre of the political implications of such studies. It has long been a view of heterodox and even some orthodox economists that, as Frank Hahn put it, orthodox economics 'can be converted into an apologia for existing economic arrangements' (cited in Lawson 2006, p.487).

This point takes us to the political presuppositions underlying Skill Bias Theory. Skill Bias Theory, from its name, as well as its modes of investigation, presupposes a theory of technological, economic and social progress. After all, while it may be no easy matter to improve education in the United States, the attempt to do so will not cause a fundamental crisis or reappraisal of the political economy of that country. The lesson from this theory is one of continuity based on inductive correlations between education and technology across time. Learning, they claim, even now equals earning and it is more important than it has ever been.

In contrast, the model that we have developed suggests discontinuity, placing the equation of learning = earning in jeopardy and raising fundamental political questions about the dominant model of the global economy.

Explanatory power and tendencies in the Global Auction

At first sight the tendencies developed by the model in the Global Auction (GA) are not that far from the predictions used by skill bias theorists. For example, that model suggests the tendency for there to be a polarisation of incomes. However, in contrast to Skill Bias Theory the polarisation explained within the GA model is within graduate incomes. What it suggests is that while an elite (typically from elite universities) will earn very high salaries, many graduates will find it more difficult to sustain well paid employment and meaningful careers, not only because they confront low-cost competition from high-skilled workers in emerging economies, but also because new technologies are being deployed in ways that enable employers to introduce a distinction between 'conception' and 'execution' to all apart from those at the apex of occupational hierarchies.

Moreover, the GA model also addresses the question of occupational polarisation of salaries. However, in contrast to the *ad hoc* explanations given by skill bias theorists, the tendency towards such polarisation is integral to the GA model. This is because there is a forward auction for global skills for those that leading corporations describe at 'talent', while for the majority there is a Dutch or reverse auction, because those at the bottom of the income distribution within occupations will be more likely to be undertaking routinised work.

The difference between the GA model and that of skill bias theorists could not be starker when we recall Acemolgu's quote above in which he argued that organisational change, the labour market and international trade had conspired to raise the demand for skilled workers, while reducing the demand for unskilled workers as these jobs are offshored to low-cost locations. In contrast, the GA model implies that labour processes relating to digital Taylorism will prove to be skill replacing and that this can now be at very high levels of skill (Markoff, 2011). Moreover, it is not only changes in the labour process but the rise of cheaper skilled labour in East Asia that has led to the offshoring of graduate level jobs. In effect, transnational companies have constructed a global labour market for highly skilled work.

To this could be added Newfield's (2010) insightful analysis of the restructuring of knowledge work in the United States, taking as his examples Microsoft and Intel. He notes that there is an abundance of knowledge workers in the United States. There are 7 million jobs for STEM subject graduates, while the universities produce 2.3 million STEM graduates, from all classes of degree, every year, suggesting that the entire STEM workforce could be replaced every three years. The issue for these large service sector companies is how to gain their knowledge at the lowest possible price. This, Newfield has argued, has led to the restructuring of labour markets for these STEM graduates, such that many are employed on temporary projects. In Britain, it has been estimated that half of STEM graduates have not gone into STEM related work.

When these changes to the labour market and labour process are combined they produce a radically different set of tendencies with respect to the future of graduate incomes. For Goldin and Katz (2008a), graduate incomes will continue to rise until the supply of graduates meets demand and will fall when there is an oversupply of graduates relative to demand. For the GA model, graduate incomes will rise or stay as they are for an elite of graduates, while for the remainder their incomes, and indeed work conditions, will stagnate or decline.

Of course experience of the real world suggests that these contrasting predictions and tendencies are too bald. But it is precisely because of the cross-cutting generative mechanisms and tendencies that exist in the economic, social and political world that outcomes are likely to be more equivocal. This leads to two considerations. Because explanatory theory is primary in critical realism, the first concerns the explanatory potential to make sense of these more complex outcomes. The second concerns the criteria by which data sets and analyses have been admitted into this debate.

Theoretical and empirical considerations in appraising the two theories

Theoretical considerations

When it comes to the criteria for comparing the relative power of different explanations, Bhaskar (1978) draws an implicit distinction between explanatory breadth and depth in order to distinguish knowledge from ideology in claiming that orthodox economics comprises a form of ideology. As Lawson (2006) makes clear this is a doubtful claim to make. Nevertheless, Bhaskar does provide clues as to how to understand this key tool in the armoury of theory appraisal. If we enlist the support of Lakatos (1970) in making judgements about theories then we can suggest the following: explanatory breadth relates to the range of phenomena that a theory can explain, depth relates to whether one theory can explain all the content of a rival theory, explain additional elements and possibly can explain the social origins and political interests of its rival theory/ies.

In looking at the GA model and that of Skill Bias Theory, the former may be seen as potentially more powerful because the development and application of technology takes place in a particular political, social and economic context. For example, the technological basis for economic growth in the post-World War II period was the application of Fordist production line technology. However, in order for the productive capacity of this technology to be realised, corporate structures had to be built to develop the R&D, marketing and sales for mass-produced goods. At the same time, workers had to be able to buy into mass consumption and this required a political settlement between the state, employers and trade unions in order to ensure that workers wages were high enough to buy consumer goods.

The interesting point about Fordism is that those who worked on the production line were low skilled but relatively well paid. So the claim that technology was skill biased during the twentieth century is not derived from the technology of the production line nor the skills of production line workers but from the army of white-collar workers that ensured the mass sales of consumer goods.

Now the explanatory power of the GA model comes from the insight that the economic, social and political structures that enabled the success of technologies such as Fordism have now fundamentally changed, and with them the possibility of the application of Skill Bias Theory solely to a national context. In the latter half of the twentieth century it might seem that the national champions that were dying in Detroit were being replaced by the West Coast campuses of Apple and Microsoft. But global capitalism has overtaken any such possibility. The very technologies these corporations have developed have ensured the reach of a global economy in which many white-collar jobs are being outsourced, simultaneously with the advent of digital Taylorism and, we can predict, the concomitant decline in the demand for some of the technical skills and expertise that graduates were once employed to exercise.

Of course, in principle, these are empirical claims both with respect to our understanding of the labour market as well as the decline in graduate level work. Both are open to testing, although, in practice, gaining appropriate data sets to test competing theories is difficult. What is clear from the GA model is that the changing graduate labour market can no longer be studied in national isolation. It may be that there are national initiatives which seek to raise the demand for graduates, through, for example, the creation of green jobs. In this case, Skill Bias Theory could incorporate such an initiative in an *ad hoc* way and it could continue to tell a story consistent about the skill bias of technology. What it would omit would be reference to the generative mechanisms and tendencies outlined in the GA model, and this is important because, whatever government intervention amounted to, the underlying tendencies, according to the GA model, would remain and would continue to pose a threat to the demand for high-skilled work, unless in some unanticipated way such an initiative altered both the nature of technology and the national boundaries within which it operated.

What the GA model is able to do is to provide a set of conceptual resources, including an account of changing economic, social and political structures that can make sense of the way workers as agents not only reproduce and transform structures but in this case are transformed by these structures. The model can provide an explanation of a fundamental rupture in the education–labour market relationships, whereas Skill Bias Theory has assumed continuity.

Given the incommensurable differences in these two accounts how can evidence be evaluated with respect to these different approaches?

Empirical considerations

While qualitative research was used to develop the account of generative mechanisms in the GA model, these mechanisms should produce a set of tendencies that are manifest in quantitative data patterns. In principle, this should apply to graduate incomes. However, as we have noted, there is considerable work to be done in understanding the relationships between global, national and local labour markets. Countries differ in their articulation of the relationship between education and the labour market (Hansen, 2011), as they do in industrial structure, regulations and the role of trade unions. All these factors would need to be carefully teased out to make sense of the trends in relation to graduate incomes.

It will be clear from the above discussion that an explanation for trends in graduate income for either theory is likely to be complex. In this context, while the sophisticated forms of falsification, such as that advanced by Lakatos (1970), are desirable, we may, in the early phases of an appraisal of the empirical merits of these theories, require simpler principles for appraisal that can focus on the broad trends and data patterns that can tell us something of their initial plausibility. For example, we might develop a principle that if in a broad sense data patterns and trends run contrary to the predictions or tendencies of one of the two theories then that would throw fundamental doubt on its empirical worth. This approach has two purposes: it serves as an impetus to explanation. It also acknowledges Lakatos' point about the elaborate theoretical and empirical defences that defy naïve falsificationism, while seeking empirical parameters within which more fine grained appraisals may take place. In case it is thought that applying such a principle is as far we need to go, we should be mindful of what Lakatos calls the protective belt or non *ad hoc* strategies that can be employed to defend a research programme: in this case an obvious defence would be that relating to time. Predictions and tendencies are clearly time related and it may be that trends that run counter to what might be expected constitute a short-term anomaly.

There are broad trends that we can identify for both the GA model and for Skill Bias Theory. For example, if a significant percentage of starting graduate incomes continued to rise in the United States and Britain, then this could be seen as breaching the default expectation of the GA model which would anticipate that while the incomes of those around the 90th percentile might increase that would not be the case for the majority of graduates. By the same token, Skill Bias Theory would predict that if the supply of graduates increased then starting salaries may decline, whereas if they do not then according to this theory graduate starting salaries will either remain at present levels or increase, depending on how changes in skill bias technologies are understood.

Given these considerations, can current studies be used as examples of these empirical processes, bearing in mind that both theories have generated predictions or tendencies with respect to future graduate incomes.

The graduate premium

When looking at the majority of studies relating to graduate income, it seems that the primary concern has been to see if there is a graduate premium. This is entirely consistent with the ideology of the knowledge economy (Brown *et al.*, 2011) and, indeed, more narrowly, Skill Bias Theory, in which it has been assumed that the electronic revolution and new forms of business organisation will lead to an increasing demand for highly educated labour.

The notion of a graduate premium can be used to address one question: whether it may be worth attending university or college in order to gain a higher income than would be the case if students entered the labour market after secondary or high school or undertook further vocational education or training.

However, a graduate premium on its own tells us nothing about the demand for graduate workers in relation to concepts of the knowledge economy or of technology. It may well be that the premium is created by a decline in the wages of non-graduate labour, if graduates were then being employed to undertake work previously done by non-graduates; in other words a 'bumping down' effect (Pryor and Schaffer, 2000) created by the lack of demand for graduate level work.

This possibility raises a further key point about comparing graduate and non-graduate wages. The problem is that these gross categories need to be disaggregated to capture the key dynamics relating to the question of the knowledge economy, technology and the demand for graduate work. Given the tendencies that are derived from the GA model, disaggregation of data is crucial to understand whether all graduates have experienced a rise in wages or only those at approximately the 90th percentile. It is also important to disaggregate the data to understand the polarisation of incomes within occupational groups. There are two points here. Skill Bias Theory predicts that nearly all graduates have seen a rise in their incomes due to the demand created by new technology. And perhaps because this proposition has seemed so obvious, as has the claim concerning the graduate premium, the majority of the studies in this tradition do not disaggregate data to examine this prediction: this holds true for the work of both Acemoglu (2002) and Goldin and Katz (2008a). The second point is that there may be a degree of substitution between those qualified as graduates and those who do not have a degree. This does not count against Skill Bias Theory because it could be argued that perhaps labour markets are not wholly rational in the way recruitment is undertaken. However, there are more powerful theoretical interests involved in this question. If the substitution takes place because of bumping down then that tells us something about the demand for graduate work. And, if a significant proportion of graduates from two-year community colleges earn more than four-year university or college graduates (Demos, 2010) this also tells us something about the demand for graduate work.

In the GA model we presented the analysis of trends in graduate wages at entry to the labour market between 1973 and 2007 undertaken by Mishel *et al.* (2009). What these trends show is that, of those entering the labour market with a four-year degree, women consistently earned less than men, which challenges some of the standard explanations for why women earn less than men, such as those relating to biological reproduction. From roughly 1989, wages for men and women at the 90th percentile increased rapidly. For those at the median they have flatlined throughout this period for men and risen a little for women. Those at the 10th percentile have also flatlined.

Our interest in these trends is that they chart precisely the period when the electronic/IT revolution took place. Yet, apart from those at the 90th percentile the effects of demand on graduate wages does not tell a story consistent with that of skill bias theorists – and at a time when in the latter part of this period the supply of graduates is in decline relative to an assumed demand. These trends do, however, tell a more consistent story with respect to the GA model. Similar research undertaken by Lauder *et al.* (2005) in Britain, for a period between the mid-1980s and 2001 also showed a flatlining of graduate incomes, but with graduates' working time increasing by a half a day a week. These trends predated the moves towards offshoring and the emergence of digital Taylorism.

Perhaps the study that most clearly exemplifies the differences that emerge when different questions are asked is that of Baum *et al.* (2010). This is perhaps one of the most detailed studies of the relative earnings of graduates and non-graduates in the United States. It shows two factors of significance: that there is a graduate premium and that returns to education are greater the higher the qualification achieved, with professional degrees registering the most significant returns. This then speaks directly to the issue of a graduate premium. However, the study also shows earning trends by gender and education between 1971 and 2008, a similar time frame to that of Mishel *et al.* (2009). The trends that both studies identify are also remarkably similar. But in contrast to the former study they examine trends for workers between the ages of 25 and 34. For men of all education levels there is a decline in earnings during this period, while for women with a Bachelor's degree there is a slight uptick; for all other women there has been a decline in earnings. What their analysis shows is that there can be a graduate premium but that the incomes of graduate men has declined over this period and increased slightly for graduate women. In turn this raises fundamental questions as to the viability of the technology explanation of Skill Bias Theory.

A more recent study in the United States which examines the effects of the Great Recession on income and employment for graduates charts a decline in both (Godofsky *et al.*, 2011). We do not claim that this provides convincing support for the GA model. But it does raise at least possibilities relating to the two theories worth considering. First, Skill Bias Theory would predict that post-recession the demand for graduate work would not only return to previous levels but increase. The GA model would imply that if there is a post-recession, the demand for graduate level work will not return to previous levels because employers will use the 'cover' of the recession to either offshore jobs or introduce digital-Taylorist techniques. In other words, the recession gives employers the opportunity to cut costs and that may be true of government agencies, as well as the private sector.

Studies that show increased dispersion of graduate incomes are also consistent with the GA model. Green and Zhu (2010) investigated over-qualification and its impact on university premia in earnings. They found that the dispersion of returns to graduate education had widened between 1994 and 2006. They also found a significant increase in over-education based on the self reports of employees. Green and Zhu claim that in most cases those who are over-qualified for their current position do not feel their skills are fully utilised (what they call formal over-education). They find a considerable pay penalty for those over-qualified and it has been rising over time. Moreover, a Eurostat study found that European wages are more disparate among the highly educated (Eurostat, 2009, p.131).[7]

While studies of this kind can be cited for or against these two theories, and in support of Skill Bias Theory we could cite Autor (2010), our concern in this discussion has been in terms of the kinds of evidence that speak to the contrasting theories and the further forms of evidence that might address the differences in prediction and tendency that could be adduced – as for example in the discussion of post-recession trends in graduate work and incomes. We would also caution against meta-analyses that draw general conclusions while riding roughshod over the theoretical and methodological differences between studies (Haig, 1996).

Conclusion

In this discussion we have sought to distinguish two theories and their respective methodologies, showing how they frame different research aims, explanatory structures and 'predictions'. It shows that even the concept of prediction is understood quite differently. The methodologies employed lead to differing kinds of interpretation of the data, such as the growing polarisation within occupations. However, while this might lead to the conclusion of radical incommensurability, this is not the case, since, as we have sought to show, a careful sifting of empirical studies show how they might address the empirical claims of the two theories. In essence, there is a touchstone (Lakatos, 1970) with respect to a common appreciation of how data can lead to an empirical, if not theoretical, adjudication between the theories.

In seeking to show how this adjudication can be achieved we have painted with a broad brush and there is still much to be discussed. This would include a greater specification of the differences between global, national and local differences in labour markets that can impact on the trends we have analysed. At the same time, the key question of what constitutes graduate-level work and how it can be best understood requires further discussion (Lauder *et al.*, 2005). What we do hope to have achieved is the initiation of a debate about theory appraisal in a crucial area in which the future of the middle classes in Western societies is at stake.

Notes

1 While this generative model can identify tendencies that have hitherto not been related, for example offshoring and graduate incomes, it should be stressed that the production of this model itself requires further explanation in terms of the distinctive generative mechanisms of knowledge capitalism. To assume that the trends we have identified are self evident would be to lapse into precisely the kind of orthodox economic empiricism that we reject.

2 Following Lawson, the term orthodox economists rather than neo-classical economists is used. However, our account of what constitutes orthodox economics differs from Lawson's account in respect of the different views of power that orthodox and critical realists can entertain. See below.

3 Given the distinction we have drawn between models and theories, in the following, for ease of exposition but with this distinction in mind, we use the terms theories and models interchangeably.

4 This is the task we are now embarking on.

5 Although Krugman has now changed his views on this issue.

6 Human capital theorists explain this 'lack' of highly educated individuals on intelligence or genetics (Lauder, 1990), which raises largely discredited explanations as to why particular groups are less endowed with intelligence, whereas skill bias theorists point, as we have seen, to limitations in the education system, which may affect some groups more than others.

7 Exceptions are the Scandanavian countries (minus Iceland).

References

Acemoglu, D. (2002) 'Technical change, inequality and the labour market', *Journal of Economic Literature*, XL(March): 7–72.

Archer, M. (2003) *Structure, Agency and the Internal Conversation*, Cambridge: Cambridge University Press.

Autor, D. (2010) *The Polarization of Job Opportunities in the US Labor Market: Implications for Employment and Earnings*. Available at: www.americanprogress.org/issues/2010/04/pdf/job_polarization.pdf.

Baum, S., Ma, J. and Payea, K. (2010) *Education Pays 2010: The Benefits of Higher Education for Individuals and Society*, The College Board. Available at: http://trends.collegeboard.org/downloads/Education_Pays_2010.pdf.

Becker, G. (2006) 'The age of human capital', in Lauder, H., Brown, P., Dillabough, J.-A. and Halsey A.H. (eds) *Education, Globalization and Social Change*, Oxford: Oxford University Press.

Bhaskar, R. (1978) *The Possibility of Naturalism*, Brighton: Harvester Press.

Blinder, A. (2009) 'Offshoring: Big deal or business as usual?', in Bhagwati, J. and Blinder, A. (eds) *Offshoring of American Jobs: What Response from US Economic Policy?* Cambridge, MA: MIT Press.

Boarini, R. and Strauss, H. (2007) *The Private Internal Rates of Return to Tertiary Education: New Estimates for 21 OECD Countries*. OECD Economics Department Working Papers No 591, Paris: OECD. Available at: www.olis.oecd.org/olis/2007doc.nsf/LinkTo/NT000059E2/$FILE/JT03238193.PDF.

Bowles, S. and Gintis, H. (1976) *Schooling in Capitalist America*, London: Routledge & Kegan Paul.

Braverman, H. (1974) *Labour and Monopoly Capital: The Degradation of Work in the Twentieth Century*, New York: Monthly Review Press.

Brown, P. and Hesketh, A. (2004) *The Mismanagement of Talent: Employability and Jobs in the Knowledge Economy*, Oxford: Oxford University Press.

Brown, P., Green, A. and Lauder, H. (2001) *High Skills: Globalization, Skill Formation and Competitiveness*, Oxford: Oxford University Press.

Brown, P., Lauder, H. and Ashton, D. (2011) *The Global Auction: The Broken Promises of Education, Jobs and Income*, New York: Oxford University Press.

Demos (2010) 'Graduated success: Sustainable economic opportunity through one- and two-year credentials', Wheary, J. and Orozco, V., New York.

Eurostat (2009) *The Bologna Process in Higher Education in Europe: Key Indicators on the Social Dimension and Mobility*, Luxembourg: Office for Official Publications of the European Communities. Available at: http://epp.eurostat.ec.europa.eu/cache/ITY_OFFPUB/KS-78-09-653/EN/KS-78-09-653-EN.PDF.

Fleetwood, S. (1999) *Critical Realism in Economics: Development and Debate*, London: Routledge.

Fleetwood, S. (2010) 'Sketching a socio-economic model of labour markets', *Cambridge Journal of Economics*, 35: 15–38.

Frank, R. and Cook, P. (1996) *The Winner-Takes-All Society*, New York: Penguin.

Godofsky, J., Zukin, C. and Van Horn, C. (2011) *Unfulfilled Expectations: Recent College Graduates Struggle in a Troubled Economy*, New Brunswick, NJ: Rutgers University, John J. Heldrich Centre for Workforce Development.

Goldin, C., and Katz, L. (2008a) *The Race Between Education and Technology*, Cambridge, MA: Harvard University Press.

Goldin, C. and Katz, L. (2008b) 'Gender differences in careers, education and games. Transition: Career and family life cycles of the educational elite', *American Economic Review, Papers and Proceedings*, 98(2): 363–369.

Gomory, R. and Baumol, W. (2000) *Global Trade and Conflicting National Interests*, Cambridge, MA: MIT Press.

Green, F. and Zhy, Y. (2010) 'Overqualification, job satisfaction, and increasing dispersion in the returns to graduate education', *Oxford Economic Papers*, 62(4): 740–763.

Haig, B.D. (1996) 'Grounded theory as scientific method', in A. Neiman (ed.) *Philosophy of Education 1995: Current Issues*, Urbana, IL: University of Illinois Press, pp.281–290.

Haig, B.D. (2005) 'An abductive theory of scientific method', *Psychological Methods*, 10: 371–388.

Hansen, H. (2011) 'Rethinking Certification Theory and the Educational Development of the United States and Germany', *Research in Social Stratification*, Special Issue edited by Bills, D. and Brown, D., forthcoming.

Heckman, J. (2008) *Schools, Skills and Synapses*, Discussion Paper No. 3515, Bonn: The Institute for the Study of Labour (IZA).

Krugman, P. (1994) 'Past and prospective causes of high unemployment reducing unemployment', *Federal Reserve Bank of Kansas City, Economic Review*, Fourth Quarter, 1993, 37.

Lakatos, I. (1970) 'Falsification and the methodology of scientific research programmes', in Lakatos, I. and Musgrave, A. (eds) *Criticism and the Growth of Knowledge*, Cambridge: Cambridge University Press.

Lauder, H. (1990) 'The new right revolution and education', in Middleton, S., Codd, J. and Jones, A. (eds) *New Zealand Education Policy Today*, Wellington: Allen and Unwin.

Lauder, H., Egerton, M. and Brown, P. (2005) 'Report on graduate earnings: Theory and empirical analysis', report to the Independent Study into the Devolution into the Student Support System and Tuition Fee Regime, Cardiff: The Welsh Assembly.

Lawson, T. (1997) *Economics and Reality*, London: Routledge.

Lawson, T. (2003) *Reorienting Economics*, London: Routledge.

Lawson, T. (2006) 'The nature of heterodox economics', *Cambridge Journal of Economics*, 30: 483–505.

Lukes, S. (2005) *Power: A Radical View*, 2nd edition, Basingstoke: Palgrave Macmillan.

Markoff, J. (2011) 'Looks like a job for an e-lawyer', *The Observer/New York Times*, 13 March.

Michaels, E., Handfield-Jones, H. and Axelrod, B. (2001) *The War for Talent*, Boston, MA: Harvard Business School.

Mishel, L., Bernstein, J. and Shierholz, H. (2009) *The State of Working America, 2008/2009*, Ithaca, NY: Cornell University Press.

Newfield, C. (2010) 'The structure and silence of the cognotariat', *Globalisation, Societies and Education*, 8(2): 175–189.

OECD (2010) *Education at a Glance*, Paris: OECD.

Pryor, F. and Schaffer, D. (2000) *Who's Not Working and Why? Employment, Cognitive Skills, Wages and the Changing US Labour Market*, Cambridge: Cambridge University Press.

Taylor, F. (1911) *The Principles of Scientific Management*, New York: Harper and Brothers.

Weber, M. (1948) 'The Chinese literati', in Gerth, H. and Wright Mills, C. (eds) *From Max Weber: Essays in Sociology*, New York: Oxford University Press, pp.416–442.

4 'Openness' and the global knowledge commons

An emerging mode of social production for education and science

Michael A. Peters

Introduction

This chapter documents the potential for the open access (OA) of knowledge, information and debate to create a new public space and culture that could underpin education, democracy and the economy. The implication of this discussion of OA is that it could release the knowledge, creativity and research to develop highly skilled productive economies to the benefit of the many rather than the few. However, the developments in OA, which are documented below need to be balanced against the possibilities that the same technologies that enable OA can be used to generate economic crises (Hoogvelt, this volume, Chapter 2), arbitrage the cost of skilled labour and de-skill knowledge-based jobs across the globe (Lauder, Brown and Tholen, this volume, Chapter 3). We are at a point in history where the liberating potential of OA is finely balanced against a set of opposing forces.

On 14 February 2008 Harvard University's Faculty of Arts and Sciences adopted a policy that required faculty members to allow the university to make their scholarly articles available free online.[1] The new policy made Harvard the first university in the United States to mandate open access to its faculty members' research publications and marked the beginning of a new era that will encourage other US universities and universities around the world to do the same. Open access means putting peer-reviewed scientific and scholarly literature on the internet, making it available free of charge and free of most copyright and licensing restrictions, and removing the barriers to serious research. Open access has already transformed the world of scholarship and its pace continues with major accord, statements and manifestos that record the commitment worldwide to the possibilities of open access to establish a global science and education commons, reinventing and reinvigorating the notion of the public sphere. Since the early 2000s major OA statements, including Budapest in 2002, have multiplied and the movement has picked up momentum developing a clear political ethos. Harvard's adoption of the new policy follows hard on the heels of open access mandates passed by the National Institute of Health (NIH) and the European Research Council (ERC). Open access, open publishing and open archiving of peer-reviewed journal articles, reports and shared scientific data bases is now building into an irreversible worldwide movement to establish a scientific and educational global public sphere. As universities around the world follow Harvard's lead and also innovate to make freely available learning materials through open archiving to anyone, including students and faculty from developing and transition countries, the movement also at the philosophical and political levels begins to extend and develop through technological affordances and political will the original concepts of freedom, self-organization and public good that characterized civil society. Harvard's adoption of the open archiving mandate is similar in scope to the step taken by MIT to adopt OpenCourseWare (OCW) in 2001 and establish the institutional means to begin global sharing of open learning resources. These initiatives are emblematic of a myriad of new arrangements, foundations, and institutions that utilize Web 2.0 technologies and principles of new social media. They are part of emergent interlocking and overlapping *knowledge ecologies* that will determine the shape of learning, scholarly publishing, scientific collaboration and the future of the university challenging commercial publishing business models and raising deeper questions about learning, scientific and content development processes as well as practical questions of resourcing and sustainability.

The Ithaka Report, *University Publishing In A Digital Age* (2007) indicates that there have been massive changes in the creation, production and consumption of scholarly resources with the "creation of new formats made possible by digital technologies, ultimately allowing scholars to work in deeply integrated electronic research and publishing environments that will enable real-time dissemination, collaboration, dynamically-updated content, and usage of new media" (p.4). These changes in content creation and publication "alternative distribution models (institutional repositories, pre-print servers, open access journals) have also arisen with the aim to broaden access, reduce costs, and enable open sharing of content" (p.4).[2] Open publishing, open archiving, open education are essential parts of the wider movement of OA that builds on the nested and evolving convergences of open source, open access and open science, and also emblematic of a set of still wider political and economic changes that ushers in a mode of social production as an alternative to the neo-liberal global economy that has proved both fragile and volatile, as the ongoing effects of the 2007–8 world recession, credit and banking crisis demonstrates so well.

The present era can be called the "open" era (open source, open systems, open standards, open archives, open everything) just as the 1990s were called the "electronic" decade (e-text, e-learning, e-commerce, e-governance) (Materu, 2004). And yet it is more than just a "decade" that follows the electronic innovations of the 1990s: it is a change of philosophy, ethos and practices, a set of interrelated and complex changes that transforms markets and the mode of production, ushering in a new collection of values based on openness, an ethic of participation and deepening of peer-to-peer collaboration. In the "Postscript" to *Building Knowledge Cultures: Education and Development in the Age of Knowledge Capitalism* we made the argument that:

there has been a shift from an underlying metaphysics of production – a "productionist" metaphysics – to a metaphysics of consumption and we must now come to understand the new logics and different patterns of cultural consumption in the areas of new media where symbolic analysis becomes a habitual and daily activity. Here the interlocking sets of enhanced mobility of capital, services, and ideas, and the new logics of consumption become all important. These new communicational practices and cross-border flows cannot be effectively policed. More provocatively we might argue, the global informational commons is an emerging infrastructure for the emergence of a civil society still yet unborn.

(Peters and Besley, 2006)

In the Postscript we also emphasized the link of this new logic of consumption to a classical concept of freedom as an essential aspect for transforming digital network practices into knowledge cultures, and we commented upon the political economy of information and its eco-cybernetic rationalities that accompany an informational global capitalism comprised of new multinational information utilities that threaten to privatize and commercialize knowledge and monopolize the new knowledge spaces. These info-utilities based on systems-scale economies are more dangerous than the economies of scale that characterized industrial capitalism and are clearly capable of colonizing the emergent ecology of info-social networks, preventing the development of knowledge cultures based on non-proprietary modes of knowledge production and exchange.

This chapter builds on these insights and makes the argument for the emergent paradigm of open education (OE) and open science (OS). The first term was used in the phrase "open educational resources" and came into use at a conference hosted by UNESCO in 2002 that defined it as "the open provision of educational resources, enabled by information and communication technologies, for consultation, use and adaptation by a community of users for noncommercial purposes." As the OECD report (2005, pp.30–31) comments "open educational resources are digitised materials offered freely and openly for educators, students and self-learners to use and reuse for teaching, learning and research".

While this is a useful definition I prefer to systematically relate the notion of open education to "open knowledge production systems" as a basis for creating, building and nurturing "knowledge cultures," a term that serves as a critique of the knowledge economy/knowledge society distinction (Peters and Besley, 2006). This kind of approach allows a better analysis of the new political economy and emerging paradigm of "social production" of which open education and open science is a part.

This chapter first plots the dimensions of the emerging paradigm of *open education* by discussing the idea of open science in relation to an emerging global knowledge commons. It then reviews and develops the notion of "the mode of social production" developed by Yochai Benkler (2006), Michel Bauwens (2005) and many others, before making some concluding observations.

Open courseware

The Cape Town Open Education Declaration subtitled "Unlocking the promise of open educational resources" arose from a meeting convened in September 2007 declaring: "We are on the cusp of a global revolution in teaching and learning. Educators worldwide are developing a vast pool of educational resources on the Internet, open and free for all to use." The declaration goes on to argue:

> This emerging open education movement combines the established tradition of sharing good ideas with fellow educators and the collaborative, interactive culture of the Internet. It is built on the belief that everyone should have the freedom to use, customize, improve and redistribute educational resources without constraint. Educators, learners and others who share this belief are gathering together as part of a worldwide effort to make education both more accessible and more effective.

The Declaration states that open education "is not limited to just open educational resources ... [but] also draws upon open technologies that facilitate collaborative, flexible learning and the open sharing of teaching practices that empower educators to benefit from the best ideas of their colleagues." It goes on to provides a statement based on a three-pronged strategy designed to support "open educational technology, open sharing of teaching practices and other approaches that promote the broader cause of open education."[3]

"Open education" has emerged strongly as a new mode of social production in the global knowledge commons. Several major reports have documented existing developments and new tools and technologies, heralded the utopian promise of "openness" in global education extolling its virtues of shared commons-based peer-production, and analyzed the ways in which it contributes to skill formation, innovation and economic development. In 2007 three substantial reports were released that reviewed open education as a movement and assessed its benefits: the OECD's (2005) *Giving Knowledge for Free: The Emergence Of Open Educational Resources*;[4] the Open e-Learning Content Observatory Services (OLCOS) project and report entitled *Open Educational Practices and Resources*;[5] and a report to The William and Flora Hewlett Foundation, *A Review of the Open Educational Resources (OER) Movement: Achievements, Challenges, and New Opportunities* (eds Atkins, Brown and Hammond, 2007).[6] These three reports share similar emphases, each focusing on "openness" and the promise of the new technologies and their educational benefits.

The Executive Summary gives us a flavor of the potential of OE[7] and the utopian educational promise that graces these three reports:

> An apparently extraordinary trend is emerging. Although learning resources are often considered as key intellectual property in a competitive higher education world, more and more institutions and individuals are sharing digital

learning resources over the Internet openly and without cost, as open educational resources (OER).

(OECD, 2005, p.9)

The report then concerns itself with the following questions: What are open educational resources? Who is using and producing OER and how much? Why are people sharing for free? What are the provisions for copyright and open licences? How can OER projects be sustained in the long run?

In asking these questions, we should consider not only the possibilities for collaborative interaction and learning that the technology now affords but also the downsides. The reports, it might be argued, are too wedded to a technological account of open education and to an engineering notion of information that blind them to the criticisms that have been and can be mounted against various conceptions of "openness," "information" and the cybernetic society based upon it. They also might be criticized for not recognizing the problem of *structured ignorance* – "information overload," "misinformation," and "disinformation" – that accompanies the commercial exploitation of edutainment technologies (Goodman, 1986); the lack of context for entertaining claims for open education in order to understand fundamental changes to liberal political economy; and the relation of OE to traditional goals of education policy to notions of freedom, equality, access, and distribution of public goods.

Open science, the public domain and the global knowledge commons: declarations and manifestos

Open science and open education, then, are part of the worldwide OA movement that makes digital content freely available and focuses on peer-reviewed academic journals, extending the historic principles of peer review as the basis of the global knowledge commons. Increasingly, public funding agencies require open access to publicly funded research, and universities and other knowledge institutions are encouraged to deposit all journal article, dissertations and theses in their own OA repository. Peter Suber, the philosopher, commentator and archivist for open access, provides a comprehensive timeline and defines OA as follows: "Open-access (OA) literature is digital, online, free of charge, and free of most copyright and licensing restrictions."[8] Clearly, OA is bigger than *access*, including *grey literature, open data, social software, free culture,* and *digital libraries and repositories.* In fact, one could argue that open science is a direct descendant of the enterprise of peer-reviewed science strongly wedded to concepts of civil society as it developed institutionally in the late seventeenth and eighteenth centuries.

Open access, the public sphere and civil society

The concept of the public sphere is closely related to the emergence of the concept of "civil society" as a space of open communication and social self-organization oriented to the public good. The modern form took shape in the seventeenth century largely through the development of a series of interrelated knowledge institutions, including the birth of learned societies, the development of the modern research university, the research library, the museum of natural history, and the research laboratory that formed a knowledge network. While the earliest societies, some thirty of them, were established in the period 1323–1599, overwhelmingly in Italy (19 of 30) but also in France, England, Ireland, Scotland and Spain, a further 43 societies were established in the period 1600–1699, again predominantly in Europe (mostly in Italy but with some societies being founded in Germany). It was during this period that the Royal Society of London was established (in 1660), strongly influenced by the philosophy of Francis Bacon, especially "experimentall learning" developed in his *The New Atlantis*. This was the birth of experimental science in England. During the period between 1679 and 1683, Elias Ashmole established the Ashmolean Museum as a scientific institution at the University of Oxford, which housed the first chemical laboratory in the United Kingdom. The Royal Society known as the "invisible college" started as a group of some twelve "scientists," including John Wilkins, Robert Hooke, Christopher Wren, William Petty and Robert Boyle who met regularly in London from 1645 onwards, forming a "College for the Promoting of Physico-Mathematical Experimental Learning", and was later granted a Royal charter by King Charles II in 1662 for "the improvement of natural knowledge". Early meetings were almost always devoted to experiments.

The history of civil society as related to a public sphere develops from diverse sources in works of Locke, Ferguson, Rousseau and Hegel that hark back to the idea of open communication among free citizens in the medieval city as a basis for decisions about how to pursue the public good. In the pragmatist tradition Dewey (1927) argued for the potential of reason through industrial media, defending a version of his open inquiry based on the scientific community, and Pierce (1878) argued that the formation of consensus on the basis of openness was the best guarantee of scientific truth, a position not entirely different from Habermas' (1962) use of the public sphere as a means to theorize democracy. The emancipatory potential of "the ideal speech community" is a meta-discourse where claims can be discussed rationally in the absence of force or any form of coercion, and where only the force of argumentation alone is compelling. This is to draw a strong connection between civil society and the use of public reason, which critically depends on access to education as a means of equalizing speaking and acting chances within a democracy (Calhoun, 1992). As Habermas (1992, p.367) states: "The core of civil society comprises a network of associations that institutionalizes problem-solving discourses on questions of general interest inside the framework of organized public spheres". This model is best exemplified, I would argue, in the notion of the scientific community that is based on free and open inquiry and norms of peer review, collaboration, and cooperation in the name of knowledge as a public good and public good science.

The notion of open science is relatively recent nomenclature. As I have previously argued:

"Open science" is a term that is being used in the literature to designate a form of science based on open source models or that utilizes principles of open access, open archiving and open publishing to promote scientific communication. Open science increasingly also refers to the open governance and more democratized engagement and control of science by scientists and other users and stakeholders. Sometimes other terms are used to refer to the same or similar conceptions of science – "wiki science" and "science 2.0" – that focus on "technologies of openness" that not only promote more effective forms of scientific communication but also increasingly the sharing of large data bases ("linked data") and "cloud computing".

(Peters, 2010, p.15)

The Science Commons dedicated to making the Web work for science made the following recommendations on open science in 2008:

Open Access to Literature from Funded Research. By "open access" to this literature, we mean that it should be on the internet in digital form, with permission granted in advance to users to "read, download, copy, distribute, print, search, or link to the full texts of articles, crawl them for indexing, pass them as data to software, or use them for any other lawful purpose, without financial, legal, or technical barriers other than those inseparable from gaining access to the internet itself."

Data from Funded Research in the Public Domain. Research data, data sets, databases, and protocols should be in the public domain. This status ensures the ability to freely distribute, copy, re-format, and integrate data from research into new research, ensuring that as new technologies are developed that researchers can apply those technologies without legal barriers. Scientific traditions of citation, attribution, and acknowledgment should be cultivated in norms.

Access to Research Tools from Funded Research. By "access" to research tools, we mean that the materials necessary to replicate funded research – cell lines, model animals, DNA tools, reagents, and more, should be described in digital formats, made available under standard terms of use or contracts, with infrastructure or resources to fulfill requests to qualified scientists, and with full credit provided to the scientist who created the tools.

Invest in Open Cyberinfrastructure. Data without structure and annotation is a lost opportunity. Research data should flow into an open, public, and extensible infrastructure that supports its recombination and reconfiguration into computer models, its searchability by search engines, and its use by both scientists and the taxpaying public. This infrastructure should be treated as an essential public good.[9]

The growing interconnectedness of the Web has also passed into a new phase that Tim Berners-Lee calls "linked data", an aspect of the "semantic web" used to describe a method of exposing, sharing, and connecting data.[10] Science is traditionally an open endeavor where the system of peer review is the core practice that anticipates the mode of social production.

Benkler and Nissenbaum emphasize a form of social production that is facilitated by an infrastructure to provide collective knowledge goods:

> Commons-based peer production is a socio-economic system of production that is emerging in the digitally networked environment. Facilitated by the technical infrastructure of the Internet, the hallmark of this socio-technical system is collaboration among large groups of individuals, sometimes in the order of tens or even hundreds of thousands, who cooperate effectively to provide information, knowledge or cultural goods without relying on either market pricing or managerial hierarchies to coordinate their common enterprise.
>
> (Benkler and Nissenbaum, 2006, p.394)

Benkler (2006) indicates that a set of related changes in the information technologies entailing new social practices of production has fundamentally changed how we make and exchange information, knowledge, and culture, and he envisages these newly emerging social practices as constituting a new information environment that gives individuals the freedom to take a more active role in the construction of public information and culture.

Benkler's view can be seen to belong to the broader tradition of thought that theorizes the co-production of public goods through newly enabled forms of "community" that are non-constraining and occur without central planning or the agency of the state.

The potential for OA to bring out a new educational political and economic culture is clearly articulated in the Public Domain Manifesto (2010), which begins with a reference to James Boyle:

> Our markets, our democracy, our science, our traditions of free speech, and our art all depend more heavily on a Public Domain of freely available material than they do on the informational material that is covered by property rights. The Public Domain is not some gummy residue left behind when all the good stuff has been covered by property law. The Public Domain is the place we quarry the building blocks of our culture. It is, in fact, the majority of our culture.
>
> (Boyle, 2008, p.40f)

The manifesto defines the public domain as "the wealth of information that is free from the barriers to access or reuse usually associated with copyright protection, either because it is free from any copyright protection or because the right holders have decided to remove these barriers." It goes on to describe the role and social and economic advantages of the public domain insisting on its status as a cultural right:

> It is the basis of our self-understanding as expressed by our shared knowledge and culture. It is the raw material from which new knowledge is derived and new cultural works are created. The Public Domain acts as a protective

mechanism that ensures that this raw material is available at its cost of reproduction – close to zero – and that all members of society can build upon it.
Having a healthy and thriving Public Domain is essential to the social and
economic well-being of our societies. The Public Domain plays a capital role
in the fields of education, science, cultural heritage and public sector information. A healthy and thriving Public Domain is one of the prerequisites for
ensuring that the principles of Article 27 (1) of the Universal Declaration of
Human Rights ("Everyone has the right freely to participate in the cultural
life of the community, to enjoy the arts and to share in scientific advancement and its benefits.") can be enjoyed by everyone around the world.[11]

Concluding observations

In this chapter I have analyzed and argued for the "openness" that characterizes
emergent global knowledge commons, exemplified in the establishment and rapid
growth of open education and open science. I have been more concerned to make
the case for open education and open science and I have not had the space to
relate these issues to the wider historical context and political economy in any systematic way. It is clear that openness has played a central role in the history and
philosophy of the public good in the developing tradition in liberal politics of the
civil society. I have tried to make this line of argument credible and sketched
aspects of its history, but a more comprehensive approach would require a critical
review of the defense of liberal society and of the ideological nature of the "open
society" as proposed by Karl Popper, Friedrich von Hayek and George Soros –
the dominant view that prevailed in the post-War period. Such a review would
need to contextualize Popper in the era of the Cold War against the background
of state phobia of late 1940s, and the rise of neoliberalism in Germany, France
and the USA, and focus on Popper's links to Hayek and the Mont Perelin
Society. This kind of critical intellectual history would bring out both the differences and dangers of different conceptions of "openness", the distinction between
open society and open democracy on the one hand versus open markets on the
other. It would also plot the rise of the "information utility" and new forms of
"information imperialism" within knowledge capitalism. Clearly, there is a sense
where criticisms of the liberal defense of openness also point to the limitations of
liberal political economy in regard to questions of "open governance" in an era of
globalization, the state's and the corporation's massive new powers of surveillance,
and problems of numerical identity and the digital self. Perhaps most importantly,
the production and consumption of global public knowledge goods are engaged
in a fierce struggle against the imposition of intellectual property rights, the priva-
tization of education and the monopolization of information and knowledge.

Notes

1   This chapter is based on a paper originally presented at the Economic and Social
    Research Council (ERSC, UK) Seminar Series on 'Education and the Knowledge
    Economy', University of Bath, 6–7 March 2008.

2   The Association of College and Research Libraries (ACRL) recently released their research agenda for scholarly publishing around eight themes: The impact and implications of cyberinfrastructure; Changing organizational models; How scholars work; Authorship and scholarly publishing; Value and value metrics of scholarly communications; Adoptions of successful innovations; Preservation of critical material; and Public policy and legal matters. See: www.acrl.ala.org/scresearchagenda/index.php?title=Main_Page (accessed).

3   The full declaration can be found at www.capetowndeclaration.org/read-the-declaration (accessed 2 October 2011).

4   Available electronically at: www.oecd.org/document/41/0,3343,en_2649_201185_38659497_1_1_1_1,00.html (accessed 2 November 2009).

5   Available at: www.olcos.org/cms/upload/docs/olcos_roadmap.pdf (accessed 2 October 2011).

6   Available at: www.oerderves.org/wp-content/uploads/2007/03/a-review-of-the-open-educational-resources-oer-movement_final.pdf (accessed 2 October 2011).

7   I prefer the term OE to OER because it embraces the notion of *practices* as well as the notion of sharing educational resources and also because it gels with open source, open access, and open science (as well as open innovation).

8   See: www.earlham.edu/~peters/fos/overview.htm (accessed 2 October 2011).

9   See: http://sciencecommons.org/wpcontent/uploads/esof_recommendations_onepage_medres.pdf (accessed 2 October 2011).

10 See the Web Design Issues Note by Berners-Lee at: www.w3.org/DesignIssues/LinkedData.html (accessed 2 October 2011); see the whitepaper at: http://virtuoso.openlinksw.com/Whitepapers/html/VirtLinkedDataDeployment.html (accessed 2 October 2011); and Berners-Lee on the next Web at TED (video) at: www.ted.com/index.php/talks/tim_berners_lee_on_the_next_web.html (accessed 2 October 2011).

11 See: www.publicdomainmanifesto.org/manifesto (accessed 2 October 2011).

References

Bauwens, M. (2005) "The political economy of peer production, ctheory.net", at: http://www.ctheory.net/articles.aspx?id=499.

Benkler, Y. (2006) *The Wealth of Networks: How Social Production Transforms Markets and Freedom*, New Haven, CT: Yale University Press.

Benkler, Y. and Nissenbaum, H. (2006) "Commons-based peer production and virtue", *Journal of Political Philosophy*, 14(4): 394–419.

Boyle, J. (2008) *The Public Domain: Enclosing the Commons of the Mind*, New Haven, CT: Yale University Press.

Calhoun, C. (ed.) (1992) *Habermas and the Public Sphere*, Cambridge, MA: MIT Press.

Dewey, J. (1927) *The Public and its Problems*, Columbus, OH: Ohio State University Press.

Goodman, P. (1986) *Amusing Ourselves to Death: Public Discourse in the Age of Show Business*, Harmondsworth: Penguin.

Habermas, J. (1962/1991) *The Structural Transformation of the Bourgeois Public Sphere: An Inquiry into a Category of Bourgeois Society* (trans. Burger, T.), Cambridge, MA: MIT Press.

Habermas, J. (1992) *Between Facts and Norms*, Cambridge, MA: MIT Press.

Ithaka Report (2007) *University Publishing In A Digital Age*, July 26, 2007 Laura Brown, Rebecca Griffiths, Matthew Rascoff, Preface: Kevin Guthrie. At www.ithaka.org/strategicservices/Ithaka%20University%20Publishing%20Report.pdf.

Materu, P. (2004) *Open Source Courseware: A Baseline Study*, Washington: The World Bank.

OECD (2005) "Giving knowledge for free: The emergence of open educational resources", at: www.oecd.org/dataoecd/63/25/38851849.pdf.

Peirce, C.S (1878/1992) *The Essential Peirce: Selected Philosophical Writings, 1867–1893*, Bloomington, IN: Indiana University Press.

Peters, M.A. and Besley, A.C. (2006) *Building Knowledge Cultures: Education and Development in the Age of Knowledge Capitalism*, Boulder, NY: Lanham; Oxford: Rowman & Littlefield.

Peters, M.A. (2010) "On the philosophy of open science", *Review of Contemporary Philosophy*, 9: 15–53.

5 Learning and contradiction across boundaries

Harry Daniels

This chapter is concerned with the development of theories of professional learning as the situations in which professionals work are transformed. The arguments were developed in the course of a study of professional learning during the formation of multiagency services for children in the United Kingdom (see Daniels *et al.*, 2007). This setting was one in which professionals were struggling to forge an understanding of the work of their colleagues in allied but professionally boundaried services. They were confronted by some overt, explicit contradictions in priorities, beliefs and approaches. The study revealed that they also needed to recognise and resolve contradictions that may have remained tacit, implicit or invisible had some form of intervention not taken place. It will draw on the work of Yrjo Engeström and his colleagues from Helsinki who have developed an interpretation of activity theory which has its origins in early twentieth century Russian social science (see Daniels, 2008 and 2001 for details). He has recently asked the following questions of our understanding of learning:

- Is learning primarily a process that transmits and preserves culture or a process that transforms and creates culture?
- Is learning primarily a process of vertical improvement along some uniform scales of competence or horizontal movement, exchange and hybridization between different cultural contexts and standards of competence?
- Is learning primarily a process of acquiring and creating empirical knowledge and concepts or a process that leads to the formation of theoretical knowledge and concepts?

(Engeström and Sannino, 2010, p.2)

From the perspective of this chapter the answers are that learning, in our current cultural and historical moment, is most appropriately and productively thought of as primarily a process that:

- transforms and creates culture;
- involves horizontal movement, exchange and hybridisation between different cultural contexts and standards of competence;
- leads to the formation of theoretical knowledge and concepts.

The case for these assertions will be made by first introducing the policy context in which the research took place, then moving onto a discussion of changes in the nature of work and then onto an account of an understanding of learning which is grounded in activity theory.

The policy context

The UK Government has given priority to tackling social exclusion which may be typified as loss of access to the most important life chances that a modern society offers, where those chances connect individuals to the mainstream of life in that society. This can happen when people or areas suffer from a combination of linked problems such as unemployment, poor skills, low incomes, poor housing, high crime, bad health and family breakdown (Cabinet Office, 2001). These problems are regarded as linked and mutually reinforcing, and it is recognised that they can combine to create a complex and fast-moving vicious cycle. The Social Exclusion Unit (SEU) was set up in 1997 to help improve government action to reduce social exclusion by producing 'joined-up solutions to joined-up problems'. This initiative has given rise to many attempts to counter the long recognised difficulties of joining-up policies across departments. It has also established the need for joint working between Local Authorities (LAs) and a range of other partners through the development of local strategic partnerships (LGA, 2002, 2001). The 2002 spending review prioritises multiagency support in schools and announces a multiagency behaviour strategy which includes the formation of behaviour and education support teams (BESTs) (DfES 2002a, b).

A major concern is that many services are shaped by their histories and organised for the convenience of the provider not the client (Cabinet Office, 2001). In the context of policy and practice for the SEU priority theme of 'Children, families and schools' it is clear that difficulties with cross and interagency working persist and that formulation of policy alone may not be enough to effect the required changes in practice (e.g. Audit Commission, 2002). The Audit Commission report (2002, p.52) suggests that there is a general consensus that agencies need to work more closely together to meet the needs of young people with special educational needs (SEN), but different spending priorities, boundaries and cultures make this difficult to achieve in practice. Clearly new forms of professional practice need to be developed.

The Tavistock review of research on post-16 pedagogy notes that studies of work-based learning (WBL) tend to be pragmatic or instrumental in focus and lacking in a theoretical drive and that findings on how to implement WBL in practice are fragmented (Cullen *et al.*, 2002). Atkinson *et al.* (2002) report a study of multiagency working which identified a number of key skills and factors but did not examine the development of practices in which professional learning took place. They identified five different forms of multiagency activity but did not place these activities within a coherent theory of work. Barr (1999) carried out systematic reviews of education and training in health and social care in order to identify ways in which interagency working could be developed. Demarcations and hierarchical relationships between professionals in hospitals were neither sustainable nor appropriate in the outside community; they argued that new ways of working had to be found which crossed preconceived boundaries. Services were needed which could respond more flexibly to the needs of clients on their own terms in situations which professionals could no longer control. As professionals came together, rivalries and misconceptions about respective roles became evident. The review concluded that professionals needed to *learn* how to work collaboratively.

Collaboration between agencies working for social inclusion also now emphasises collaboration with service users. Powell, in an overview of partnership in the welfare services, suggests that user involvement is more likely to flourish in interagency partnerships where the principles and ethics of collaboration have been explored and understood (Powell, 1997), while the Children's and Young People's Unit is promoting the capacities of young people to shape local services (CYPU, 2000). Professional learning and the development of user engagement are central policy concerns.

Actual government initiatives have included Sure Start, which works with children and their families from birth (Glass, 1999); the Children's Fund, which set up local partnerships to encourage interagency collaborations across services working with children aged five to thirteen (Edwards *et al.*, 2006); On-Track, which focuses on children and crime prevention in targeted areas (France *et al.*, 2004); Local Network Funding (DfES, 2005); and extended schools (Cummings *et al.*, 2004), which offer support for families, activities for children, community access and quick access to other services.

Changes in the nature of work

As the nature of work changes so there is a demand for appropriate theories of work and its organisation and the learning that is required to participate and subsequently learn in these new forms of practice (Cullen *et al.*, 2002; Barley and Kunda, 2001). These theories suggest that detailed studies of work should be reintegrated into organisational science in order to provide a solid empirical basis for post-bureaucratic theories of organising. Organisational changes geared towards cross-boundary collaboration and client participation require new forms of negotiated professional practice (Nixon *et al.*, 1997). Without a substantive understanding of the historically changing character of the work done in a given organisation, theories of organisational and professional learning are likely to remain too general and abstract to capture the emerging possibilities and new forms of learning.

In analysing and developing the capacity of services to learn and work with productive flexibility for social inclusion, we will draw on recent developments in learning and the transformation of work emanating from the Harvard Business School. Victor and Boynton (1998) identify five types of work in the history of industrial production: craft, mass production, process enhancement, mass

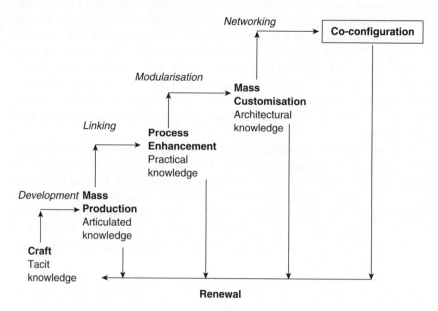

Figure 5.1   Historical forms of work (adapted from Victor and Boynton, 1998).

customisation, and co-configuration (Figure 5.1). Each type of work generates and requires a certain type of knowledge and learning. They suggest that progress occurs through learning and the leveraging of the knowledge produced into new and more effective types of work.

Victor and Boynton (1998) argue that what craft workers know about products and processes rests in their personal intuition and experience about the customer, the product, the process, and the use of their tools. When they invent solutions, they create tacit knowledge that is tightly coupled with experience, technique and tools. This is the kind of knowledge that teachers who regard themselves as 'intuitive' would develop and use.

Through the articulation of the tacit knowledge of craft work, organisations may develop a machine-like system that mass produces on the basis of the knowledge it has 'mined' from craft work and reformulated as the 'best way to work'. This has been witnessed in attempts to codify and articulate 'best practice' in forms which are open to mass training and surveillance, e.g. aspects of the Literacy Strategy in the United Kingdom.

Just as in the shift from craft to mass production, progress beyond mass production is created by learning. Mass production workers follow instructions, yet also learn about work through observation, sensing, and feeling the operations. They learn where the instructions are effective and where they are not. This learning leads to a new type of knowledge, practical knowledge. Linking is the transformation that bridges mass production by leveraging practical knowledge and creates the work that Victor and Boynton call process enhancement. It involves setting up a team system in which members focus on process improvement, which promotes the sharing of ideas within the team, and which fosters collaboration across teams and functions. This has been witnessed when initiatives such as the Literacy Strategy are implemented in schools.

The next move within their model involves the incorporation of the concept of precision alongside that of quality. The producer or service provider begins to try and identify precisely what it is that the client requires. This practice of mass customisation progresses along a transformation path termed modularisation. The new knowledge generated by doing process enhancement work is leveraged and put into action as the organisation transforms its work to mass customisation. This transformation is based on architectural knowledge, the understanding of work required to make the transformation to mass customisation. Recent moves in the development and adaptation of curriculum and pedagogy in the 14–19 sector in the United Kingdom witness this kind of work.

Practices of mass customisation may be renewed when the available variety of options is exhausted. There may be the need to return to craft work in order to leverage out new information, recognising that no universal formula can meet all client demands for precision. The crucial difference between this work and the move to co-configuration is that mass customisation tends to produce finished products or services whereas the emphasis of the next form of work is on the development of the product or service.

Co-configuration is identified as the form of work which is currently emerging in complex multi-professional settings.

> The work of co-configuration involves building and sustaining a fully integrated system that can sense, respond, and adapt to the individual experience of the customer. When a firm does co-configuration work, it creates a product that can learn and adapt, but it also builds an ongoing relationship between each customer–product pair and the company. Doing mass customization requires designing a product at least once for each customer. This design process requires the company to sense and respond to the individual customer's needs. But co-configuration work takes this relationship up one level – it brings the value of an intelligent and 'adapting' product. The company then continues to work with this customer–product pair to make the product more responsive to each user. In this way, the customization work becomes continuous. ... Unlike previous work, co-configuration work never results in a 'finished' product. Instead, a living, growing network develops between customer, product, and company.
>
> (Victor and Boynton, 1998, p.195)

In other words, co-configuration is more than just smart, adaptive products. 'With the organisation of work under co-configuration, the customer becomes, in a sense, a real partner with the producer.' (ibid., 1998, p.199). Co-configuration typically also includes interdependency between multiple producers forming a strategic alliance, supplier network, or other such pattern of partnership which collaboratively puts together and maintains a complex package which integrates material products and services and has a long life cycle.

In practices of co-configuration there is a need to go beyond conventional team work or networking to the practice of knotworking (Engeström *et al.*, 1999). Knotworking is a rapidly changing, distributed and partially improvised orchestration of collaborative performance which takes place between otherwise loosely connected actors and their work systems to support clients. In knotworking various forms of tying and untying of otherwise separate threads of activity takes place. Co-configuration in responsive and collaborating services requires flexible knotworking in which no single actor has the sole, fixed responsibility and control. It requires participants to have a disposition to recognise and engage with the expertise distributed across rapidly changing workplaces. As Engeström and Middleton (1996) suggest, expertise in such contexts is best understood as the collaborative and discursive construction of tasks, solutions, visions, breakdowns and innovations.

Co-configuration is a very demanding mode of work and production. It offers radical strategic advantages when the objects of work demand it. Engeström has shown that in examples of medical care in Finland an increasing percentage of patients have multiple chronic illnesses for which standardised, single-diagnosis care packages are inadequate. In Helsinki, 3.3 per cent of the patients use 49.3 per cent of all health care expenses, and 15.5 per cent of patients use 78.2 per cent of all resources. A significant proportion of these patients are so expensive because they drift from one caregiver to another without anyone having an overview and overall responsibility for their care. Similarly, the Audit Commission (2002) has shown that 68 per cent of SEN expenditure is focused on the 3 per cent of pupils who have formal statements of SEN. Whilst one would expect higher levels of need to attract a greater proportion of available resources, it is argued that the way in which funding is provided may fail to support inclusive practice and often does not result in 'joined up' working. Co-configuration work is a strategic priority because the different practitioners within services and agencies and the service users (students and parents) need to learn to produce together well-coordinated and highly adaptable long-term care and/or education trajectories.

Co-configuration presents a twofold learning challenge to work organisations. First, co-configuration itself needs to be learned (learning for co-configuration). In divided multi-activity fields (e.g. health, education, social services, youth offending teams), expansive learning takes shape as renegotiation and reorganisation of collaborative relations and practices, and as creation and implementation of corresponding concepts, tools, rules, and entire infrastructures. This occurs within and between agencies. Second, organisations and their members need to learn constantly from interactions with the user or client (learning in co-configuration). Even after the infrastructures are in place, the very nature of ongoing co-configuration work is expansive; the product/service is never finished.

These two aspects – learning for and learning in – merge in practice. The learning that is taking place is therefore both personal and organisational. These two aspects of learning are evident in organisational, interactional and discursive practice in knotworking in inter-professional working.

Learning in co-configuration settings is typically distributed over long, discontinuous periods of time. It is accomplished in and between multiple loosely interconnected activity systems and organisations, representing different traditions, domains of expertise, and social languages.

A precondition of such successful co-configuration work is dialogue in which the parties rely on real-time feedback information on their activity. The interpretation, negotiation and synthesising of such information between the parties requires new, dialogical and reflective knowledge tools as well as new, collaboratively constructed functional rules and infrastructures (Engeström and Ahonen, 2001). Much of the recent ethnographic research in professional and industrial work has focused on following professional and client actors constructing their activities, social worlds and accepted truths by means of talk and text (e.g. Kunda, 1992; Darrah, 1996). However, there is a risk in focusing exclusively on actors. The professionals and their discursive interactions may appear as all powerful in their activities and social worlds. To an increasing degree, professional work and discourse are socio-spatially distributed among multiple organisational units and form long chains of interconnected practical and discursive actions. Actors become dispersed and replaceable which renders the focus on actors increasingly vulnerable as a research strategy.

Contradictions

Engeström drew on Il'enkov (1977) to emphasise the importance of contradictions within activity systems as the driving force of change and thus development. Contradictions are not the same as problems or conflicts. Contradictions are historically accumulating structural tensions within and between activity systems (Engeström, 2001, p.137). Activities are open systems.

> When inner contradictions are conscious, they become the primary driving forces that bring about change and development within and between activity systems. Generally overlooked is the fact that contradictions have to be historically accumulated inner contradictions, within the things themselves rather than more surface expressions of tensions, problems, conflicts, and breakdowns.
>
> (Roth and Lee, 2007, p.203)

Engeström defines the 'primary inner contradiction' of use and exchange value as a 'Level 1 contradiction': one that exists within each constituent component of the central activity. When an activity system adopts a new element from the outside (for example, a new technology or a new object), it often leads to an aggravated secondary contradiction, where some old element collides with the new one. Such contradictions generate disturbances and conflicts, but also drive attempts to change the activity. For Engeström a tertiary contradiction is apparent when a more sophisticated external object attempts to supplant an existing object within an activity system. Inter-systemic quaternary contradictions are also envisaged. Contradictions within activity become 'a guiding principle of empirical research' (Engeström, 2001: p.135).

The Center for Activity Theory and Developmental Work Research (2007) website summarises this account of contradiction as follows:

Level 1: Primary inner contradiction (double nature) within each constituent component of the central activity.

Level 2: Secondary contradictions between the constituents of the central activity.

Level 3: Tertiary contradiction between the object/motive of the dominant form of the central activity and the object/motive of a culturally more advanced form of the central activity.

Level 4: Quaternary contradictions between the central activity and its neighbour activities.

Engeström argues (2001) argues that as the contradictions of an activity system are aggravated, some individual participants begin to question and to deviate from its established norms. In some cases, this escalates into collaborative envisioning and a deliberate collective change effort. An expansive transformation is accomplished when the object and motive of the activity are reconceptualised to embrace a radically wider horizon of possibilities than in the previous mode of the activity.

Expansive learning

In many theories of learning, the learner (or learners) acquires some identifiable knowledge or skills in such a way that a corresponding, relatively lasting change in the behaviour of the subject may be observed. It is assumed that the knowledge or skill to be acquired is itself stable and open to reasonably unambiguous definition and articulation. The assumption is that in the practice of learning there is a teacher who knows what has to be learned. The situation we are studying is one in which subjects are learning something that is not known. The knowledge that has to be learned is being learned as it is being developed. Therefore there is no one in the role of teacher.

In the original formulation of expansive learning, Engeström (1987) acknowledges the importance of this form of learning and draws on Bateson's (1972) formulation of levels of learning. Down (2004) provides a summary of Bateson's levels as shown in Table 5.1.

Engeström draws attention to learning level III. He argues that this form of learning involves reformulation of problems and the creation of new tools for

Table 5.1 Bateson's levels of learning

	Description	Example
Level I	Conditioning through the acquisition of responses deemed correct within a given context	Learning the correct answers and behaviours in a classroom
Level II	Acquisition of the deep-seated rules and patterns of behaviour characteristic to the context itself	Learning the 'hidden' curriculum of what it means to be a student
Level III	Radical questioning of the sense and meaning of the context and the construction of a wider alternative context	Learning leading to change in organisational practices

Source: http://www.cade-aced.ca/icdepapers/down.htm

engaging with these problems. This ongoing production of new problem solving tools enables subjects to transform the entire activity system, and potentially create, or transform and expand, the objects of the activity (Engeström 1987, pp.158–159).

Expansive learning and enhanced professional practice occurs in activity settings which enable expansion of the object of activity. Expansive learning involves the creation of new knowledge and new practices for a newly emerging activity; that is, learning embedded in and constitutive of qualitative transformation of the entire activity system. Such a transformation may be triggered by the introduction of a new technology or set of regulations, but it is not reducible to it. This type of learning may be seen as distinct from that which takes place when existing knowledge and skills embedded in an established activity are gradually acquired and internalised as in apprenticeship settings or when existing knowledge is deployed in new activity settings, or even when the new knowledge is constructed through experimentation within an established activity. All three types of learning may take place within expansive learning, but these gain a different meaning, motive and perspective as parts of the expansive process. A full cycle of expansive transformation may be understood as a collective journey through the zone of proximal development of the activity (Engeström, 1999). His argument is:

> The essence of [expansive] learning activity is production of objectively, societally new activity structures (including new objects, instruments, etc.) out of actions manifesting the inner contradictions of the preceding form of the activity in question. [Expansive] learning activity is mastery of expansion from actions to a new activity. While traditional schooling is essentially a subject-producing activity and traditional science is essentially an instrument-producing activity, [expansive] learning activity is an activity-producing activity.
>
> (Engeström, 1987, p.125)

Engeström has been developing conceptual tools to understand dialogues, multiple perspectives and networks of interacting activity systems. He draws on Bahktin's (1986, pp.84, 81) ideas on dialogicality and multivoicedness in order to move beyond the limitations of the second generation of activity theory, which was concerned with the analysis of single activity systems. The idea of networks of activity, within which contradictions and struggles take place, in the definition of the motives and object of the activity calls for an analysis of power and control within developing activity systems. Engeström (1999) provides the following example:

> [Object] moves from an initial state of unreflected, situationally given 'raw material' (object 1; e.g. a specific patient entering a physician's office) to a collectively meaningful object constructed by the activity system (object 2; e.g. the patient constructed as a specimen of a biomedical disease category and thus as an instantiation of the general object of illness/health), and to a potentially shared or jointly constructed object (object 3; e.g. a collabora-tively constructed understanding of the patient's life situation and care plan). The object of activity is a moving target, not reducible to conscious short-term goals.
>
> (Engeström, 1999, p.136)

Boundary objects, translation, and boundary crossing

Engeström also argues that it is important to extend beyond the singular activity system and to examine and work towards the transformation of networks of activity (Engeström, 2000). He advocates exploration of the concept of boundary crossing to analyse the 'unfolding of object-oriented cooperative activity of sev-eral actors, focusing on tools and means of construction of boundary objects in concrete work processes' (Engeström, 1999, p.391). The concept of boundary crossing offers a potential means of conceptualising the ways in which collabora-tion between workers from different professional backgrounds might generate new professional practices (Engeström and Kerosuo, 2003; Engeström *et al.*, 1995). Standard notions of professional expertise imply a vertical model, in which practitioners develop competence over time as they acquire new levels of profes-sional knowledge, graduating 'upwards' level by level in their own specialisms. By contrast, boundary-crossing suggests that expertise is also developed when practi-tioners collaborate *horizontally* across sectors.

Engeström *et al.* developed the concept of knotworking to describe the 'con-struction of constantly changing combinations of people and artefacts over lengthy trajectories of time and widely distributed in space' (Engeström *et al.*, 1999, p.345). They described knotworking as follows:

> Knotworking is characterized by a pulsating movement of tying, untying and retying together otherwise separate threads of activity. The tying and disso-lution of a knot of collaborative work is not reducible to any specific

individual or fixed organizational entity as the center of control. The center does not hold. The locus of initiative changes from moment to moment within a knotworking sequence. Thus, knotworking cannot be adequately analyzed from the point of view of an assumed center of coordination and control, or as an additive sum of the separate perspectives of individuals or institutions contributing to it. The unstable knot itself needs to be made the focus of analysis.

(Engeström *et al.*, 1999, pp.346–347)

They pointed out the difference between knotworking which operates at the individual and collective levels. Thus 'intersubjectivity is not reducible to either the *inter*action between or the *subjectivity* of each participant. Both are needed' (Engeström *et al.*, 1999, p.354). Boundary zones allow practitioners to express multiple alternatives, challenge the concepts that are declared from above by using their own experienced concepts, and through these debates create a new negotiated model of activity (Engeström *et al.*, 2005). In this respect expansive learning is dialogical; it helps to tie knots between different activity systems and find a common perspective by moving sideways using the existing knowledge and practitioners' experiences, as well as their visions for the future (Engeström, 2004). Taken together the concepts of boundary crossing and knotworking are attempts to theorise the actions that take place as networks of activity are transformed.

Engeström has also drawn on Cussins' (1992) theory of cognitive trails which he and Kerosuo suggest serve as anchors and stabilising networks that make divided activity networks and their multi-organisational terrains knowable and livable (Engeström and Kerosuo, 2007). Cognitive trails are constantly created and recreated in the flow of a person's experiences (Engeström, 2006). They are a form of embodied cognition created as people move through space and time.

Trails are both person-made and world-made, and what makes persons and worlds. Trails are in the environment, certainly, but they are also *cognitive* objects. A trail isn't just an indentation in a physical surface, but a *marking* of the environment; a signposting for coordinating sensation and move-ment, an experiential line of force. Hence the marking is both experiential and environmental.

(Cussins, 1992, pp.673–674)

Cognitive trails 'mark' the landscape in which people have acted and they act as a means of support for future action. Although it is not an entirely correct ana-logy, when I was first trying to understand this concept I thought about 'Songlines' or dreaming tracks described in the novel by Bruce Chatwin (1987) which are remembrances which support navigation through what might ostensi-bly be seen as a featureless landscape in rural Australia. Cussins' description emphasises the way in which, once created, cognitive trails function as guides for future action.

Each trail occurs over time, and is a manipulation or a trial or an avoidance or capture or simply a movement. It is entirely context-dependent ... Yet a trail is not transitory (although a tracking of a trail is): the environmental marking persists and thereby the ability to navigate through the feature-domain is enhanced.

(Cussins, 1992, p.674)

These inscriptions facilitate development of new forms of action in the relative unknown territory that is developed when boundaries as crossed. Engeström extends this notion when he deploys the metaphor of mycorrhizae, the invisible subterranean structure of fungus, to describe the emergence and functioning of knotworking (Engeström, 2006). Once developed, mycorrhizae can lie dormant for lengthy periods, but are able to grow mushrooms, i.e. unite successfully heterogeneous partners in order to work together symbiotically, when the conditions are right (Engeström, 2006). Similarly cognitive trails required for knotworking may stay unused for periods, but become re-activated by different innovatively collaborating and improvising actors when new contradictions and new learning challenges for the activity system occur. The subterranean structure has a meaning only in relation to the plants it grows, but the growing of plants (i.e. transformation of activity systems) cannot be understood without taking into account the mycorrhizae-like base (Märtsin, 2007). It is through this kind of metaphorical discussion that Engeström seeks to theorise and understand what might be happening when subjects cross the boundaries that are created in complex activity system networks as they seek to develop and promote new ways of working and being.

In Daniels and Warmington (2007) we suggested that cognitive trails, knotworking and boundary crossing could be regarded as tools for reconfiguring collective labour power. We argue that the notion of labour power may also prove to be a useful addition to the activity theory model of the 'setting of development' with specific reference to the notion of 'subject'.

The categories of use- and exchange-value that Engeström (2001, p.137) identifies as 'the primary contradiction of activities in capitalism' derive from Marx's depiction of commodification. In offering explanation of the internal relationship between use- and exchange-value, Engeström customarily invokes Leont'ev's example of a medical practitioner's work. However, this example of a commodity is only partly helpful, since Marx, in *Capital* (Marx, 1976/1883) and its precursor, *Grundrisse* (Marx 1973/1858), posits *two* categories of commodity: the 'general class of commodities', of which Leont'ev's medicines is an example, and the 'other great class of commodity', which he terms *labour-power*. The latter is described as a potential force: a resource residing in the subject (and in the subject's tool appropriation). It includes an array of qualities: not just skills and knowledge forms but also attitudes, motivation and self-presentation. The definition of 'labour-power' might include the potential or the disposition to form those inter-subjective resources such as 'cognitive trails', 'confidence pathways' and 'trust cohorts' (Cussins, 1992; Knorr-Cetina, 1999).

Education, training and work-related learning are forms of social production of labour-power potential. This has implications for the practical application of activity theory in work-related research, since it suggests that, above and beyond the specific, directly functional object of a particular activity (the realisation of specific workplace projects), the 'meta-object' of a workplace activity system is the expansion of labour-power potential (Warmington, 2005). The development of Vygotsky's activity theory in the subsequent work of Leont'ev and Engeström is rooted in a concern with the *collective* aspect of labour-power. Engeström's notion of expansive learning (in work settings) and his analytic focus on the second and third generations of activity theory implies the meta-object of working on the quality of labour-power: in particular, the quality of cooperation between labour-powers within activity systems ('second generation') and between related activity systems ('third generation').

Object-orientated activity is rendered contradictory because it constitutes both directly functional work and the social production of labour-power, which is always riven by contradictions. These contradictions are experienced by the subject (with its inhabiting labour-power), as the subject negotiates objects, rules, tools, communities and divisions of labour that are themselves contradictory (because they are elements of this double activity and expressions of labour in capitalism). Contradictions are generated because, within the labour process, the human is simultaneously marginal and central within the activity system: simultaneously actor and labour-power resource (cf. Roth *et al.*, 2005, p.7).

Research interventions that apply activity theory in workplace learning studies are immersed in the contradictory double form of object-orientated activity systems: (1) the object of directly functional work; and (2) the goal that is the social production of labour-power. Given this, it is unsurprising that Engeström (2001, p.134) speaks of object-oriented actions as 'always, explicitly or implicitly, characterized by ambiguity, surprise, interpretation, sense making, and potential for change' and urges us to abandon the presupposition that knowledge and skills acquired in the workplace are 'stable and reasonably well defined' (Engeström, 2001, p.137). For, in so far as the meta-object of an activity system is the social production of labour-power, it must be contradictory and, in potential, 'infinitely' expansive. These instabilities pervade the contemporary sphere of 'service industries', the 'knowledge economy', 'reflexivity' and 'learning organisations', wherein workplace activities are as much about the social production of the unstable and unfinished commodity of labour-power as they are about marshalling concrete labour to produce general commodities.

There is clearly still much to be done if we are to develop a theory or theories of learning that are of value in our struggle to understand and gain some control over the rapidly changing landscape of work and its demands. This will involve the incorporation of affective aspects of human functioning into what has, too often, remained an overly cognitive endeavour. As Engeström and Sannino argue:

> The theory of expansive learning currently expands its analysis both up and down, outward and inward. Moving up and outward, it tackles learning in

fields or networks of interconnected activity systems with their partially shared and often contested objects. Moving down and inward, it tackles issues of subjectivity, experiencing, personal sense, emotion, embodiment, identity, and moral commitment. The two directions may seem incompatible. Indeed, there is a risk that the theory is split into the study of collective activity systems, organizations and history on the one hand and subjects, actions and situations on the other hand. This is exactly the kind of split the founders of activity theory set out to overcome.

(Engeström, and Sannino, 2010, p.21)

Engeström has referred to the 'agony' that confrontation with changes in professional practice and identity may entail (Engeström, 2005). Another potential way of conceptualising this 'agony' is that it is the lived experience of contradictions between the efforts of organisations to manage and innovate cooperation between labour-powers, the demands that this places upon subjects in terms of how they are required to activate their labour-power potential within the labour process, and subjects' own, wilful control over activating their 'actual' labour within the labour process. The Russian writer Vasilyuk discussed the particular internal work by means of which 'a person overcomes and conquers a crisis, restores lost spiritual equilibrium and resurrects the lost meaning of existence' (Vasilyuk, 1991, p.10).

In Engeström's latest interventionist research he has noted that whilst individual practitioners were happy to construct new models and tools for changing their work they sometimes appeared reluctant to proceed with implementation (Engeström, 2006). This resistance to the construction of new professional identities presents a challenge to the overly cognitive orientation of much activity theory-based research. In the last year of his life, Vygotsky turned his attention to a new unit of analysis, namely, *perezhivanie*.

This idea has been largely ignored in the development of activity theory. It was refined in the writing of Vasilyuk when he introduced the notion of experiencing defined as a particular form of activity directed towards the restoration of meaning in life (Vasilyuk, 1991). He contrasted his activity theory-based understanding with that of a reflection of a state in the subject's consciousness and with forms of contemplation. The general working hypothesis of learning itself requires expansion to include notions of experiencing and identity formation within an account that includes a systematic and coherent analysis of the wider social structuring of society as an inseparable part of the analysis. This direction provides the possibility of understanding the kinds of learning that are taking place as the economy and its workplaces are transformed.

References

Atkinson, M., Wilkin, A., Stott, A., Doherty, P., and Kinder, K. (2002) *Multiagency working: A detailed study*, LGA Research report 26, Slough: NFER.
Audit Commission (2002) *Statements and Assessments of SEN: In Need of a Review*, London: Audit Commission.

Bakhtin, M.M. (1986) *Speech Genres and Other Late Essays*, trans. Vern W. McGee, ed. Caryl Emerson and Michael Holquist, Slavic Series 8, Austin, TX: University of Texas Press.

Barley, S R. and Kunda, G. (2001) 'Bringing work back in', *Organization Science*, 12(1): 76–95.

Barr, H. (1999) 'Evaluating interprofessional education: Two systematic reviews for health and social care', *British Educational Research Journal*, 25(4): 533–544.

Bateson, G. (1972) *Steps to an Ecology of Mind*, Chicago, IL: University of Chicago Press.

Cabinet Office (2001) 'Preventing social exclusion', www.cabinet-office.gov.uk/seu/publications/reports/html/pse/pse_html/01.htm.

Center for Activity Theory and Developmental Work Research (2007) Website: http://www.bath.ac.uk/csat/.

Chatwin, B. (1987) *Songlines*, London: Penguin.

Children and Young People's Unit (2000) *Tomorrow's Future: Building a Strategy for Children and Young People*, London: CYPU.

Cullen, J., Hadivassiliou, K., Hamilton, E., Kelleher, J., Sommerlad, E. and Stern, E. (2002) 'Review of current pedagogic research and practice in the fields of post-compulsory education and lifelong learning', report submitted to the Economic and Social Research Council by the Tavistock Institute, February.

Cummings, C., Dyson, A., Papps, I., Pearson, D., Raffo, C. and Todd, L. (2005) *Evaluation of the Full Service Extended Schools Initiative: End of First Year Report*, Research report 680, London: DfES.

Cussins, A. (1992) 'Content, embodiment and objectivity: The theory of cognitive trails', *Mind*, 101: 651–688.

Daniels, H. (2001) *Vygotsky and Pedagogy*, London: Routledge.

Daniels, H. (2008) *Vygotsky and Research*, London: Routledge.

Daniels, H. and Warmington P. (2007) 'Analysing third generation activity systems: Labour-power, subject position and personal transformation', *Journal of Workplace Learning*, 19(6): 377–391.

Daniels, H., Leadbetter, J. and Warmington P. with Edwards, A., Brown, S., Middleton, D., Popova, A. and Apostolov, A. (2007) 'Learning in and for multi-agency working', *Oxford Review of Education*, 33(4): 521–538.

Darrah, C.N. (1996) *Learning and Work: An Exploration in Industrial Ethnography*, New York: Garland.

Department for Education and Skills (2002a) *Spending Review: Investment for Reform*, London: DfES.

Department for Education and Skills (2002b) 'Safer school partnerships: Guidance', issued jointly by Department for Education and Skills, Home Office, Youth Justice Board, Association of Chief Education Officers and Association of Chief Police Officers (Ref: DfES/0485/2002).

Department for Education and Skills (2005) *Learning from the Information Sharing and Assessment Trailblazers*, London: DfES. Available online at: http://www.everychildmatters.gov.uk/_files/5E8CB225811E2C2A02D8E3CA93D5AA81.PDF.

Down, C. (2004) *Situated Learning: Perceptions of Training Practitioners on the Transfer of Competence Across Workplace Contexts*, PhD, School of Education, Portfolio of Design and Context, RMIT. Available online at: http://research-bank.rmit.edu.au/eserv/rmit:6311/Down.pdf.

Edwards, A, Barnes, M., Plewis, I. and Morris, K. (2006) *Working to Prevent the Social Exclusion of Children and Young People: Final Lessons from the National Evaluation of the Children's Fund*, Research report 734, London: DfES.

Engeström, Y. (1987) *Learning by Expanding: An Activity-Theoretical Approach to Developmental Research*, Helsinki: Orienta-Konsultit. Available online at: http://lchc.ucsd.edu/MCA/Paper/Engestrom/expanding/toc.htm.

Engeström, Y. (1999) 'Innovative learning in work teams: Analysing cycles of knowledge creation in practice', in Engeström, Y. *et al.* (eds) *Perspectives on Activity Theory*, Cambridge: Cambridge University Press.

Engeström, Y. (2000) 'Making expansive decisions: An activity-theoretical study of practitioners building collaborative medical care for children', in Allwood, K.M. and Selart, M. (eds) *Creative Decision Making in the Social World*, Amsterdam: Kluwer.

Engeström, Y. (2001) 'Expansive learning at work: Toward an activity theoretical reconceptualization', *Journal of Education and Work*, 14(1): 133–156.

Engeström, Y. (2004) 'New forms of learning in co-configuration work', paper presented to the Department of Information Systems 'ICTs in the contemporary world' seminar, LSE, London, January.

Engestrom, Y. (2005) *Developmental Work Research: Expanding Activity Theory in Practice*, Berlin: Lehmanns Media.

Engeström, Y. (2006) 'Development, movement and agency: Breaking away into mycorrhizae activities', in Yamazumi, K. (ed.) *Building Activity Theory in Practice: Toward the Next Generation*, Osaka: Kansai University Press, pp.1–43.

Engeström, Y. and Ahonen, H. (2001) 'On the materiality of social capital: An activity-theoretical exploration', in Hasan, H., Gould, E., and Larkin, P. and Vrazalic, L. (eds) *Information Systems and Activity Theory. Vol. 2: Theory and Practice*, Wollongong: University of Wollongong Press.

Engeström, Y. and Kerosuo, H. (2007) 'From workplace learning to inter-organizational learning and back: The contribution of activity theory', *Journal of Workplace Learning*, 19(6): 336–342.

Engeström, Y. and Middleton, D. (eds) (1996) *Cognition and Communication at Work*, Cambridge: Cambridge University Press.

Engeström, Y. and Sannino, A. (2010) 'Studies of expansive learning: Foundations, findings and future challenges', *Educational Research Review*, 5: 1–24.

Engeström, Y., Engeström, R. and Kärkkäinen, M. (1995) 'Polycontextuality and boundary crossing in expert cognition: Learning and problem solving in complex work activities', *Learning and Instruction*, 5: 319–336.

Engeström, Y., Engeström, R. and Vahaaho, T. (1999) 'When the center does not hold: The importance of knotworking', in Chaiklin, S., Hedegaard, M. and Jensen, U.J. (eds) *Activity Theory and Social Practice: Cultural-Historical Approaches*, Aarhus, Denmark: Aarhus University Press, pp.345–374.

Engeström, Y., Pasanen, A., Toiviainen, H. and Haavisto, V. (2005) 'Expansive learning as collaborative concept formation at work', in Yamazumi, K., Engeström, Y. and Daniels, H. (eds) *New Learning Challenges: Going beyond the Industrial Age System of School and Work*, Osaka: Kansai University Press, pp.47–77.

France, A., Hine, J., Armstrong, D. and Camina, M. (2004) *The On-Track Early Intervention and Prevention Programme: From Theory to Action*, Online report 10/04, London: Home Office.

Glass, N. (1999) 'Sure Start: The development of an early intervention programme for young children in the United Kingdom', *Children and Society*, 13: 257–264.

Il'enkov, E.V. (1977) *Dialectical Logic: Essays on its History and Theory*, Moscow: Progress.

Knorr-Cetina, K. (1999) *Epistemic Cultures: How Sciences Make Knowledge*, Cambridge, MA: Harvard University Press.

Kunda, G. (1992) *Engineering Culture: Control and Commitment in a High-tech Corporation*, Philadelphia, PA: Temple University Press.

Local Government Association (2001) *All Together Now? A Survey of Local Authority Approaches*, London: Local Government Association.

Local Government Association (2002) *We Can Work It Out: In Depth Research into Development and Policy Issues for Local Strategic Partnerships*, London: Local Government Association.

Märtsin, M. (2007) 'From triangles to runaway-objects and mycorrhizae activities: An overview of the Engeströmian version of activity theory', Mimeograph Centre for Sociocultural and Activity Theory, University of Bath.

Marx, K. (1973/1858) *Grundrisse*, London: Penguin.

Marx, K. (1976/1883) *Capital: A Critique of Political Economy*, Volume 1, London: Penguin.

Nixon, J., Martin, J., McKeown, P. and Ranson, S. (1997) 'Towards a learning profession: Changing codes of occupational practice within the new management of education, *British Journal of Sociology of Education*, 18(1): 5–28.

Powell, R. (1997) Understanding partnership: Agency collaboration and the service user', in Pithouse, A. and Williamson, H. (eds) *Engaging the User in Welfare Services*, Birmingham: Venture Press.

Roth, W.M. and Lee, Y.J. (2007) '"Vygotsky's neglected legacy": Cultural-historical activity theory', *Review of Educational Research*, 77(2): 186–232.

Roth, W.M., Hwang, S.W., Goulart, M. and Lee, Y.J. (2005) *Participation, Learning and Identity: Dialectical Perspectives*, Berlin: Lehmanns Media.

Vasilyuk, F. (1991) *The Psychology of Experiencing: The Resolution of Life's Critical Situations*, Hemel Hempstead: Harvester.

Victor, B. and Boynton, A.C. (1998) *Invented Here: Maximizing your Organization's Internal Growth and Profitability*, Boston, MA: Harvard Business School Press.

Warmington, P. (2005) 'From activity to labour: Commodification, labour-power and contradiction in activity theory', paper presented at Contradictions in Activity Symposium, 1st International Congress of the International Society for Cultural and Activity Research (ISCAR), Seville, 20–24 September.

Part II
Knowledge and the economy

6 The educational transformation of work

A synthesis

David P. Baker

> Laborers have become capitalists not from a diffusion of the ownership of corporation stocks, as folklore would have it, but from the acquisition of knowledge and skill that have economic value.
>
> > (Theodore W. Schultz, 1961 – Presidential Address to the American Economic Association)

> Schools used to be for educating people, for developing minds and characters. Today, as jobs depend more and more on certificates, degrees and diplomas, aims and motives are changing. Schooling has become more and more a ritualized process of qualification-earning ... ritualistic, tedious, suffused with anxiety and boredom, destructive of curiosity and imagination; in short, anti-educational.
>
> > (Ronald Dore, 1976)

The ubiquitous massive growth and spread of education has transformed the world into a schooled society – a wholly new type of society where dimensions of education reach into, and change, nearly every facet of human life (Baker, forthcoming). As educational expansion, most recently the expansion of mass higher education, continues unabated into the twenty-first century, formal education not only transforms individuals, it reconstitutes the very foundations of society through a pervasive culture of education with a legitimate capacity to reconstruct work and its central components, such as ideas about human productive abilities, new organisations and management, widespread professionalism and expertise, and the emerging educated workplace. The implications of the educational revolution and its resulting schooled society are applied to the narrow version of human capital theory and education-as-myth sociological theory – two widely employed theories of education and work over the past 40 years. And a theoretical synthesis that takes into account the empirical realities of the schooled society is proposed.

From the 1960s to the 1980s, as the mass education revolution heated up, enrolment rates in lower- and upper-secondary and higher education expanded, and many educators, economists, sociologists and experts of national development predicted dire consequences from a worldwide oversupply of educated youth working in jobs beneath them. In wealthy nations the poster-boy for seemingly run-away over-education was the embittered PhD driving a taxi for a living, while in less wealthy nations it was the angry young man with an upper-secondary diploma who could not find a prestigious job in the nation's civil service.[1]

As the first wave of the masses began to swell into educational opportunities formerly reserved mostly for elites, it threatened the upper levels of the older educational order, which had been tightly connected to a small number of elite jobs. The assumption was that the expanding enrolment would mean that as more students received higher levels of educational degrees than in the past, the upper reaches of the labour market would become full; and with their expectations for an elite future dashed, the over-educated might turn disaffected and unruly. Over-education was considered a looming social problem, even as a kind of disease on the verge of epidemic proportions.

Ironically, at precisely the same period in which the fears of an oversupply of the educated began to circulate widely within intellectual and policy circles, and also the education revolution unfolded apace, a radically new theory about labour in modern economies was born. Human capital theory's innovative ideas, and the research agenda that these ideas fostered, rapidly became a dominant force in the study of economics and the application of economic principles to development of nations' economies.

Human capital and the diploma disease are two polar opposite views of the relationship of education to modern society, serving as bookends around the debate over the nature of work in the schooled society. The ideas originating from each influence how the opposing camps of intellectuals think about education today, which in turn influences how policy-makers make decisions about education programmes and its practice in the world's school systems.

As extremes, these two perspectives produce a certain amount of stereotyping of the 'real relationship' between the education revolution and the world of work. And as often happens in such cases, over-reliance on stereotypes leads to some misconception. Some would have it that there is no relationship between what schooling does for students and what they need in jobs, while others see a narrow one-to-one correspondence between the two. Yet for the naysayer there is growing evidence that not only does educating people change their productivity, having greater numbers of educated people in the workplace changes the nature of work itself. And for the yea-sayer the evidence suggests that the relationship between schooling and work is more complicated and probably less efficient than they imagine, or wish.

Two models of education and work

The relationship between education and work is much studied and there are significant conceptual and empirical literatures from any number of academic disciplines on this central connection in modern society. Nevertheless, some might wonder what all the fuss is about since from everyday observations there are all kinds of indications that education and work are related. And indeed that is what a virtual mountain of systematic research shows in nation after nation, then as well as now, and without exception across the whole literature: all else equal, on average workers with more education make more income than less educated workers. The 'education premium in wages', as this finding has become known, is assumed to reflect an underlying difference in the marginal productivity of workers because of their education. Or in other words, all other economic factors equal, education makes a better worker. But does education really mean more productivity? And if so, how does it generate this change? After nearly four decades of research, answers to these two central questions about education and work are still fiercely debated. By and large, the whole debate boils down to two contrasting models of the nature of the relationship, each one fundamentally different from the other in terms of what takes place in school and its relevance to the world of work.[2]

On one side are the human capitalists who brought education in out of the cold of classical and even neo-classical economics and placed it into the mainstream of economic analysis. For them, education is directly and inseparably tied to work through the ability of individuals to invest in their own productivity through skill acquisition from either formal education or on-the-job training (e.g. Becker, 1993; Schultz, 1961). Even though the human capital literature is full of discussions of 'skill', what it really means in almost every case is 'skill acquired through education'.[3] The main version of the human capital model takes schooling at its face value as an imparter of useful capabilities to individuals; schooling does what it is 'supposed to' in an everyday sense. The human capital model only assumes that what actually happens inside schools is for the most part useful work skill acquisition, so it never really brings this key assumption into question. As tautological as it may be, the fact that there is an education premium in wages in the labour market is enough for the human capitalist to assume that market forces choose workers with greater productivity, and hence education must be the main causal factor behind the wage gap. Even though the human capital perspective was radical for its time, since its inception a generalised form of it has become common, so much that it is now called the 'human capital perspective' on education and work.

The other side of the debate takes formal education to be a kind of myth or even a grand rip-off: schooling does not for the most part do what it is 'supposed to'. It does not impart useful skills as much as it is a rather expensive societal sorting machine telling employers which students have the ability and attitude to work (e.g. Spring, 1988). The titles of Paul Willis' and Jay MacLeod's popular ethnographies of the education of working class British and American youth – *Learning to Labour* and *Ain't No Makin' It* – lean heavily on this idea: Schooling is far more allocative than truly educational. What can be referred to as the 'education-as-myth' perspective, along with its cruder version of the diploma disease, attempts to debunk schooling as an educational transforming process by arguing that it only sorts and allocates individuals into the world of work based on their innate ability and socialisation. Beyond sorting, what goes on in school in the guise of learning is mostly irrelevant and even oppressive (Giroux 2000). Like the human capitalists, the education-as-myth model assumes it too knows what happens in schools, yet it rarely looks inside the black box.

Most economic research on the schooled society originates from a general human capital perspective, while most sociological research is guided by the cynical education-as-myth position. Hence these two major research literatures infrequently, if ever, influence one another. And interestingly, given the important role that formal education plays in each research literature, both positions ignore the power of education as an institution to not only train and allocate students, but also to transform our understanding and expectations for peoples' capabilities, the nature of work, and even what is usable knowledge for economic value. Interestingly, too, there is a fair amount of new research indicating a more complex reality than either of these two models suggests, and it can be argued that this complex reality stems precisely from the broader neo-institutional impact of the schooled society on how we work and think about work (Baker, forthcoming; Meyer, 1977).

Recognising this complexity leads to a kind of new synthesis of the two models. Schooling does in fact include the learning of skills that transform the individual, and when there are mass numbers of educated in the workforce this then transforms the work world. At the same time, schooling sorts and allocates individuals with increasing legitimate authority and this rising authority reconstitutes the main cultural ideas of the productive worker, the workplace and the nature of jobs.

It should be noted that this has been a result of a process of accretion more than a big bang and, as such, the forces behind the trend take some unpacking to clearly see how they operate. The evidence supporting this synthesis stems from several sources.

First, clear evidence shows how wrong the dire predictions were that the education revolution would produce extensive over-education and thus social upheaval. Higher education expansion has not led to any of the problems assumed to stem from over-education by so many sociologists and educationalists.

Second, contrary to older visions of jobs and skills, extensive new evidence suggests that as more waves of educated individuals flooded the workplace, increasingly in larger formal organisations, there were sustained shifts towards jobs with more managerial, communicative components, which yielded a spread of a kind of mass professionalisation of work. This is in large part driven by a new image of the worker and training and skill that was, and continues to be, transformed by the education revolution in the form of educationally produced authoritative knowledge from the university, along with the credentialing of expanding ranks of experts who specialise in a proliferating set of functions and activities in the heavily organised workplaces of the late twentieth century.

Third, new research on technology adoption and the content of jobs in firms shows that the education level of employees causes substantial changes in basic job activities in firms more than the reverse causal direction, which is the one usually assumed.

And fourth, several lines of research show that the schooled employee of the schooled occupation in the schooled workplace does not just come about because of changes in many individuals' skill sets. Rather, what is necessary for these new arrangements to come about is a profound change in the beliefs and values about the capabilities, expectations and qualities of educated people.

In what follows the arguments are developed for this new synthesis between the education revolution and the nature of work in the schooled society.

The evidence about the educational transformation of work

Why the expectations of the education-as-myth proponents did not happen is illustrated in the story of the rise of professionals and managers in wealthy nations' economies. There is a vast sociological literature on the rise of the professions and professionals, a major sub-theme of which is that in modern society profession becomes a pervasive form, or more accurately a model that is spreading through the organisation of work well beyond the ancient traditional ones such as medicine, law and theology. It is widely hypothesised that one of the cornerstones of expanding professionalisation is formal education, particularly access to, and expansion of university-based education (e.g. Parsons, 1971). If this is true, then as mass education expands into higher education, one should see growth in jobs taking on more qualities of professions, as well as the roles of workers in these jobs taking on more qualities of professionalism. And this is exactly what has occurred for a substantial part of the American and many other nations' workplaces.

Two economists of the US Bureau of Labor Statistics, Ian Wyatt and Daniel Hecker, recently compiled the most comprehensive, comparable set of information on trends in occupation groups over the twentieth century to date (Wyatt and Hecker, 2006).[4] Census data have always included information about the occupational categories (menial workers, technical workers, professionals, etc.) of jobs that American workers have done over the last century, but because of different definitions and the emergence of new job categories over time, it was difficult to accurately compare trends across time. Wyatt and Hecker painstakingly developed a standard set of occupational categories that can be used to compare across censuses; thus for the first time there is a full picture of changes in the American labour forces during the time of the rise and acceleration of the schooled society in the USA.

As Figure 6.1 shows, the most striking change over the century is the radical increase in the occupational group termed 'professionals, technical and kindred workers' which increased their share of the overall labour market from about 4 per cent in the early part of the twentieth century to 23 per cent by the beginning of the twenty-first century, an expansion from 1.7 million to over 30 million workers!

Unpacking this overall trend, Wyatt and Hecker show that a multifaceted transformation of the American economy went hand in hand with the rising

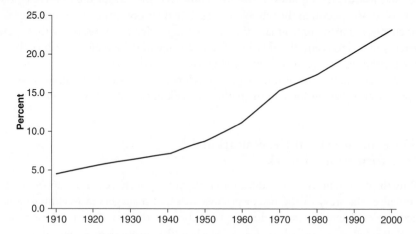

Figure 6.1   Proportion of total employment of professional, technical and kindred
            workers, 1910–2000. Note: Data for 1930 are an average of 1920 and
            1940 data because 1930 data were unavailable when this article was
            written. Source: Wyatt and Hecker (2006, 44).

supply of more advanced educated individuals streaming into the labour market
(Goldin and Katz, 1996). Technological production, particularly the introduction of computers in the workplace around 1970, the growth in size and complexity of formal organisations, the growth in healthcare, education, social
service and government, each contributed to the professionalisation of the workplace; or in other words, the increase in jobs for people with special expertise to
use university-generated authoritative knowledge, mostly trained and credentialed through formal advanced education.

   Correspondingly, computer specialists grew 95 times as a proportion of total
employment between 1960 and 2000; engineers grew nine times from 1910 to
2000; accountants and auditors grew 13 times over the century; healthcare professionals grew five times; educators at the university level grew 12 times, and
teachers, a large single category of white-collar workers, grew 1.4 times (Wyatt
and Hecker 2006).

   Certainly a proportion of this expansion is due to increases in technical components of jobs (see below), but a fair amount of it is due to the growth in jobs
that take on professional – read educated – qualities. Among Wyatt and Hecker's
list of labour market transformations, perhaps the most relevant to the impact
the education revolution had on the mass spread of professionalisation into the
workforce is the growth in the number, size and internal complexity of formal
organisations. In other words, organisations that have formal decision-making,
explicitly articulated rules and universalistic principles, offices holders, and operate under general bureaucratic and highly rationalised means–goals procedures,
as opposed to informal organisations such as traditional small firms, families or
clan, are increasingly prevalent.

As founders of the study of the modern organisation, Arthur Stinchcombe and James March insightfully observed as early as 1965 that a schooled society raises 'practically every variable which encourages the formation of organizations and increases the staying power of new organizations' (Stinchcombe and March, 1965, p.150). Specialised formal organisations are widely found across the globe organising all kinds of human activity to a degree unheard of in traditional society. The world is now made up of formal organisations that, regardless of their mission and societal sector, are based on essentially the same cultural model, a model whose popularity has grown over time, and thus operate in a similar fashion (e.g. Boli and Thomas, 1999; Carroll and Hannan, 1999; Chandler and Mazlish, 2005; Dobbins *et al.*, 1993; Drori *et al.*, 2006). In the 1950s, the earliest students of the rise of formal organisations in modern society barely envisioned a future that has come to pass, but even then they were confident that the emerging schooled society constructed the bedrock upon which a proliferation of formal organisations would flourish.

If one could collect information on the kind of places in which the vast army of late twentieth-century educated professionals and technicians work, there is no doubt they would predominately be employed in formal organisations instead of self-employed or small family-run businesses. This means that more people, across all kinds of education levels, work within formal organisations. Including all for-profit corporations and other economic organisations, as well as non-profit organisations; the shear density of populations of formal organisations results in extensive networks of organisations interacting among themselves, and is a major facet of modern society. But moreover, the emergence of the modern organisations, coinciding exactly with early waves of masses entering secondary and post-secondary institutions, makes it the premiere model of workplace characteristics that were originally adopted by, and now are widely expected by, individuals with advanced education.

Organisational sociologist Walter Powell's insightful study of the emerging institutionalised organisational design of corporations and hence the landscape of labour finds 'how rapidly the social technology of organising work has changed' over the past 50 years (Powell, 2001, p.68). The dimensions of this new social technology have recently been thoroughly documented in a multi-part study of the globalisation of formal organisations by Gili Drori, John Meyer, Hokyu Hwang and nine other neo-institutional scholars (Drori *et al.*, 2006). They find that the new modern organisation has three central qualities largely based on the schooled society's leveraging of the organisational capacity of humans.

The first component, and the one that is most obviously a direct result of the schooled society, is the extensive degree and broad scope of personnel professionalism permeating throughout the modern organisation. Personnel professionalism means two things. First, not only are leading core professionals of the organisation educated and formally credentialed, but so are increasing numbers of others who work there. Education provides not only the people with the skills to function in the modern organisation, but it certifies them as such. Maybe most important is that the system of credentials, in terms of degrees giving access to sets of activities and management responsibilities inside the organisation, has become thoroughly blended with the hierarchy of the modern organisation.[5] Second is that with the notion of personnel professionalism comes a workplace based on ideas towards personnel as responsible individuals who are 'thinking and choosing actors, embodying professional expertise and capable of rational and creative behavior' (Luo, 2006, p. 230), all qualities that have become embedded in the education systems of most nations as attributes expected of everyone. This is in direct contrast to the average workplace earlier in the twentieth century where workers were seen as 'adjuncts of machines, coarse, unclean, unreliable, and prone to drunkenness' (Common *et al.*, 1921, as quoted in Luo, 2006, p.230).

The second component is the increase of intensive rationalisation within the modern organisation. Rationalisation of human activities as an explicit organisational strategy flourished in the early bureaucracies of the nineteenth century, and the social technology of the modern organisation now applies rationalised means–ends activity with more authority to ever more aspects of the social order (e.g. Perrow, 1986; Weber, 1978). Just as the modern organisational form is applied to a wider set of human activities once considered outside the reach of formal organisation, intensive rationalisation is applied to ever more aspects internal to organisations. The rise of accounting and auditing, fundraising, elaborate legal contracts, corporate social responsibility, human relations and strategic planning are just a few examples of now heavily rationalised internal activities of all formal organisations in which an expert culture reigns supreme.

The connection to the schooled society and the world of work is obvious. The underlying belief in a schooled society is that these rationalised domains are to be trusted only to educationally credentialed individuals in educationally created areas of expertise. Hence, the rise in these rationalised internal activities as 'naturally' connected to professionalised occupations, with clear career ladders shared across organisations, standard ethics, technical procedures and professional associations – i.e. the accountants, the auditors, the fundraisers, the legal staff, corporate social responsibility experts, directors of planning and so forth are organisational professionals interchangeable across organisations engaged in all kinds of areas of activity (Drori *et al.*, 2006; Shanahan and Khagram, 2006).

The last component is that the modern organisation has become horizontal in its authority structure. Authority and responsibility are far more widely distributed within organisations than in the past, meaning that aspects of more jobs take on managerial components. The wide-scale impact of this change on the composition of job skills is discussed below, but for example, this change in organisations (along with the rapid overall increase in numbers of organisations) has meant that Americans employed as managers grew from 6.5 per cent of the workforce in 1910 to 14.2 per cent in 2000, or an absolute growth from 2.5 million to just over 18 million managers (Wyatt and Hecker, 2006). In terms of historical changes in job skills in the USA, Howell and Wolff (1991, p.488) find that many jobs have greatly expanded in terms of the interactive skills required of workers, and in particular this means 'the relative authority, autonomy, and degree of responsibility for people and things' – or, in short, managerial skills of various types.

The nature of job skills in the schooled society

If it can be argued that the schooled society has created more jobs in more workplaces that are compatible with the educated worker, it should be true that the very content of jobs themselves have changed as well. Even though this is not commonly assumed to have happened, there is significant evidence that it has.

The most traditional human capital conception of education and skill demands of jobs is that the former services the latter. Somehow jobs change and their skills levels go up or down, or more accurately low- or high-skilled jobs are added or subtracted to the overall labour market, and education (individual's costs to acquire it) adjusts accordingly, and if everything goes right, formal education supplies the appropriately skilled workers for the skill mix of the labour market at any particular time. Seen from this perspective, education does nothing more than produce workers with the skills demanded by the labour market; in other words it has little effect on work itself beyond the training of individuals. For the traditionalist on education and work, the education revolution does nothing more than make productive workers more plentiful, but it does not fashion different jobs.

What if the world of work is not mostly fixed in some preconceived 'natural' fashion and instead expands and adapts given large-scale changes in the characteristics of the work force? Thinking about the education revolution as not only so many people receiving more schooling, but also as a massive transformation of the ideas about people as workers, leads to a very different conclusion about the relationship between education and work. Demand for skilled labour means more than just a change in recruiting and training; it means redesigning the jobs themselves to fit the capabilities and mentalities of high-skill – read highly educated – workers. Recent research on shifting job skills and their relationship to the education revolution shows precisely this.

Working with the same information from the measure of the DOT but with a longer time series from 1960 to 1985 and with a detailed systematic approach to the measures, two more labour economists, David Howell and Edward Wolff (1991), find that across a consistent set of 264 occupations and 64 industries three major changes occurred over the past four decades. First, not surprising, is a persistent decline in the demand for physical motor skills in American jobs. Second, no doubt part of the education fostered managerial revolution examined above, is a sharp rise in interactive skills for working with co-workers. And last is the growth in the cognitive skills of analytical reasoning and synthetic reasoning.

This last finding is particularly telling of the wider impact of education on the workplace. The rise of a culture of academic intelligence that is at the heart of the schooled society is among the most fundamental impacts that mass education has made on modern society (Baker, forthcoming; Young, 2008). It would be a strange world if after most people were socialised in formal school instruction lasting from 12 to 16-plus years of their lives during which they learned these skills and value them in themselves and others, that the world of work did not reflect this change. And by 'reflect' one means more than the mere addition of some higher-level cognitive jobs. Instead, given the large-scale transformation that the education revolution has brought in how people think about thinking, one would expect a similar transformation of the entire workplace. And this is just what Howell and Wolff find.

Benefiting from earlier research on the DOT (e.g. Spenner, 1983; Zuboff, 1988), these researchers calculated two measures of the cognitive skills required in jobs: one is the combined GED[6] measures (mathematics, language and reasoning skills) to form an indicator of analytical reasoning; and the second is a measure of the substantive complexity of the job to form an indicator of the synthetic reasoning, i.e. putting different ideas and concepts together in new ways (also referred to in cognitive development as effortful thinking and new problem-solving). It is notable that both of these skill sets rely heavily on the components of fluid IQ that have been so thoroughly institutionalised as key academic intelligence capabilities through mass education (Baker *et al.*, 2010; Blair *et al.*, 2005). And this is true in the labour market as well.

Howell and Wolff find that from 1960 to 1985 occupations with the highest level of substantive complexity grow from a fifth of all studied occupations to just fewer than 30 per cent. And over the same time, jobs with the lowest levels of substantive complexity dropped to 15 per cent. Similarly, the jobs with higher cognitive complexity attracted large gains in employment growth. Added to these trends over this period is the growth of the entire service sector, which has higher than average skill requirements relative to the manufacturing sector (Howell and Wolff, 1991, table 6).

Also Howell and Wolff find that among the industries with the greatest growth in cognitive job skills there is the least amount of inequality in skill across jobs – in other words, 'upgrading of cognitive skill is associated with narrowing cognitive skill requirements across jobs' (Howell and Wolff, 1991, 498). And this is true even though the American labour market continues to have areas of significant inequality in wages and job conditions. As mass education has spread an ideology of the universal individual with developed thinking skills, change in the nature of some jobs has reflected this shift.

This is not to say that because of the rising skill levels, particularly in the areas of substantive complexity and formal education skills reflected in the GED, all of this is a positive change for workers. Along with these trends in the USA there is also growing inequality in income across education levels, the segregation of females into lower paying part-time jobs (but many demanding considerable cognitive skill levels), and growing inequality between low- and high-skill educated parts of the labour market (e.g. Massey and Hirst, 1998).

It is also true that those who have not played the education game well increasingly suffer in the labour market. Starting in the late 1970s and continuing into the 1990s in the USA, the real wages of workers with 12 or fewer years of schooling fell by 26 per cent and have never recovered since. A similar pattern has clearly happened throughout the labour markets of other economically developed nations and most likely is now happening in less developed economies too (e.g. Berman *et al.*, 1998; Hanson and Harrison, 1995). In the current world economy, the once embittered taxicab driver with a PhD, the symbol of what turned out to be the benign diploma disease of the 1970s, is now very likely to be fully employed in a higher-level job at a good wage; it is the under-educated taxicab drivers taking him to work that are at much greater risk of economic uncertainty than before.

Nevertheless there is compelling evidence to indicate that the content of jobs has changed and that a substantial portion of this change is exactly as one would predict from the growing emphasis on cognitive skills in mass education.

There is an emerging research literature indicating that the schooled society has had a profound impact on many dimensions of technology, including how it is incorporated into work. Largely in the pages of the *Quarterly Journal of Economics*, economists of labour and national development have established an insightful set of empirical findings about the relationship among education of workers, technology and the organisation of the work inside firms.

This research is motivated in part by an intriguing counter-intuitive finding about the expansion of higher education and what economists refer to as the 'college wage premium', or how much more salary college-educated workers make (Autor *et al.*, 1998). The puzzle is as follows: in the USA from 1940 to 1970 college-educated workers in the labour force grew by 2.73 per cent each year, and then from 1970 on increased annually by 3.66 per cent. As the large American baby boom was finishing high school and heading to college, these rates represented a massive change in the educational composition of the labour force that continues into the present. So to economists it made sense that from just before World War II as the supply of college-educated workers rapidly increased, their skills became less and less unique, and so following the law of supply and demand, the college wage premium fell as expected from an advantage of 55 per cent more wage for a college graduate than high school graduates in 1970 to 41 per cent by 1981. But as the supply of college-educated workers in the workforce rose even faster after the watershed year of 1970, the college wage premium did not continue to decrease; instead, paradoxically, it turned and increased so that by 1995 the college graduates were earning 62 per cent more. Yet given the relationship between labour supply and demand (as reflected in wages) this should not have happened, so why did it?

A big part of the answer to this paradox is what education does to individuals and in turn what that means for the use of technology in the workplace. Recently, labour economists have been exploring a phenomenon known as complementary technology, or the process by which the educated worker transforms the workplace through the expectations of what he/she is capable of and hence what technologies will be most productive and profitable (Acemoglu 1998).

When most think about the relationship between technology and the skill capabilities of workers, they think about technology as replacing, not complementing, workers. And there is a long history of just such a relationship; throughout the eighteenth century most innovative technology – spinning jennies, weaving machines, printer cylinders and the later assembly lines, etc. – replaced workers (Acemoglu 1998). And the same process can still be found in today's workplaces; like, for example, when computers replaced some skilled jobs that are now done by less-skilled workers. But this is not the only way technology influences the workplace. There are now a number of examples of how technology complements the rising education of workers and makes employing them more profitable.

Further, it is not just any technology that is complementary with more edu-cated workers, rather it is what labour economists refer to as 'pervasive skill-biased' – read pervasive educated-biased – technology that is responsible for the comple-mentary relationship with education that is transforming the workplace (Autor *et al.*, 1998; Berman *et al.*, 1998; Murnane and Levy, 1996). And this is what a number of studies of firms, technology, and worker education have shown.

Claudia Goldin and Lawrence Katz have shown that much of economic devel-opment has been a spiralling interplay between rising human (i.e. educational) capital of the working populations and technological change (Goldin and Katz, 2010). Noting ironically that virtually the entire American literature on labour history rarely mentions the education of production workers, they find that the education-biased process that seems so newly pronounced in recent decades, actually began in turn-of-the-twentieth-century manufacturing.

Goldin and Katz's review of federal archival documents on labour from the second decade of the twentieth century illustrates that transforming industries wanted to recruit the more educated worker not for his middle-class sensibilities and habits as the education-as-myth perspective insists, nor for narrowly defined technical skills as a traditional perspective suggests, but rather for the cognitive skills found in the emerging curriculum of academic intelligence that went hand in hand with educational expansion and also increased production. As Goldin and Katz describe it:

> Cognitive skills were valued in various trades. High school graduates were sought because they could read manuals and blueprints, knew about chemistry and electricity, could do algebra and solve formulas and ... could more effec-tively converse with nonproduction workers .... Blue-collar positions requiring some years of high school or a diploma were described as needing cognitive skills such as 'good judgment', 'skilled in free-hand drawing', 'special ability to interpret drawings [and] chemical formulas', 'general knowledge of chemi-cals used', '[ability] to mix the chemicals' ... 'knowledge of electricity and electric wire sizes and insulations', and 'general knowledge of photography'.
>
> (Goldin and Katz, 1998, p.718; quoted texts are from US Department of Labor reports from 1918 to 1921)

This historical story is important for the argument here that the unfolding of the mass education revolution had a profound impact on society. Not only is the third cycle of the revolution – the spread of mass higher education – transforming the current workplace, the earlier cycles of schooling expansion also played a role in transforming the workplace of one hundred years ago.

In reflecting on the causes of this earlier trend, Goldin and Katz speculate that the education-biased technology change was caused by the booming growth in secondary education in the USA during the first half of the twentieth century. As other labour economists, they take a narrow view of educational expansion and argue that the jobs created in these technologically changed industries created a demand for more educated workers and people undertook more education as a result. Certainly this was, and is now also, true to a degree, but is it hard to imagine a simple process of job change creating the massive expansion of secondary education for all kinds of people (females, people with dubious academic ability, secondary generation immigrant youth, and so forth).

Lastly, since the education revolution is worldwide, its impact on economies should be observed worldwide. Economists of an older generation speculated that opening trade between rich and poor nations would greatly favour unskilled workers in the latter and skilled workers would suffer, and hence be more likely to immigrate. But over the last two decades there are indications that the workplace in less-developed nations is also being upgraded through the educated worker and his/her ability to use advanced technology.

An international study of manufacturing firms and their production plants by Berman *et al.* (1998) suggest how this is happening. A rising supply of more educated people entering the labour market leads to more extensive use of education-biased technology, so that jobs within plants are rapidly being upgraded through a complementary relationship between education and technology. It is important to show, as Berman *et al.* do, that this is happening across nations within both the same industries and the same plants within those industries, as this helps to rule out exogenous factors that could influence the composition of the labour force. The trend is significant; for example, in many developed nations examined over just eight years from 1979 to 1987 there was a 71 per cent shift to more educated workers within plants; an estimated eight times more potent factor than increased trade (Berman *et al.*, 1998). And of course all of this is occurring even while more educated workers receive higher wages. Further, there is still cross-national variation in the rate of the education upgrading of the manufacturing workplace. This makes sense as the rate of educational expansion, while all in a positive direction, varies cross-nationally as well, which is further indication of the transforming power of education in the workplace (Gottschalk and Joyce, 1998). This is not to conclude that technology is only used for more enlightened production; there is considerable evidence that computers (and the expert-managers behind them) are also used for command and control functions in firms (Brown *et al.*, 2011).

Towards the educated workplace

Education goes well beyond the training of individuals in its influence on society (Baker, forthcoming; Baker and LeTendre, 2005). New research examined here indicates that the schooled society's workplace constantly adapts to the ideas of personnel professionalism within an expanding model of the formal organisation as the main context of jobs, while major control of the massive resources and power generated by technological production goes to credentialed experts. Professionalism, technical expertise and managerial skills are the defining components of the twenty-first-century job. And there is significant job skill upgrading along these lines, particularly in terms of complex cognitive skills and synthetic reasoning that were more or less unheard of in the workplace one hundred years ago. Its ability to redefine people and their capabilities, as well as technical innovation and information, is how ever-expanding mass formal education shapes work to an unprecedented degree.

Most of the research reviewed here is more critical of the education-as-myth perspective than the human capital, but the latter does not go unchallenged. In fact, while the emerging educated workplace supports some of the basic ideas behind the human capital perspective, it points to a number of limitations as well. Most human capital argumentation reads as if there is a natural order of productivity that increases as workers gain more skill. And as is shown above, there is some evidence to support this kind of process in recent decades in the US workplace, one of the most educated in the world. But a more institutional view of the constructionist powers of education also argues that there is no particular natural order of skill; rather as mass education is unleashed on society, it makes a new order of job skill. In many ways the original spirit of the education-as-myth perspective, particularly as applied by Collins' vision of a credentialed society, was on to an important insight; it just stopped short of its full implications. Namely, that education fashions a new order of work in society. Educated workers become 'productive' in an educationally defined fashion, but not as the education-as-myth perspective would have as in a phony way, because there are real ramifications of this new educational order of work. This ability of education to reshape the workplace, particularly in the large formal organisation, along the dimensions of cognitised abilities, personnel professionalism and mass managerialism in the aggregate is underappreciated by the human capital perspective.

The hypothesised kind of tight one-to-one efficiencies among new skill, wages and productivity are not so easy to find empirically, or at least not on a large scale. The relationship among education, job skill and technology is much looser, and hence evident of a fair amount of change at the micro level. There is considerable evidence that changes brought on by mass education of workers simultaneously occur (and may cause change) at the level of the job and economic sector through the educated workplace. The usual narrow human capital perspective must be expanded to take into account the ways in which formal education, both as individual human capital and a mass phenomenon, interacts with the modern economy (see also Bills, 2003). Unless it does so, its explanatory power will be far less than it could be.

The research here also suggests that the education-as-myth view needs to be put to rest, at least in its crudest application. It censors the full extent of insights of a more sociological model of education, technology and work. There is no reason why a perspective on education and work cannot hold the ideas of education as transforming work and the elaboration of an educated workplace together. Schooled individuals are capable of (accustom to and expect to use) certain kinds of skills (particularly along the lines of those related to academic intelligence) that less or unschooled individuals tend not to be. Work is increasingly organised around these skills as education is intensified through educational credentialing that is fully integrated into the formal organisations that contain most jobs. This is not to say that the educated worker is a 'naturally' more productive worker in every type of workplace, as cruder versions of the human capital view suggest. Rather, the educated worker is the definition of productive in the educated workplace. Workers and jobs change together as the full impact of the education revolution unfolds.

A new synthesis of the best of these earlier theories of education and work is in the making (see also Young 2008). A view of the full scope of evidence recognises that the education revolution transforms most individuals and creates new ideas of their capabilities in profound ways never before seen in human history, and as schooling sorts and allocates transformed individuals, it does so with increasingly legitimate social authority, which lends it ever greater power in constructing the dimensions of work.

Notes

1　For some reason most of the over-education literature focuses only on males, but if more attention had been paid to the telling combination of factors behind the similarly skyrocketing enrolments of females these experts might have realised that there is far more behind the education revolution than just a narrow competition for jobs (e.g. Baker and LeTendre, 2005).
2　I am indebted to the succinct conceptualisations of Mark Blaug (1970), Richard Rubinson and Irene Browne (1994) and Peter Wiles (1974); although dated these writings ring as true now as they did then.
3　In the original conception of human capital there were other kinds of investments such as willingness to move to areas with new jobs, and on-the-job training, but over time formal education has proved to be the main investment (Teixeira, 2009).
4　I am indebted to Peter Meyer, also of the Bureau of Labor Statistics, for leading me to this research.
5　See Abbott (1988) for the opposite argument that the formal organisation destroys professionalisation in the traditional sense.
6　GED here stands for General Educational Development and as a measure used by the US Department of Labor to categorise skills requirements of jobs it should not be confused with the GED, or the American General Education Development Diploma, the alternative secondary school degree obtained through its examination.

References

Abbott, A. (1988) *The System of Professions*, Chicago, IL: University of Chicago Press.
Acemoglu, D. (1998) 'Why do new technologies complement skills: Directed technical change and wage inequality', *Quarterly Journal of Economics*, 113(4): 1055–1089.
Autor, D., Katz, L. and Krueger, A. (1998) 'Computing inequality: Have computers changed the labor market', *Quarterly Journal of Economics*, 113(4): 1169–1213.

Baker, D. (forthcoming). The schooled society: The educational transformation of postindustrial society.

Baker, D. and LeTrendre, G.K. (2005) *National Differences, Global Similarities: World Culture and the Future of Schooling*, Stanford, CA: Stanford University Press.

Baker, D., Knipe, H., Cummings, E., Collins, J., Leon, J., Blair, C. and Gamson, D. (2010) 'One hundred years of American primary school mathematics: A content analysis and cognitive assessment of textbooks from 1900 to 2000', *Journal of Research on Mathematics Education*, 41(4): 383–423.

Becker, G. (1993) *Human Capital: A Theoretical and Empirical Analysis, with Special Reference to Education*, Chicago, IL: University of Chicago Press.

Berman, E., Bound, J. and Machin, S. (1998) 'Implications of skill-biased technological change: International evidence', *Quarterly Journal of Economics*, 113(4): 1245–1279.

Bills, D. (2003) 'Credentials, signals, and screens: Explaining the relationship between schooling and job assignment', *Review of Educational Research*, 73(4): 441–449.

Blair, C., Gamson, D., Thorne, S. and Baker, D. (2005) 'Rising mean IQ: Cognitive demand of mathematics education for young children, population exposure to formal schooling, and the neurobiology of the prefrontal cortex', *Intelligence*, 33(1): 93–106.

Blaug, M. (1970) *An Introduction to Economics of Education*, London: Penguin.

Boli, J. and Thomas, G. (1999) *Constructing World Culture: International Non-governmental Organizations Since 1875*, Stanford, CA: Stanford University Press.

Carroll, G., and Hannan, M. (1999) *The Demography of Corporations and Industries*, Princeton, NJ: Princeton University Press.

Chandler, A. and Mazlish, B. (2005) *Leviathans: Multinational Corporations and the New Global History*. Cambridge: Cambridge University Press.

Dobbins, F., Meyer, J. and Scott, R. (1993) 'Equal opportunity law and the construction of internal labor markets', *American Journal of Sociology*, 104(2): 441–476.

Dore, R. (1976) *The Diploma Disease: Education, Qualification and Development*, Berkeley, CA: University of California Press.

Drori, G., Meyer, J. and Hwang, H. (2006) *Globalization and Organization: World Society and Organizational Change*, Oxford: Oxford University Press.

Giroux, H. (2000) 'Postmodern education and disposable youth', in Trifonas, P.P. (ed.) *Revolutionary Pedagogies: Cultural Politics, Instituting Education, and the Discourse of Theory*, New York: RoutledgeFalmer, pp.174–195.

Goldin, C. and Katz, L. (1998) 'The origins of technology-skill complementarity', *Quarterly Journal of Economics*, 13(3): 693–732.

Goldin, C. and Katz, L. (2010) *The Race between Technology and Education*. Cambridge: Harvard University Press.

Gottschalk, P. and Joyce, M. (1998) 'Cross-national differences in the rise in earnings inequality: Market and institutional factors', *Review of Economics and Statistics*, 80(4): 489–502.

Hanson, G. and Harrison, A. (1995) 'Trade, technology, and wage inequality', National Bureau of Economic Research, Working Paper No. W55110.

Howell, D. and Wolff, E. (1991) 'Trends in the growth and distribution of skills in the US workplace, 1960–1985', *Industrial and Labor Relations Review*, 44(3): 486–502.

Luo, X. (2006) 'The spread of a "human resources" culture: Institutional individualism and the rise of personal development training', in Drori, G., Meyer, J. and Hwang, H. (eds) *Globalization and Organization: World Society and Organizational Change*, Oxford: Oxford University Press, pp.225–240.

Massey, D. and Hirst, D. (1998) 'From escalator to hourglass: Changes in the US occupational wage structure 1949–1989', *Social Science Research*, 27(1): 51–71.

Meyer, J. (1977) 'The effects of education as an institution', *American Journal of Sociology*, 83(1): 55–77.

Murnane, R. and Levy, F. (1996) *Teaching the New Basic Skills: Principles for Educating Children to Thrive in a Changing Economy*, New York: Free Press.

Parsons, T. (1971) 'Higher education as a theoretical focus', in Turk, H. and Simpson, R.L. (eds) *Institutions and Social Exchange: The Sociologies of Talcott Parsons and George C. Homans*, Indianapolis, IN: Bobbs-Merill, pp.233–252.

Perrow, C. (1986) *Complex Organizations: A Critical Essay*, 3rd ed., New York: Random House.

Powell, W. (2001) 'The capitalist firm in the twenty-first century: Emerging patterns in Western Europe', in DiMaggio, P. (ed.) *The Twenty-First-Century Firm: Changing Economic Organization in International Perspective*, Princeton, NJ: Princeton University Press, pp.33–68.

Rubinson, R. and Browne, I. (1994) 'Education and the economy', in Smelser, N.J. and Swedberg, R. (eds) *The Handbook of Economic Sociology*, Princeton, NJ: Princeton University Press, pp.581–599.

Schultz, T.W. (1961) 'Investment in human capital', *American Economic Review*, 51: 1–17.

Shanahan, S. and Khagram, S. (2006) 'Dynamics of corporate responsibility', in Drori, G., Meyer, J. and Wang, H. (eds) *Global Organizations*, Oxford: Oxford University Press, p.198.

Spenner, K. (1983) 'Deciphering Prometheus: Temporal change in the skill level of work', *American Sociological Review*, 48(6): 824–837.

Spring, J. (1988) *The Sorting Machine: National Educational Policy Since 1945*, White Plains, NY: Longman.

Stinchcombe, A. and March, J. (1965) *Handbook of Organizations*, Chicago, IL: Rand McNally.

Teixeira, P. (2009) *Jacob Mincer – The Human Capital Labour Economist*, Oxford: Oxford University Press and IZA.

Weber, M. (1978) *Economy and Society: An Outline of Interpretive Sociology*, Berkeley, CA: University of California Press.

Wiles, P. (1974) 'The correlation between education and earnings: The External-Test-not-Content Hypothesis', *Higher Education*, 3(1): 43–58.

Wyatt, I. and Hecker, D. (2006) 'Occupational changes during the 20th century', *Monthly Labor Review*, 129(3): 35–57.

Young, M. (2008) *Bringing Knowledge Back in: From Social Constructivism To Social Realism in the Sociology of Education*, New York: Routledge.

Zuboff, S. (1988) *In the Age of the Smart Machine*, New York: Basic Books.

7 Forms of knowledge and curriculum coherence

Johan Muller

Introduction

The approach taken in this chapter to the questions raised at the seminar on 'The Knowledge Economy and Education' is what can be called a socio-epistemic one. I take it that the forms of the disciplines and the curriculum we have today have their roots in historical struggles and innovations, as well as the diversifying division of labour, and that these shed light on much that seems to us perplexing and intractable today. I also depart from the view that the primary task is to get the big picture clear, by which I mean first trying to delineate as clearly as I am able the range of possible knowledge forms, then the range of possible curricular and qualification forms that are logically entailed. It is within this purview that I will also discuss the issues of 'vocational' knowledge and education.

My conclusions will have an affinity with those reached by Michael Young (this volume, Chapter 8) and Leesa Wheelahan (this volume, Chapter 9) on the subject of vocational knowledge. They, however, start at the other end – with the problem of vocational knowledge – and then locate it in the bigger picture, so naturally there will be some differences of emphasis. For the purposes of this chapter, I will confine myself to the higher education sector.

I will start off by enquiring into the roots of disciplinary difference; move on to how disciplinary differences are commonly discussed in the literature, mainly, but not only, that of higher education teaching and learning; consider the relation between knowledge form and curricular form; develop in the penultimate section of the chapter an account that attempts to relate occupational field, knowledge, and qualification routes; and will conclude with some questions which, with special reference to contextually relevant qualifications, consider the possibilities and limits to academic advancement, and to transferability of forms of specialised knowledge.[1]

Contests of the faculties: the roots of disciplinary difference

Disciplines as we know them today only arose in the eighteenth and nineteenth centuries. Nevertheless, the European university, in a form we can still recognise, came into existence in major cities in the twelfth century, starting with Paris and Bologna. By the mid fifteenth century there were about fifty universities in Europe, and the curriculum was remarkably uniform, from Coimbra to Cracow, so that the students were able to move with ease from one institution to another, an early Bologna-type practice called *peregrinatio academica* (Burke, 2000).

Two features gave it this uniformity. The first was the domination of the academies by the Catholic Church, mainly the Dominicans, so that by as late as the nineteenth century commentators like Samuel Taylor Coleridge still referred to academics as the *clerisy*. This was an apt name, since the European university and the English college system was conceived on the model of the monastery. The second was the organisation of knowledge in the medieval university. This organisation mapped over a double fault line, both faults historically variable, both still with us today:

- The first fault line is the distinction between 'liberal' and 'practically useful' (or 'mechanical') knowledge. The medieval university was forthrightly anti-utilitarian. Consequently, only the seven 'liberal arts' were taught in the university, not the seven 'mechanical arts' – cloth-making, shipbuilding, navigation, agriculture, hunting, healing (later surgery), and acting.
- The 'liberal arts' in turn were divided into two, forming the second fault line: the Trivium (grammar, logic and rhetoric) and the Quadrivium (arithmetic, astronomy, geometry and music).

The 'three philosophies' (ethics, metaphysics and natural philosophy [Aristotelian science]) were also taught, and faculties of Law and Medicine, faculties of the practical arts, were frequently tolerated. At the heart of the medieval university, nevertheless, was the distinction between 'liberal' and 'mechanical', a distinction which embodied a prejudice against induction, experiment, and all forms of practical knowledge; and the distinction between the Trivium and the Quadrivium, the foundational distinction between the Humanities and the nascent Sciences. In the medieval university, the Trivium had unquestioned priority.

The reason for this priority has been acutely sketched by Durkheim. The dislocation between the Trivium and the Quadrivium and the precedence of the Trivium over the Quadrivium in the medieval university depended for Durkheim (1977) upon the attempt to fuse the power of Christianity with abstract Greek thought, the Word with the World. The Trivium, governed then by Christianity (Catholicism) and concerned with inner discipline (carried by the revealed Word), was to be the condition for understanding the World; God's Word as a means for grasping the natural World, inner cultivation as a condition for outer appropriation. This was a spiritual and ethical imperative. Without it, so it was thought, the study of the outer becomes soulless, even positively dangerous. Science without the Humanities becomes a technicist Frankenstein. Starting with the first academics, the Scholastics, then taken over comprehensively by their secularising successors, the Humanists, this has been the perennial reproach directed at the Sciences by the Humanities, and the enduring ideological basis for their antagonism. Below I will examine an emblematic example of this tension, the 'two cultures' debate between C.P. Snow and F.R. Leavis.

In the sixteenth and seventeenth centuries, the secular Humanists deposed the Scholastics as custodians of the Trivium and therefore of the university. The self-styled 'Moderns' deposed the 'Ancients', but in other respects took over their past-oriented conservatism, their disdain for 'handwork' in favour of what Zilsel calls 'mouth work', and added to it the pursuit of individual distinction ('glory') and the pursuit of the 'mastery of word and letter' (Zilsel, 2003, p.229) – post modern textual pyrotechnics *avant le lettre*. The Trivium was expanded to the *studia humanitatis* (grammar, rhetoric, history, ethics and poetry), but the priority of this *studia* over all forms of worldly or outer study was fiercely upheld.

By the seventeenth century, however, the artisanal traditions of empirical procedural 'mechanical' knowledge had grown more sophisticated, and from the ranks of the artist-engineers came a new species of intellectual that opposed the elitism of the Humanists, embraced the experimental orientation of the artisans, and married this to the conceptual analytical orientation of the university-trained scholars: the age of the scientist and the 'new philosophy', also called the 'mechanical philosophy', had dawned. Roger Bacon fought the battle on his own for a while, but not for long. Soon knowledge became a future-oriented, ever-expanding enterprise, 'from the closed world (of the Scholastics and Humanists) to the infinite universe', in Alexandre Koyre's striking phrase.

The printing press played a large role. Written in the vernacular, as opposed to the Latin of the Humanists, the new philosophy spread rapidly, first outside of the universities, where it was resisted, later becoming entrenched where the expanded Quadrivium gradually but ineluctably eclipsed the Trivium. The scientists were careful to differentiate their approach from that of the artisans as well as from the Humanists; Bacon, writing in his *New Organon* (Aristotle's being the 'old' one), warned against emulating the empiric ant (the artisans) on the one hand and the scholastic spider on the other, recommending instead the bee that combined the virtues of both. For a brief time up to the eighteenth century a period of curiosity for its own sake reigned, but in the eighteenth century the application-driven heritage of the crafts asserted itself, and useful scientific knowledge became both valued and respectable. It was at this time that the idea of 'research' and the professional researcher became current, and a range of institutions that were the forerunners to modern universities of technology were established: the 'Collegium Carolinum' in Kassel, engineering academies in Vienna and Prague, and a mining academy in Hungary are just some examples (Burke, 2000).

This did not spell the end of the rift between the 'liberal' and the 'mechanical' arts, alas. Rather, it soon came to underline a new fundamental difference. This difference is brought out well by Cassirer (1943) in his discussion of the origin of the infinitesimal calculus. Newton had, in the development of his mechanics, by the late seventeenth century come up against the difficulty of dealing with motion and velocity, or more generally, change. As a working scientist, Newton's inclination was to seek a solution through analytical induction. He was by no means a crude empiricist, but he was a believer in factually based truth and he needed a solution to a practical problem. The mathematics of variable quantities must therefore, he reasoned, be based on facts, and he came up with the method of fluxions to solve his problem. Leibnitz was a philosopher and a rationalist, who held, in opposition to Newton, that all empirical truth is describable in terms of a prior rational or necessary truth, a *scientia generalis* that went beyond particular facts or special applications. Newton's problem was thus for Leibnitz a special application of a more general logical operation. From a purely logical mathematical approach, Leibnitz thus developed what came to be called the infinitesimal calculus. The calculus, as we know today, not only solved Newton's problem of variable quantities more accurately and elegantly than the method of fluxions, but much else besides.

The difference between these two giants lay in their intellectual approach, deductive in Leibnitz' case, problem-driven in Newton's. But it lay too with the internal organisation of science as a 'pure' discipline as opposed to that of 'applied' disciplines, which brings us closer to our concerns here. Scientific knowledge grows by the evolution of ever more abstract and general propositions; this is its epistemic destiny, so to speak. Applied knowledge grows through an accretion of practical solutions to particular problems. Of course it can be, and is, retrospectively rationalised in terms of its scientific generalisability. But its *raison d'être* is procedures that work; science's is principles that are true.

The rise of science and the waning of the Trivium as the unifying bridge between inner and outer was viewed with alarm and met with resistance by the epigones of the inner. What the scientific revolution of the seventeenth century accomplished was a decisive challenge by the self-styled Moderns to the 'human-centred universe' (Shapin, 1996, p.20) of the Ancients, as consecrated by Aristotelianism, which had become a hermetic dogma of *a priori* truth. After centuries of scholastic certitude, this was now shattered by the 'new philosophy' of scientific truth. The cultural shock should not be underestimated. By 1611, the clerical poet John Donne could write: 'And New Philosophy calls all in doubt', ending with: 'Tis all in pieces, all coherence gone;/All just supply, and all Relation' (Shapin, 1996, p.28).

Donne was registering a commonly felt shock at the cultural displacement of a deeply cherished worldview, whereby the outer world attained meaning only by virtue of its 'relation' to the inner. What was gone was the 'measure of man', man as the measure of nature. At the heart of it was the entirely novel notion of progression towards a not-yet-attained truth that was determined by nature not by man (or God), but could be discovered by man through rational methods and intellectual daring. With the future and man's fate loosed from the comforting embrace of classical-Christian teleology, and now embedded in a world picture of immense integrative power, the classicists, Christians and humanists of every stripe were certain civilisation was headed into a cultural abyss. The threat was felt to every form of social authority that depended on that world picture.

There have been successive waves of revolt against the dethronement of man (the inner) by science, against the perceived philistinism of morally agnostic knowledge, from the Romantics, Nietzsche, the hippies, to our contemporary constructivists and residual humanistic elitists. A thousand encounters tell the story. One, between C.P. Snow and F.R. Leavis, illustrates the undimmed ferocity of this ageless antagonism.

By the 1960s, the sciences were firmly in the driving seat in the British universities. Nevertheless, in the bastions of Oxford, Cambridge and elsewhere a humanistic mandarin elite still held a certain moral authority in the colleges and journals like *New Criterion*. Lord Snow, both a qualified scientist and a published novelist, a Cambridge man himself, presented a Rede Lecture at Cambridge, called provocatively 'The Two Cultures and the Scientific Revolution'. It was at the secularised guardians of elite 'traditional' culture that Snow aimed his provocation. Snow characterised scientific culture as optimistic and forward looking, though regarded as shallow and philistine by the cultivated literary culture of the literary elite, who Snow considered ignorant snobs. He derided the mutual incomprehension of the two cultures: 'The degree of incomprehension on both sides is the kind of joke which has gone sour' (Snow, 1993, p.11) and lamented the 'sheer loss to us all' (ibid.). The fault he laid squarely at the door of the literary intellectuals, calling them 'natural Luddites' who lacked the culture to grasp the second law of thermodynamics, a piece of general cultural knowledge he likened to knowing something about Shakespeare. He compared Britain unfavourably to the then Soviet Union, who, he said, produced educated men and women with a grasp of science and scientific culture.

The fallout was immediate, and has continued, the book version of the 'two cultures' having been reprinted 31 times by 1993. Despite his oversimplifications, Snow had hit a nerve. The most extreme response came from F.R. Leavis, doyen of the literary elite (Kimball, 1994). In a lecture first given also at Cambridge, then published in *The Spectator*, and re-published in Leavis (1972), Leavis heaped derision on Snow's 'embarrassing vulgarity of style', on his ignorance, and on his ineptness as a novelist; he is, said Leavis, as 'intellectually undistinguished as it is possible to be'. Leavis' attack drew an avalanche of responses, which called it *inter alia* 'bemused drivelling' of 'unexampled ferocity' (ibid.).

The ferocity, characteristic of the antagonism through the ages, should not obscure the terms of the response. Leavis is here clearly trying to re-wrest the governance of discernment back for the literary intellectuals, and away from the 'philistinism' of Snow and his plea for recognition of the 'culture' of science. Leavis' principal argument is to deny that science has such a thing as a 'culture'. Science cannot have a 'culture' because it has no intrinsic moral resource; it is a discourse of 'means', and cannot deal with morally loaded 'ends', which is the province of 'real culture' like literature. Snow from Leavis' point of view has thus an anti-cultural bias, which serves to mask the 'moral challenges of science' by presenting them as capable of being dealt with by science on its own. In short, Leavis responds in the spirit of the Trivium by re-invoking the necessary connection between inner and outer that formed the rationale for Trivium precedence. Snow, in this argument, is attenuating their dislocation (see also Maton, 2007).

The tide has turned decisively against the Humanists for the time being; a new rapprochement between inner and outer is needed, but is nowhere to be discerned. Scientific productivity is now the pre-eminent measure of the global university; measures of eminence obdurately favour the sciences, propelling academic drift everywhere. In the meanwhile, within the sciences, application – or relevance – is increasingly prized. We will presently return to the meanings of this historical moment.

Before concluding this section on the wellsprings of modern knowledge, a brief comment on disciplinary evolution outside Europe is in order. It has frequently been remarked that in certain respects the Islamic world matched, even led, Europe in the medieval and early modern period. There were no universities as such in Baghdad, Cairo and Damascus. Rather, the madrasas, religious schools attached to mosques, bore some resemblance to the colleges of Oxford and Cambridge. A distinction parallel to the Trivium/Quadrivium one was made between 'Islamic sciences' (study of the Q'ran, sayings of the Prophet, Muslim law, theology, poetry, and Arabic) and 'foreign sciences' (arithmetic and natural philosophy), the latter subordinate to the former. In contrast to Europe, the study circle and the curriculum were far more fluid and informal; students moved from master to master, and qualifications were also less formalised. It mattered more *who* you studied with than *what* you studied. Islamic resistance to academic institutionalisation was, as Burke (2000) says, impressive, a resistance extended to hostility to codification and to the printing press. All of these hampered the evolution and spread of Islamic learning. The madrasas of the Ottoman Empire and Istanbul followed this pattern.

This section of the chapter has been concerned to outline the lineaments of two enduring fault lines in the evolution of the disciplines as we know them. These are first, a rift between the disciplines of the inner and the disciplines of the outer – what we would call the Arts and Humanities on the one hand, and the Sciences on the other. Second, there is the rift between the 'liberal' and 'mechanical' disciplines – what we would call the 'pure' disciplines on the one hand, and the practical 'applied' disciplines on the other. Although disciplines have come and gone, although we live now in a time of unprecedented flux and fluidity, with fields of specialisation periodically opening up new regions of interdisciplinary inquiry, these fault lines continue to exert their influence on the pattern of the disciplines in the contemporary university, and on the curriculum.

Contemporary analyses of the disciplines

In 1973 Anthony Biglan (1973a, b) published a pair of papers that publicised a set of disciplinary distinctions that have been remarkably enduring. The first and most significant distinction was between disciplines that were 'hard' or 'soft'.[2] Biglan meant to mark out a continuum of characteristics of disciplines that differed as to the degree to which they operated with a 'paradigm' or not. Biglan meant by 'paradigm' exactly what Thomas Khun had originally meant by a paradigm, that is, 'the degree of consensus or sharing of beliefs within a scientific field about theory, methodology, techniques and problems' (Landahl and Gordon, 1972, p.58). There is in other words a great measure of agreement about what is known, what constitutes a novel problem, and what constitutes a legitimate way to solve it.[3] Notable about this definition is its sociological implications: it designates the degree of 'social connectedness among scholars'. Where 'paradigmicity' is high, as Durkheim had already spelt out in his analysis of increasing specialisation, this permits greater functional differentiation and hence requires greater interdependence, greater cooperation, the hallmarks of organic solidarity, making possible significant time economies. Where disciplines do not share a paradigm, we find low differentiation, low interdependence and hence low social connectedness. Cognate distinctions to 'paradigmicity' would be Toulmin's (1972) distinction between 'compact' versus 'diffuse'; Pantin's (1968) between 'restricted' versus 'unrestricted'; Merton's (1992) between high or low 'codification'; and Bernstein's (2000) hierarchical and horizontal knowledge structures.[4]

Biglan also distinguished between 'pure' and 'applied' disciplines. This distinction has not been given the same conceptual underpinning as the 'hard/soft' distinction, but has also stuck. Taken together, they form a four part continuum. Other distinctions, like that of Kolb, followed suit (Table 7.1).

Becher expanded and filled in the purview of Biglan's quaternary. He started out by distinguishing four layers of what he called academic culture: a generic common layer pertaining to all academics everywhere; a layer pertaining to Biglan's four disciplinary clusters, which Becher calls *tribes*, and two other sublayers pertaining to disciplines and sub-disciplines. The tribes are the key layer: each tribe has its own intellectual values, its own cultural domain, and its own cognitive territory. In this way Becher tries to make explicit the inescapable duality of the social and the cognitive in considering the worlds of knowledge work.

Becher sets out to characterise both the *cultural style* and *cognitive style* of each of Biglan's tribes. I summarise these in Tables 7.2 and 7.3.

This account captures something essential going on between the tribes, especially if we recall Biglan's master trope of 'paradigmicity' and 'social connectedness'. The 'hards' are higher in social connectedness, so they collaborate more in teaching, especially at the lower levels where less is contentious. Consequently, they spend far less time than the 'softs' in lesson preparation. Since their

Table 7.1 A typology of the disciplines

Biglan (1973 a, b)	Hard pure	Soft pure	Hard applied	Soft applied
Kolb (1981)	Abstract reflective	Concrete reflective	Abstract active	Concrete active
Examples	Natural sciences	Social sciences	Science-based professions	Social professions

Table 7.2 Cultural style of the tribes

Hard pure	Hard applied	Soft pure	Soft applied
Competitive Gregarious Politically well- organised Task oriented High publication rate	Entrepreneurial Cosmopolitan Role oriented Patents rather than publications Contract work	Individualistic Loosely organised Person oriented Low publication rate Funding less important	Status anxiety Prey to intellectual fashions Power oriented Low publication rate Vulnerable to funding pressures

Table 7.3 Cognitive style of the tribes

Hard pure	Hard applied	Soft pure	Soft applied
Cumulative, iterative	Purposive	Reiterative	Functional
Atomistic	Pragmatic	Holistic	Utilitarian
Pursuit of universals	Know-how via hard knowledge	Pursuit of particulars	Know-how via soft knowledge
Quantities and simplification	Mastery of environment	Qualities and complication	Enhancement of practice
Discovery/ explanation	Products/ techniques	Understanding/ interpretation	Protocols/ procedures

teaching, research and supervision is better integrated, and since they spend less time on supervision – less than a quarter of the time spent by 'softs' (Smeby, 1996; 2000) – they have far more time for research, which they see as their fundamental mission as academics. The 'softs' by contrast spend far more time both on lesson preparation and on actual teaching; they spend far more time on undergraduate teaching than on supervising postgraduates, unlike the 'hards'; and supervision is a far greater chore for the 'softs' than it is for the 'hards', because they all too often supervise outside their own specific research focus area (Neuman *et al.*, 2002). Invariably then, they end up researching and publishing less.

Other implications for the production and distribution of the disciplines are spelt out by Robert Merton. He establishes in a terse formulation his version of 'hardness' and 'paradigmicity' in terms of 'codification': 'Codification refers to the consolidation of empirical knowledge into succinct and interdependent theoretical formulations. The various sciences and specialities within them differ in the extent to which they are codified' (Merton, 1992, p.507; see also Foray and Hargreaves, 2003). Merton's definition of codification helps to reinforce the Durkheimian nostrum of the relations between cognitive relations and social relations: high theoretical interdependence entails high social interdependence; low theoretical interdependence entails low social interdependence (Muller, forthcoming). Degree of codification has a series of consequences, three of which are the following:

- Because they display a greater tendency to integrate existing knowledge, there is a higher rate of obsolescence in high codification (C +) than in low codification (C −) disciplines. One consequence is that there is a greater percentage of references to recent rather than older work in C + than is the case in C − disciplines. This has in turn an effect on disciplinary citation patterns. In the C − disciplines, citations take longer to register, and citation counts tend to be smaller.
- Because of higher agreement and interdependence, innovative work by young scholars in C + disciplines is more easily recognised than in C − disciplines, where it is easier to be overlooked, leading to what Merton calls the Matthew Effect (Merton, op.cit., p.516), from St Matthew: to him who hath shall be given, etc. Young scholars find it difficult to break into C − disciplines. One consequence is that there are age differences in discovery patterns, summed up famously by Caius Asinius Pollio in Robert Graves' *I Claudius*: 'Science is a young man's game' while 'history is an old man's game' (op.cit., fn. 39, p.513), or Merton, with the irony for which he was famous: 'This sort of thing can thus foster the illusion that good mathematicians die young, but that, say, good sociologists linger on forever' (op. cit.).

This feature is not lost on the tribesmen themselves. The theoretical physics inner circle, meeting in Copenhagen for their annual Easter conference in 1932, produced as part of their high-spirited activities a spoof on Goethe's *Faust*. Woven into the play was the theme that the 'boy geniuses' who invented quantum mechanics in 1925 were by 1932 already over the hill. Paul Dirac is given the following lines to speak: 'Old age is a cold fever/That every physicist suffers with!/When one is past thirty,/He is as good as dead!' (Dyson, 2007, p.46).

- Induction into C + disciplines entails grasping high-level propositions; into C − disciplines, into learning masses of particulars. Induction opportunity costs consequently differ: the former will always be more rapidly learnt, all things being equal, than the latter. The result is that students of the former typically learn more high-level knowledge in the same amount of time as the latter do. Of course, the latter valorise knowledge of particulars. But in a global world, power resides with generalisable knowledge, because of the master trope of innovation. The former must therefore be at an advantage, all things being equal.

   In addition, because the high level propositions of the C + discipline are broadly shared, there are high levels of agreement about disciplinary foundations. This means that any adept can teach them, and, consequently, the work is easily shared. In C − disciplines, the foundations taught often depend on the predilections of who gets allocated to teach them. When these professors move on, the foundations taught are also likely to change.

The 'applieds', as we saw already in the previous section, deal in pragmatic and useful knowledge, knowledge marshalled towards a worldly goal. Their primary pedagogic aim is to produce practitioners, and their primary research aim is to produce useful know-how. Consequently, they tend to produce far fewer research-oriented graduates, and less research published in scientific forums. They also typically turn out more unpublished (and unpublishable, because of intellectual property issues) contract research reports than either their 'pure' science or humanities peers.

Sectoral and institutional battles have arisen around the 'professional doctorate', which typically has a lighter research-based requirement – the Doctor of Business Administration and the Educational Doctorate, for example. These are more and more common, though still tenaciously resisted in some quarters because of the 'potential for diminution of the epistemic foundations of doctoral study' (Parry, 2007, p.144). These foundations are set, of course, by the 'pures', but interestingly seem to be defended most vociferously by the harder of the soft pures (like Economics), and the hard applieds (like Engineering); as Bourdieu likes to remind us, it is the dominated fractions of the dominant social formations that are most keenly attuned to relative advantage, and defend it grimly.

Questions remain, however: should all disciplines aspire to 'paradigmicity'? Is 'hardness' a normative ideal for all disciplines to which 'softness' is but a weak and premature approximation? Are the 'softs' mere cognitive juveniles in the kingdom of knowledge? Ought and will they still mature? Kuhn and Popper certainly thought so: the prefix 'pre' in Kuhn's description of the social sciences as 'pre-paradigmatic' is symptomatic. 'Hardness' in this view is a quality that, though historically conditioned, can be delayed but not denied. It is a quality that defines science and scientificity. By this view, the social sciences are deficit sciences. Exceptions are half-heartedly made for the Humanities. This is the 'mechanical' world picture, now modernised almost beyond recognition and unquestionably dominant, that the Humanists have been in revolt over ever since the dethronement of the Trivium in the Renaissance.

There is one more set of distinctions to be made about knowledge fields before we move on to the curriculum proper. The account developed above seems to suggest that the epistemic destination of all knowledge fields bar the Humanities is either progressive abstraction ('hardness') or fission (breaking off into alternative theoretical languages). There is another alternative. This is that independent disciplines may *converge* to form a new field, or *'region'*, of knowledge, comprised of a cluster of disciplines now come together to focus on a supervening purpose. This purpose may be driven by intellectual imperatives, as is the case with some new regions like biotechnology and cognitive science. More usually, regions are designed to support a domain of professional practice. In the process, they may retain their specialised distinctiveness as in certain sections of medicine and law; or they may be 'recontextualised' into a virtual generic field like 'Business Studies' (Young, 2006a, b; Wheelahan, 2007b).

The traditional professions[5] – law, medicine, engineering, accounting, architecture for example – have over the centuries developed stable ways of determining and updating the knowledge base of the profession, in concert with a strong social base in the organisation of the profession. Although these professions exercise a strong contextual grip over professional training, the university-based trainers have over time developed an impressive autonomy over their work, and they tend to present a united front to both the academy and the world. The traditional professions have thus evolved a powerful way to develop a robust *professional habitus* and *identity* in their practitioners, deep induction into the 'values of the profession, its standards of professional integrity, judgement and loyalty' (Beck and Young, 2005, p.188). Indeed, these professional identities, albeit 'projected' from the profession rather than solely 'introjected' from the discipline (Bernstein, 2000), are similarly stable and robust. Both depend upon a degree of insulation, or 'necessary distance' (Muller, 2005) from managerial or state interference.

Professions like teaching, clinical psychology and social work have joined the traditional professions, and have developed their regional knowledge bases, aspiring to the autonomy and stability of the traditionals but not (yet) in their league, both in terms of their social organisation and their disciplinary robustness. More recently, a new kind of profession, sometimes called fourth generation professions, has come to the fore which has given rise to new regions like tourism, business studies and information science. These new professions and their regional knowledge bases differ in a number of respects from the older ones. First, the profession itself is, generally speaking, more diffuse, fluid, less organised, and consequently sends out more ambiguous, frequently contradictory signals about professional requirements to the academy. The division of labour in the field is simple, occupational roles often blurred, with role specifications unclear. Coupled to this simpler social base, the associated region has a certain arbitrariness to it, which derives in part from the fact that the core knowledge base has not yet shaken down into a stable, generally accepted, incremental body of knowledge. Emblematic of this is the fact that the new regions rarely have foundational disciplines in their core curricula. The overall consequence of the relatively simple social base, the lack of an accepted body of professional knowledge, and the lack of a foundational disciplinary core, is that adepts develop a relatively weak professional identity as compared with their peers in the older professions and the disciplines.

To see why, it is useful briefly to consider the dual nature of academic identity. Identity is, like many social science objects, Janus-faced: the one face is identification, induction into a community of practice, joining a club of those with similar values and competences; the other face is individuation, developing one's unique niche or 'voice', becoming a recognised innovator in an established tradition. The first face points to identity as dependence, conformity to the community's values and standards; the second points to identity as independence and novelty, setting new standards (Henkel, 2000, 2005). A strong academic identity thus binds the social to the cognitive: it means both a strong, stable intellectual or professional community, and a robust means for recognising and generating innovation within it. The one depends upon the other.[6]

This begins to suggest why newer regions without disciplinary foundations might be weak, and might inculcate weak academic identities. Such a region may even be strong on practice-oriented 'know-how' necessary for professional tasks, but without a disciplinary core, the knowledge base will be weak on 'know-why', the knowledge condition for exploring alternatives systematically and for generating innovation (Becher and Parry, 2005). This explains why regions with strong disciplinary foundations – like engineering and medicine – are also research-rich regions; they produce people with strong academic identities able and inclined towards producing novelty through research, while regions with weak or non-existent disciplinary foundations, like tourism, do not. The curriculum planning message here is that disciplinary foundations are one key to strengthening both the identities of adepts and the research activity in the region.

Although 'regions' and 'regionalisation' are explanatory social scientific concepts, some have taken them to signify something desirable, something to be actively encouraged. For those of this persuasion, disciplines are bad, while inter-disciplinarity and regions are good, as are the curricular bedfellows of the new regions – programmes, modularisation, and the ideal of curriculum integration. In periods of social change, regionalisation and programmatisation are seen as virtuous policy ideals. Ensor (2006) has graphically shown how the Department of Education project in the late 1990s of programmatisation had decidedly mixed results at a number of the universities. The reason for this is clear: academics in stable institutions with strong academic identities located in strong disciplines or regions had the wherewithal to resist programmes, which these academics correctly perceived had the potential to undermine the disciplines. This resilience of strong academic identities has been frequently noted (Henkel, 2005; Moore, 2005). In newer or less well established institutions, such resilience is in shorter supply, and it has been noted that policies of regionalisation and programmatisation have been more likely to take hold in the newer institutions worldwide (Bernstein, 2000).

The point for present purposes is that regions and programmes are neither good nor bad in themselves. They are the appropriate form for some fields of knowledge but not for others. When regionalisation is inappropriately foisted on disciplines, it can cause long-term damage. By the same token, weak regions ill serve both the professional community and academia, and therefore deserve strengthening. But this strengthening cannot be pedagogically driven, a point returned to later.

This story began with the medieval curriculum – the Trivium and the Quadrivium – but the analysis more recently has focused on the disciplines and regions as research or knowledge-producing institutions, as we have seen above. Are disciplines and the curricula that are designed to induct students into their mysteries one and the same thing? And do these curricula have the same forms and features as their parent disciplines? The answer is not as straightforward as one might expect.

Disciplines[7] and the curriculum

We normally speak as if disciplinary knowledge and curricular knowledge are one and the same thing, as if what teachers and university lecturers teach is the discipline itself. Indeed, insofar as Becher and his co-workers refer to the curriculum they tend to make this assumption too. But there is an honourable tradition in curriculum theory and development that makes no such assumption. In this tradition it is assumed, in contrast, that the inevitable selections and arrangements that go to make up the curriculum create a quite different animal to the discipline as it is practised by adepts in the university. Dewey called the transforming process 'psychologising' the discipline; Bruner spoke of 'conversion', and Schwab of 'translation' (Deng, 2007). Bernstein (2000) called it 'recontextualisation', to emphasize the widely differing contexts of producing new knowledge in the university, and reproducing it in the classroom, particularly in schools.

Bernstein went so far as to deny that the logic of the curriculum could be derived from the logic of the discipline.[8] If this is taken to mean that recontextualisation (or 'pedagogisation') wipes out any link back to the parent discourse, then this is surely too strong. Why that should be so can be seen in studies that compare what is learnt in the school curriculum with what is required at university. Dempster and Hugo (2006) studied the new biology syllabus for the senior school phase. They found that the syllabus drafters had tried to be very sensitive in their handling of the scientific/religious debate about evolution and creationism, with the result that they had tried to accommodate both evolution and creationism. Despite the laudable democratic intents of this policy, the pedagogical result was that key resources of biodiversity were foregone, and most critically, the conceptual spine required to grasp evolution as a scientific theory was scrambled and the conceptual sequence skewed. Yet this conceptual spine is assumed to be known by the time learners get to university.

But what exactly did the syllabus writers get wrong? Chisholm *et al.* (2000) provide an answer to this question in their review of Curriculum 2005. In a manner analogous but not identical to the hard/soft distinction, they start by characterising the form of internal coherence of curricula, distinguishing between curricula which have *conceptual coherence* and those which have *contextual coherence*.[9] The former is akin to what Parry (2007) calls the 'epistemological core' of the discipline, the latter, the principle of coherence appropriate to a region. Conceptual coherence curricula have what Merton calls high codification; they presume a hierarchy of abstraction and conceptual difficulty. Contextual coherence curricula, on the other hand, are segmentally connected, where each segment is adequate to a context, sufficient to a purpose. Here, adequacy is externally guaranteed, often by a profession or professional statutory body, where in the former, adequacy is internally guaranteed.

The critical curricular implications are twofold. First, the more vertical the curriculum and the more crucial is conceptual coherence, the more sequence matters. Later elements depend upon earlier elements first being grasped (they display 'prerequisite relations' in Posner and Strike's (1976, p.681) terms). The more segmental the curriculum, on the other hand, the less sequence matters; what matters is coherence to context, where external requirements and constituencies legitimately take a greater interest in curricular focus, content and adequacy. Second, the more that conceptual coherence matters, the clearer must be the knowledge signposts, both illustratively and evaluatively. Learners must know what counts as a good answer more especially when there is no external adequacy-to-context to act as a visible corrective. Simplifying, one might say that conceptual coherence curricula are regulated by adequacy to truth (logic); contextual coherence curricula by contextual adequacy, to a particular specialised form of practice.

What the Review Committee found was that the original designers of Curriculum 2005 had proceeded as if contextual coherence was the sole, or almost only, requirement to be met in the school curriculum. Arranging the curriculum in terms of a set of segmental activities rather than in a hierarchy of concepts to be grasped is, by and large, what a radical outcomes-based (OBE) curriculum format does. The consequence for the conceptual disciplines was, and is, a curriculum whose signalling of knowledge and sequence was and is wholly inadequate.

The moral of this digression is to show that, while curriculum formats are arbitrary in the sense that designers can indeed impose patterns of their choosing, these patterns can be judged to be more or less compatible with disciplinary structure. Disciplinary form thus does impose constraints on appropriate curricular form. An important corollary is that it is just this form that imposes constraints on curricular interdisciplinarity; not that it cannot happen, but that not everything goes with everything. This general point will be sharpened below.

This section of the chapter has made a distinction between conceptual and contextual coherence curricula. Mapping that onto our previous analysis, one might be tempted to say that conceptual coherence curricula apply to 'hards' and contextual coherence curricula to 'applieds'. This is not a helpful way to think about it. Rather, 'conceptuality' denotes a quality analogous to 'verticality' (from 'hard' to 'soft' in Becher's terms); 'contexuality' likewise a quality (from 'pure' to 'applied' in Becher's terms). Put like this, there are three points to note: the first is that stipulating these features as qualities helps us see that all curricula have elements of both qualities; they differ in the mix (see Gamble, 2006; Wheelahan, 2007b for a persuasive defence of the importance of the mix for all curricula). More particularly, as we saw above, regions and contextual coherence curricula benefit from having a conceptual coherence or disciplinary core. Second, the applied disciplines and regions, and contextual coherence curricula, have so far been less well spelt out than have their vertical/conceptual counterparts. Third, 'appliedness' or 'contextuality' is a quality in need of further explication if it is to be of use in understanding curriculum planning in comprehensive institutions. The chapter now turns to this task.

The curriculum: contextual and conceptual

A useful way to broach this issue is by asking the question: What kind of qualified person do we want to produce? We have seen above that the recently promulgated

South African Higher Education Qualifications Framework (HEQF, 2007) distinguishes between two modal types of curriculum and qualification; one that aims to produce disciplinary adepts, and is thus formative or research-based; the other that aims to produce knowledgeable professionals, and is thus oriented more to the demands of the workplace. This is fine as far as it goes. But there is clearly not just one kind of professional practice and these differ in ways that are critical for curricular planning. Above, I distinguished between old and new professions. In Table 7.4 I distinguish between three kinds of professional fields on the basis of their relative mix of conceptual and contextual coherence features.

There are a number of points to be made about this table:

• This occupational spread can be seen as a form of continuum – essentially from conceptual to contextual - but it is not a simple continuum. Within each occupational field, occupations vary as to the disciplinary core in their knowledge base. It is easy to see in the 'academic work' field: the knowledge base of physics is more vertical than that of anthropology, say. Equally, doctors have a more vertical knowledge base than social workers, fitters than cabinetmakers, hospitality than tourism workers (see further below).

By the same token, we can see *within* each knowledge base – more pronounced in some fields than in others – a distinction or tension between a more conceptual and a more contextual form of disciplinary practice. For example, in teacher education, there are those for whom the practice of teaching is primary, and its improvement should best be pursued by learning-by-doing, by classroom-based innovation; on the other hand, there are those who wish to produce generalisable knowledge by means of random clinical trials and experiments (Foray and Hargreaves, 2003; Muller, 2006). In anthropology, we sometimes find two different departments in the same university, as at Stanford University, one leaning more to science, the other more to the humanities. And of course, the respective clans publish in different journals.

These tensions are sometimes a clash between 'hard' and 'soft' factions (as in economics); sometimes recognisably another local bout between the rival Trivium and the Quadrivium priesthoods, between Snow's two cultures (as in anthropology), and sometimes even a bit of both (as in teaching). The battle is at times waged in methodological terms (qualitative versus quantitative); more interestingly for present purposes, it is at times waged in curricular terms. A current example is the debate about the problem-based mode of the medical curriculum. Its proponents are clearly trying to bend the medical stick towards the contextual side by emphasising the contextual problem to be solved rather than the disciplinary knowledge to be learned. Consequently, they design the curriculum in terms of external contextual coherence instead of internal conceptual coherence. This flouts the sequential requirements of the vertical parent knowledge structures (anatomy, for example), in the same way as we saw with school biology above (Dempster and Hugo, 2006), and students end up with gaps in their

Table 7.4 Occupational fields and knowledge

	Particular occupations	General occupations	Traditional and some 4th generation professions	Academia; 4th generation professions
Occupations	E.g. travel agents, hospitality workers	E.g. engineering trades (fitters, boilermakers), HR operators	E.g. engineers, lawyers, architects, HR managers, doctors, teachers, social workers	Researchers, new white collar welfare and service workers
Knowledge	Practical knowledge	Practical knowledge plus some applied theory	Applied theory plus practical experience	Theoretical progression of the discipline
Induction	On-the-job-training, some apprenticeship	Apprenticeship	External internship (e.g. pupilage, housemanship)	Internal internship (e.g. postdoctoral work, tenure)
Regulation	Moderate to weak sectoral regulation (e.g. hairdresser's practical test)	Moderate sectoral regulation (e.g. trade tests)	Strong sectoral regulation (e.g. board exams)	Moderate to strong disciplinary regulation (peer review)

knowledge (Kirschner *et al.*, 2006). As we saw in the previous section in the discussion around Curriculum 2005, there are limits to contextualising (or segmentalising) the curriculum of a vertical discipline, if perverse effects are to be avoided. In this sense, the vertical discipline, like the empire it is, strikes back.

This is absolutely critical in the design of curricula. The more vertical the discipline, the greater are the conceptual coherence adequacy requirements in the curriculum. These include necessary coverage and appropriate pacing, but foremost amongst them is *sequence*. The adequacy requirement of sequence demands that the curriculum maintains a certain necessary congruence with the vertical spine of the parent discipline. Where this congruence is scrambled – whether by modularisation, unit standardisation, problem-based stipulation or any other technical means that contextualises the curriculum in such a way that renders the conceptual sequence invisible or out of sequence – then learning is put at risk in one of two ways: either crucial conceptual steps are missed, in which case learning stops; or vital chunks of knowledge are missed, leaving knowledge gaps.

- This spread could be said to denote a continuum from mental work to manual work, but it is misleading to describe it in those terms. The knowledge society means that each occupation and its attendant knowledge base will increasingly be under pressure to augment its quantum of conceptual knowledge, to become at least partly mental. This is because generalisable innovation relies on conceptual knowledge, as we saw above, and it is this kind of innovation that the global economy prizes most at all levels of the division of labour. This is not to say that all knowledges will in future become equally conceptual, or that work-based PhDs will soon be in the offing, as some in the vocational field fondly but mistakenly hope (Mehl, 2007). Rather, it is to argue that some conceptual knowledge could become a component of all forms of occupational knowledge, for epistemological, economic and social justice reasons (Gamble, 2006; Wheelahan, 2007a). It is highly unlikely that the ranking in the continuum above will change; the payoff we can expect will be a strengthened cognitive core to the knowledge base, and a firmer academic identity. We might note that, within the 'particular occupations' sector, some vocational knowledges, like Consumer Studies, are currently more receptive to conceptual augmentation than others, like Tourism, that remains very largely procedural. It should be borne in mind that even at the extremes of the continuum, actual knowledges are always to some extent hybrid: there is procedural knowledge required to work in a laboratory; and there is some conceptual knowledge required in particular occupations, even if it is largely tacit (Gamble, 2004). But this does not contradict the principal point that some curricula are more conceptual, others more contextual; or that the main knowledge ensemble bears a relation to the division of labour in the target occupational field.
- The form of induction into the knowledge will differ as to its relative conceptuality or contextuality. The more conceptual the curriculum has to be,

the more formally set will be the entry requirements, the curriculum specifications, the qualification, and the form of practical apprenticeship; the more contextual the curriculum, the less formal and less extensive will be the entry requirements and the formal curriculum, and the more extensive the apprenticeship and the value of on-the-job practice, learning-by-doing (Young, 2006a). As we saw above, the more contextual, the less sequential will be the curricular requirements, the more segmental or 'modularisable' the curriculum. Here too, struggles to bend the stick towards more formal curricula requirements – in the interests of achieving parity of esteem if not remuneration – are apparent, particularly in the non-formal adult education and training field. An entire institutional maze of institutions, the Sector Education and Training Authorities (SETAs) has been established in South Africa to 'pedagogise' what is essentially contextually tacit procedural knowledge. The assumption here is that it is possible to drive conceptuality pedagogically. This assumption is mistaken. Conceptuality is driven by conceptual innovation in the knowledge structure itself, in the field of knowledge production; it cannot be 'recontextually' driven in the curriculum, in the field of knowledge reproduction, without producing perverse effects. These perverse effects are everywhere apparent in the distressing shambles of the SETAs and the depressing proliferation of virtual qualification tracks within traditional trades like hairdressing.

- The disciplines are *internally* regulated by professional societies, editorial boards, and other institutions that formalise peer review. In this sense they still adhere to the nineteenth century vision of the 'republic of science' (Polanyi, 1962), although globalisation increasingly questions this autonomy and demands displays of contextual relevance. The curricula and qualifications of the worldly professions and occupations are regulated by a variety of accreditation boards and councils, who oversee both the formal curricula and the competency levels of the qualifiers. These are sometimes sectorally organised (in medicine, accountancy and law for example), sometimes state-run (social work, teacher education). In general, the more the knowledge base is contextually rooted – in the practice itself – and the less conceptuality in the knowledge base, the less organised will be the regulation; hospitality is regulated mainly for chefs; tourism hardly at all. This will change, but it will be a long time before entrance is as strictly regulated as it is for accountants by the charted accountants' board examination, for example.

These four qualification routes to the world of productive labour are not bounded in any absolute way. We have seen above that the tensions between the four are fractally mirrored within each occupational cluster, sometimes within each learning area serving the occupational cluster. Nevertheless, I will argue below that each occupational type or cluster forms a distinctive conceptual/practice node that implicitly prescribes a curricular and qualification best practice. This can be seen if we map qualification types onto the four occupational fields (Figure 7.1).

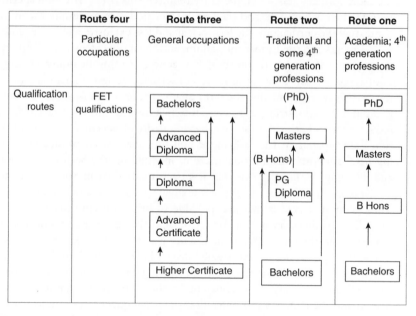

Figure 7.1   Occupational fields and qualifications.

- In the right-hand column we can recognise the lineaments of the traditional arts and science curricula – the contemporary version of the 'liberal' arts. The real difference now – and it is a big difference – is that since the nineteenth century this curriculum's purpose has steadily shifted from general-formative to innovation-focused, from well-rounded to research-competent, from undergraduate to postgraduate. The PhD is now accepted as the capstone qualification. This has been the case for some time now in the hard 'pure' disciplines, but is increasingly the case for the soft 'pures' and the Humanities as well.

There are some commentators who see this as higher education continuing to cling to the features of 'traditional academic performance' (van Vught, 2007). In truth, the dominance of research in the academic mission of the 'pures' is less than a century old. What these commentators probably mean by 'traditional' is 'dominant', since this feature is incontestably the dominant feature towards which higher education generically is enjoined to aspire, as the global ratings by the Academic Ranking of World Universities (ARWU) and the *Times Higher Education Supplement* make clear (Vaughn, *et al.*, 2007).

The more that national funding formulae underwrite this dominance in an undifferentiated way, the more will academic drift be a central trend in the higher education system.

- In route two, producing the traditional and some new professions, the intensive Bachelors with professional capping up to Masters is the basic pattern.

In disciplines like Medicine, there will be some tension between a research route that proceeds to the PhD along the column one pattern, and a professional route with the Masters as the preferred qualification for professional updating. This is certainly the preferred route in the more rapidly developing knowledge-based fourth generation professions. Contextual requirements of these professions will probably lead the professional contextual agencies to resist the conversion of the qualification route to Masters into one that is research-dominant. Nonetheless, the 'professional doctorate' remains under consideration in some of these fields. Architecture is an example, where the Commonwealth academic community together with the Royal Institute of British Architects (RIBA) is currently locked in debate as to whether the professional PhD should be purely research-based or not (Carter, 2007).

- In route three, the occupational requirements are more prominently to the fore, and consequently occupational specialisation occurs far earlier than in route two, where the traditional general-formative ideal still shapes the undergraduate curriculum. In route three, the Bachelors becomes a minority option: the majority will enter the labour market with a pre-Bachelors qualification. While folklore has it that academics are hard-pressed to distinguish the respective purposes of qualifications in route two as compared with those in route three – as in Engineering, for example – a route two qualification clearly requires both a better entry qualification and offers less constrained occupational possibilities than does route three with its more contextual focus.

- In route four we find the qualifications stream that has one foot in secondary and the other in tertiary, largely further education. These qualifications are the most occupationally specific, far more so even than their secondary counterparts. The school-based Tourism curriculum has, for example, more general-formative features than its more senior route four successor, which places a far greater stress on on-the-job training. This is because the secondary qualification gives access to route three as well as route four qualifications; and route three gives access to the Bachelors and beyond, while route four gives no direct access to the Bachelors.

In all of this, the *purpose* of the qualification is paramount, and must be clearly established from the outset. The question is not: Should they not be the same since they are all (for example) engineering? Rather it is: What kind of graduate should this qualification produce? While it is true that there are hundreds of occupations for which we prepare graduates, it is also true that there are only four modal qualification routes. The 'what kind of graduate?' question can thus be answered only by determining which qualification route is most appropriate, and vice versa.

Some concluding comments

There are many issues left unresolved, or insufficiently unpacked. Of these I will in conclusion deal with just two, each of which is sometimes seen through a lens of social justice. The first has to deal with the question of *vertical academic mobility*, of proceeding further, of 'upskilling' from a relatively low vocational knowledge base to relatively higher reaches of the educational and occupational hierarchy. On the one hand, this is sometimes regarded as an inbuilt limitation of qualifications with a vocational knowledge base, part of the unfair low status of such qualifications; on the other, it is regarded as a matter of social justice, and the curriculum ought, by moral right, to give access to mobility upwards. To do this, a curriculum ought, as a matter of fairness, include abstract knowledge of the kind that would, if desired, grant the academic conditions for access upwards.

When this becomes a demand of, say, the trade unions, it may be relatively modest – 'from artisan to engineer' is one such – or it may be overweeningly ambitious – 'from sweeper to engineer', in the slogan of the South African trade unions that impelled us towards a disastrous form of qualifications framework that aimed to produce 'equivalence' and 'articulation', but of course did neither. One implication of the argument of this chapter is that there is no general rule that can decide the matter, certainly not a general moral rule. For each qualification pathway, the following must, from a knowledge perspective, be determined: What is the degree of specialisation required? What are the conceptual demands of the knowledge to be acquired? The greater the degree of specialisation, the more sequence matters, the more specific will the entry levels of competence have to be. If these are not in place, then bridging courses may be needed to supply them, which is the way the German system deals with the question of 'articulation': not as a matter of curriculum or framework design. A further difficulty may well be that, in a newly regionalised field like tourism, where the division of labour is still rather simple and the knowledge base generic and unspecialised, there may just not be an appropriate conceptual foundation obviously to hand. Should one say that this curriculum is ethically obliged to include a borrowed conceptual foundation to ensure at least the possibility of mobility? Or would the German solution of bridging courses if and when the need arises not meet the case just as well? Which is to put differently the point made earlier: while we may agree that weak regions stand in need of strengthening, this is not a goal, not even a socially just goal, that can be achieved solely by curriculum means.

The second related issue has to do with the relative *transferability of specialised knowledge*. It is sometimes said, even if a vocational field has yet to develop specialisations, and mobility possibilities in the simple division of labour of that field are stunted, that the presence of at least some (borrowed) kind of conceptual foundation makes possible opportunities to transfer to another field with perhaps other or greater possibilities. This presumes that abstract knowledge is abstract knowledge is abstract knowledge, that there is some quality of conceptuality that is generic. There are two things to say to this. The first is that if a generic conceptual discipline is conceivable, it could only be mathematics for the Sciences and language for the Humanities; the possibilities are most certainly not endless. The second is that the more specialised a discipline becomes, generally speaking the less transferable it becomes. This is because it now pertains to a highly specialised niche in the division of labour. One might certainly opt out into another field altogether, but in a certain sense at least, one would be starting again. Very few people do that, and it is hardly ever a matter of social justice.

Notes

1 A part of this chapter was first written for an unpublished report to the SANTED Project, CEPD.
2 The terms 'hard' and 'soft' were not Biglan's own. They had been used first by Bertrand Russell in 1929, and in the sociology of science, by Storer (1967) and Price (1970) before Biglan.
3 Expressed epistemologically, this means that, although an observation can be given two interpretations, the difference between these can always be resolved by reference to a 'touchstone', thus forestalling the kind of incommensurability so often found in the 'soft' disciplines (Mackenzie, 1998, pp.34, 35).
4 Some of these features apply to the Humanities, but many do not. The knowledge structures of the Humanities do not display Bernstein's 'verticality', for example; only the natural and social sciences do.
5 It should be borne in mind that professional fields have many occupational niches at different levels of the division of labour; medicine trains surgeons and nurses, and much in between.
6 How the globally dispersed contemporary disciplinary communities actually 'work' as communities has only recently been posed as a puzzle worth examining (Muller, 2008).
7 For purposes of this section, 'disciplines' refer to disciplines and disciplinary regions, as distinguished from curricula.
8 'Pedagogic discourses can never be identified with any of the discourse it has recontextualised' (Bernstein, 1996, p.47).
9 This binary is admittedly rather crude, because it again partly omits the Humanities (see Mackenzie, 1998, fn.18, p.46). Posner and Strike (1976) distinguish five major curriculum design drivers: concept related; world related; learning related; enquiry related; and utilisation related. For present purposes, our equivalent of their concept and utilisation related distinctions suffice.

References

Becher, A. and Parry, S. (2005) 'The endurance of the disciplines', in Bleiklie, I. and Henkel, M. (eds) *Governing Knowledge: A Study of Continuity and Change in Higher Education – festschrift in honour of Maurice Kogan*, Dordrecht: Springer.

Beck, J. and Young, M. (2005) 'The assault on the professions and the restructuring of academic and professional identities: A Bernsteinian analysis', *British Journal of Sociology of Education*, 26(2): 183–197.

Bernstein, B. (1996) *Pedagogy, Symbolic Control and Identity*, London: Taylor & Francis.

Bernstein, B. (2000) *Pedagogy, Symbolic Control and Identity*, 2nd ed., New York: Rowman & Littlefield.

Biglan, A. (1973a) 'The characteristics of subject matter in different academic areas', *Journal of Applied Psychology*, 53(3): 195–203.

Biglan, A. (1973b) 'Relationships between subject matter characteristics and the structure and output of university departments', *Journal of Applied Psychology*, 53(3): 204–213.

Burke, P. (2000) *A Social History of Knowledge: From Gutenberg to Diderot*, Cambridge: Polity Press.

Carter, F. (2007) 'Fractured pedagogy: The design and implementation fault line in architectural knowledge – a conceptual and historical analysis', unpublished Masters dissertation, University of Cape Town.

Cassirer, E. (1943) 'Newton and Leibnitz', *The Philosophical Review*, 52(4): 366–391.

Chisholm, L. *et al.* (2000) *A South African Curriculum for the Twenty First Century*, Pretoria: Department of Education.

Dempster, E.R. and Hugo, W. (2006) 'Introducing the concept of evolution into South African schools', *South African Journal of Science*, 102(3/4): 106–112.

Deng, Z. (2007) 'Transforming the subject matter: Examining the intellectual roots of pedagogical content knowledge', *Curriculum Inquiry*, 37(3): 279–295.

Durkheim, E. (1977) *The Evolution of Educational Thought: Lectures on the Formation and Development of Secondary Education in France*, London: Routledge.

Dyson, F. (2007) 'Working for the revolution', *New York Review of Books*, LIV (16): 45–47.

Ensor, P. (2006) 'Curriculum', in Cloete, N. *et al.* (eds) *Transformation in Higher Education: Global Pressures and Local Realities*, Dordrecht: Springer.

Foray, D. and Hargreaves, D. (2003) 'The production of knowledge in different sectors: A model and some hypotheses', *London Review of Education*, 1(1): 7–19.

Gamble, J. (2004) 'Tacit knowledge in craft pedagogy: A sociological analysis', unpublished PhD thesis, University of Cape Town.

Gamble, J. (2006) 'Theory and practice in the vocational curriculum', in Young, M. and Gamble, J. (eds) *Knowledge, Curriculum and Qualifications for South African Further Education*, Pretoria: HSRC Press.

Henkel, M. (2000) *Academic Identities and Policy Change in Higher Education*, London: Jessica Kingsley.

Henkel, M. (2005) 'Academic identity and autonomy revisited', in Bleiklie, I. and Henkel, M. (eds) *Governing Knowledge: A Study of Continuity and Change in Higher Education – Festschrift in Honour of Maurice Kogan*, Dordrecht: Springer.

HEQF (2007) *Higher Education Act, 1997* (Act No. 101 of 1997), Pretoria: Department of Education.

Kimball, R. (1994) 'The "two cultures" today', *The New Criterion*, 12: 6.

Kirschner, P., Sweller, J. and Clark, R. (2006) 'Why minimal guidance during instruction does not work: An analysis of the failure of constructivist, discovery, problem-based, experiential and inquiry-based teaching', *Educational Psychologist*, 41(2): 75–86.

Kolb, D.A. (1981) 'Learning styles and disciplinary differences', in Chickering, A. (ed.) *The Modern American College*, San Francisco, CA: Jossey Bass.

Landahl, J.B. and Gordon, G. (1972) 'The structure of scientific fields and the functioning of university graduate departments', *American Sociological Review*, 37: 57–72.

Leavis, F.R. (1972) 'Two cultures? The significance of Lord Snow', in *Nor Shall my Sword: Discourse on Pluralism, Compassion and Social Hope*, New York: Barnes & Noble.

Mackenzie, J. (1998) 'Forms of knowledge and forms of discussion', *Educational Philosophy and Theory*, 30(1): 27–49.

Maton, K. (2007) 'Knowledge–knower structures in intellectual and educational fields', in Christie, F. and Martin, J.R. (eds) *Language, Knowledge and Pedagogy: Functional Linguistic and Sociological Perspectives*, London: Continuum.

Mehl, M. (2007) 'Reflections on the National Skills Conference', Powerpoint presentation to the National Skills Conference, Johannesburg, 18-19 October.

Merton, R. K. (1992) *The Sociology of Science: Theoretical and Empirical Investigations*, Chicago, IL: The University of Chicago Press.

Moore, R. (2003) 'Between covenant and contract: The negotiation of academic pedagogic identities', *Journal of Education*, 30: 81–100.

Muller, J. (2005) 'The world is not enough: Knowledge in question', *South African Journal of Higher Education*, 19(3): 497–511.

Muller, J. (2006) 'Should educators be wary of evidence?', Proceedings of a Double Symposium on Evidence-based Practice, Pretoria: Academy of Sciences of South Africa.

Muller, J. (2008) 'Recognition and standing in the disciplines', paper presented to the 5th Basil Bernstein International Symposium, Cardiff University, July.

Muller, J. (2011) 'The essential tension: An essay on sociology as knowledge', in Frandji, D. and Vitale, P. (eds) *Knowledge, Pedagogy and Society*, Oxford: Routledge.

Neumann, R., Parry, S. and Becher, A. (2002) 'Teaching and learning in their disciplinary contexts: A conceptual analysis', *Studies in Higher Education*, 27(4): 406–417.

Pantin, C. (1968) *The Relations between the Sciences*, Cambridge: Cambridge University Press.

Parry, S. (2007) *Disciplines and Doctorates*, Dordrecht: Springer.

Polanyi, M. (1962) 'The republic of science', *Minerva*, 1(1): 54–73.

Posner, G. and Strike, K. (1976) 'A categorisation scheme for principles of sequencing content', *Review of Educational Research*, 46(4): 665–690.

Price, D. de Solla (1970) 'Citation measures of hard science and soft science, technology and non-science', in Nelson, C. and Pollack, D. (eds) *Communication Among Scientists and Engineers*, Lexington, MA: Heath Lexington Books.

Shapin, S. (1996) *The Scientific Revolution*, Chicago, IL: University of Chicago Press.

Smeby, J.-C. (1996) 'Disciplinary differences in university teaching', *Studies in Higher Education*, 21(1): 67–79.

Smeby, J.-C. (2000) 'Disciplinary differences in Norwegian graduate education', *Studies in Higher Education*, 25(1): 53–67.

Snow, C.P. (1993) *The Two Cultures*, Cambridge: Cambridge University Press.

Storer, N. (1967) The hard sciences and the soft: Some sociological observations, *Bulletin of the Medical Library Association*, 55: 75–84.

Toulmin, S. (1972) *Human Understanding: Vol. 1: The Collective Use and Evolution of Concepts*, Oxford: Clarendon Press.

Van Vught, F. (2007) 'Diversity and differentiation in higher education systems', paper presented at the CHET Differentiation Seminar, Erinvale, 16 November.

Vaughn, C., Reddy, D., Noakes, T. and Moran, V. (2007) 'A commentary on the intellectual health of the nation', *South African Journal of Science*, 46(4): 665–690.

Wheelahan, L. (2007a) 'How competency-based training locks the working class out of powerful knowledge: A modified Bernsteinian analysis', *British Journal of Sociology of Education*, 28(5): 637–651.

Wheelahan, L. (2007b) 'The role of theoretical knowledge in vocational qualifications in Australia – a blended Bernsteinian and critical realist analysis', unpublished PhD thesis, University of Monash.

Young, M. (2006a) 'Conceptualising vocational knowledge: Some theoretical consid-
erations', in Young, M. and Gamble, J. (eds), *Knowledge, Curriculum and
Qualifications for South African Further Education*, Cape Town: Human Sciences
Research Council.

Young, M. (2006b) 'Reforming the Further Education and Training curriculum: An
international perspective', in Young, M. and Gamble, J. (eds), *Knowledge,
Curriculum and Qualifications for South African Further Education*, Cape Town:
Human Sciences Research Council.

Zilsel, E. (2003) *The Social Origins of Modern Science*, Dordrecht: Kluwer Academic
Publishers.

8 Education, globalisation and the 'voice of knowledge'

Michael Young

Introduction

This chapter starts from a problem that is perhaps better expressed as a contradiction. On the one hand 'knowledge' has undoubtedly become the major organising category in the educational policies of international organisations and many national governments. Global similarities are increasingly apparent – whether they are expressed with reference to knowledge itself, to the knowledge society, to knowledge workers or The Knowledge Promotion, as the recent reforms of Norwegian secondary education are referred to.[1] On the other hand the category 'knowledge' appears to be used in an almost entirely rhetorical way; the meaning of knowledge is at best implicit[2] and at worst virtually empty of content. One consequence is that such policies deny or disregard the idea that access to knowledge in the strong sense that involves its claims to reliability is central to the whole purpose of education. Thus, what I shall refer to in this chapter as the 'voice of knowledge' (Moore 2007), as a distinctive factor shaping educational policy, is lost. If I have accurately identified this trend and it continues, it is a highly problematic heritage that we leave to future generations – namely that there is no explicit knowledge that it is important enough to be 'transmitted' to the next generation. It is a heritage that has none of the visibility of the environmental or sustainability crises, although arguably, addressing it is fundamental to whether we are able to deal with either.

The aim of this chapter is to explore this apparent contradiction and to begin to develop an alternative that takes the idea of the 'voice of knowledge' seriously. An issue that I touch on, but only by implication, is whether significant strands of the social sciences (and sociology in particular) may be part of the problem of denying a 'voice' for knowledge rather than being the basis for offering a viable alternative for the future (Young and Muller, 2007, 2009).

The chapter has six sections. The first section provides a number of examples of how knowledge is interpreted in international educational policies and raises the question: Why knowledge? What purpose does such a focus on knowledge have in today's educational policies? My examples are drawn from the educational policies of international organisations such as the World Bank and new national curricula and national education policies (my illustrations are from

Norway and England). I also refer briefly to the work of the Portuguese sociologist, Boaventura de Sousa Santos, a leading critic of globalisation, to indicate the terms within which the debate about education and the knowledge economy among globalisers and anti-globalisers has largely been set. My argument is that, despite treating knowledge as a main organising category, international and national policy makers *and their critics* in effect bypass what I (following Rob Moore) mean by the 'voice of knowledge'.

The second section begins to make explicit what the idea of the 'voice of knowledge' in educational policy might mean. It starts from a paper by Moore (Moore, 2006), in which he draws on the critical realist tradition in the philosophy of science and establishes the epistemological basis for the idea of the 'voice of knowledge' in education. However, in my view, despite its strengths, critical realism does not move us very far towards conceptualising a more adequate role for knowledge in educational policy.

The third section builds on Moore's ideas by arguing that the key idea implicit in a realist theory of knowledge is *knowledge differentiation*. This idea is elaborated through a brief account[3] of the ideas of the French philosopher, Gaston Bachelard. The fourth section considers the educational implications of the idea of the social differentiation of knowledge with reference to the work of Durkheim, Vygotsky and Bernstein, and the fifth section builds on this to explore five forms of knowledge differentiation as they apply to the curriculum. The concluding section returns to the idea of the 'voice of knowledge' as a shaper of educational policy.

Knowledge as the new global narrative

The striking thing about the many publications of international organisations and governments that refer to knowledge and the knowledge economy is that they do not feel the need to ask the question: What is this knowledge that we are referring to? Its meaning is simply taken for granted. As Susan Robertson (Robertson, 2007) puts it in a recent paper which started me thinking about this issue: 'Who can be against knowledge?' It is not therefore surprising, she writes, 'that the idea of knowledge articulates with the left as well as the right'. In UK terms this use of 'knowledge' was a characteristic of the former government's New Labour doctrine – it included everything, it sounded progressive (or at least modernising) but it said nothing substantive.

It is the word knowledge, rather than the related term 'information' that has caught on as the key category in the new education policy literature. I suspect that the reason for this is that, despite its multiple meanings and absence of any referents, the word *knowledge* does retain a public association with ideas such as certainty, reliability, and objectivity and even truth. Reference to knowledge therefore provides a kind of authority for policies that do not have to be justified in other ways. The authority of the term knowledge is taken over but not the basis of its claims.

A brief glance at documents produced by international organisations and governments indicates that the idea of knowledge acts as a licence for a whole range of educational policies that have little directly to do with knowledge in the more specifically epistemological sense. Two examples of widely supported educational policies illustrate this point. The first is the emphasis on maximising learner choice and the associated tendency for learning to become little more than another form of consumption. In a world dominated by learner choice, knowledge looses all its authority. The second example is the popularity of the slogans 'personalised learning' and 'individual learning styles' and the gradual replacement of the terms education, school and college with their assumed elitism by learning and learning centres. This is not to underplay the importance of learners having an active role in any educational process at any level. It is rather to highlight the importance of distinguishing between the everyday or common sense knowledge that is acquired by individual learners in specific contexts and the idea that we acquire powerful knowledge (Young, 2009) to take us beyond our everyday experiences (Karpov and Heywood, 1998). If this distinction is blurred or seen as unimportant, the role of teachers is reduced to little more than facilitation and support, and we are not a million miles away from the idea of 'user-generated knowledge' that is associated with YouTube and Facebook (Keen, 2007).

My argument is that an empty and rhetorical notion of knowledge and the increasing tendency to blur distinctions between the production of knowledge and its acquisition, and between knowledge and skills – the latter unlike the former being something measurable and targetable – becomes a way of denying a distinct 'voice' for knowledge in education. Furthermore excluding such a 'voice' from educational policy most disadvantages those learners (and whole societies, in the case of developing countries), who are already disadvantaged by circumstances beyond the school.

Illustrations of this 'emptying of content' can be found in the educational policies of many countries; I will mention two briefly – England, before the election of the Conservative-led Coalition government in 2010, and Norway. What has been even extended by the new government is that, the control of public education in England has been centralised under the newly named Department for Education (DFE). Local authorities, examination boards and research councils have increasingly taken on the role of agencies delivering government policy and the intermediary bodies such as the QCDA (Qualifications and Curriculum Development Authority) are being progressively abolished. The DFE, like all government departments, is now regulated under a Public Service Agreement (PSA) which governs the funds they receive from the Treasury.[4] The PSA for Education has five objectives broken up into 14 sub-objectives. All refer to generic targets and none make reference to any specific knowledge or curriculum content. Another illustration that is more obviously closer to what goes on in schools and colleges comes from the requirements laid down by the government for the new diplomas for 14–18 year olds.[5] These requirements set out in considerable detail the packaging, module combinations, credit levels and pathways for the diplomas, but make only minimal reference to content. Targets which are based on a common set of levels, and common units for measuring volume of learning, have priority over reference to specific contents. The implications are that what might be assumed to be distinctive to formal education – the acquisition of specific knowledge – is treated as relatively unimportant. Institutions are held accountable and students assessed in terms of outcomes that are not content-specific.

The new Norwegian[6] curriculum reforms follow a similar trend. They are known, significantly, as The Knowledge Promotion (op. cit. for website reference). The new Norwegian curriculum is defined by five basic skills and a seven-part quality framework; each of the twelve criteria has to be reflected in the teaching of the different subjects; subject syllabuses no longer prescribe specific contents. It is this combination of basic (generic) skills and a quality framework, not the knowledge content of subjects, which is built into the legislation, drives teaching, and defines what students have opportunities to learn, and how they are assessed,

A rather different example of the evacuation of knowledge is found in the publications of the radical Portuguese sociologist, Boaventura de Sousa Santos, now largely based at Wisconsin. It illustrates how the approach taken to knowledge by at least some the left-wing critics of globalisation and the role of international agencies leads to a similar evacuation of content. De Sousa Santos' works are widely read in Brazil and he has played a key role in the Global Social Forum. In Brazil I have heard him spoken of as the new Paulo Freire. What he refers to as his 'epistemology of absent knowledges' claims to go beyond what he sees as the 'blindness' of Western science. He refers to it in a paper in the *European Journal of Social Theory* in the following terms:

> the epistemology of absent knowledges starts from the premise that *social practices* are *knowledge practices* ... nonscience-based practices, rather than being ignorant practices, *are practices of alternative rival knowledges*. There is *no apriori reason to favour one form of knowledge against another*.
>
> (De Sousa Santos, 2001)

Starting from a critique of mainstream economics, de Sousa Santos is trapped in a framework that associates epistemologies with particular social groups or world regions. The result is a concept of knowledge that equates it oversimplistically with power,[7] and is as empty, despite its radical rhetoric, as that of the World Bank.

The 'voice of knowledge'

What then might the idea of the 'voice of knowledge' that I have argued is increasingly absent in educational policies mean? I begin with what Moore identifies as its four elements. It must, he argues be:

1 *critical* – be open to revision and embody a fallibilist notion of truth;
2 *emergentist* – in recognizing that knowledge is not reducible to the conditions of its production or the activities and interests of those involved;

3 *realist* – in recognizing that the objects of knowledge of both the natural and social worlds are realities that (a) are independent of our perception of the world and (b) provide limits to how we can know about the world;

4 *materialist* – in recognizing that knowledge is produced (and acquired) in specific historically created modes of production, or in Bourdieu's terms, intellectual fields.

(Moore, 2007)

Knowledge, it follows, from a realist perspective and in the sense that I as an educationalist use the word,[8] can be differentiated from the meanings we construct to make sense of the world in our everyday lives; it is not created by learners or even by learners with their teachers; it is acquired.

Although these propositions form a sound basis for any serious enquiry into the role of knowledge in education, the terms in which they are set are too general for them to be a basis on their own, for drawing any conclusions about educational and more specifically, curriculum policy. I will comment briefly on each proposition and suggest that the key underlying concept that can be derived from them and needs developing is the *differentiation of knowledge*.

Proposition 1 refers to *fallibility*. The idea of fallibility or 'openness to critique and revision' is usually associated with the natural sciences. However, it is no less important in the humanities and social sciences. Different concepts of fallibility arise from the ways in which different knowledge domains subsume the particular under the general (Joe Muller and I discuss this in an earlier paper (Young and Muller, 2007)). However fallibility is always understood as being 'within a tradition or a discipline'. The dangers of breaking the link between 'openness to critique' and a tradition within which critique is located are well demonstrated by Anthony Kronman, the former Dean of Humanities at Yale. In his book *Education's End: Why Our Colleges and Universities Have Given up on the Meaning of Life* (Kronman, 2007) Kronman describes how after the 1960s many humanities faculties in the USA rejected any notion of tradition and focused only on critique; this left them, he argues, open to the most extreme forms of relativism and political correctness.

Proposition 2 refers to *emergence*. This is the idea that powerful knowledge is the product of social conditions or contexts that do not wholly determine it. Examples might be the science laboratory or the classroom. Archives, libraries and the internet can also be conditions for the emergent properties of knowledge to be generated. However this does not take place, as is sometimes assumed, in isolation from teachers or members of other 'communities of specialists'. These originating 'contexts' will leave their mark on the knowledge acquired and produced in them. However what makes 'powerful knowledge' powerful is its independence or autonomy from the specific contexts of its origin. Let us take an example. The English chemist Robert Boyle needed to be wealthy enough to build the laboratory on his estate in which he discovered what became known as Boyles Law. However today's aircraft designers do not need to read Steven Shapin's account of the gentry culture (Shapin, 1995) of which Boyle was a part to understand and apply his law about how gas volumes change under pressure.

Emergence is a less straightforward idea in the social sciences. For example, Max Weber's concept of ideal types has emergent properties, which explains why it remains fruitful to this day. However, only a few sociologists will be familiar with the debates Weber had with the Marxists in the German Social Democratic Party which led him to formulate the idea. Contemporary sociologists could well gain additional sociological insights into Weber's ideas by reading Marianne Weber's account of his life in ways that would not be true for physicists reading Shapin's account of Boyle's life, however interesting they might find it.

Proposition 3 refers to the *real* basis of knowledge; in other words that our claims to knowledge are not just claims; they say something about the world that is not dependent on how we conceive of it. If the sociology of knowledge is to say anything about the curriculum it must provide a theory that distinguishes between knowledge and non-knowledge – whether this is expressed as experience, opinion, belief or common sense. Likewise, if the nature of the objects of knowledge (our theories) limits what we can know about reality, we need to know how they are differentiated between different domains when we come to make decisions about the curriculum.

Proposition 4 refers to the *materiality* of knowledge production and acquisition – that these processes do not take place anywhere but in particular social contexts with specific rules and forms of organisation. This idea of the materiality of knowledge production points to the importance of research into different forms of specialist knowledge communities and their role (and often their lack of role) in the design of curricula. In the United Kingdom, vocational education programmes preparing students for different occupational fields vary widely in how they interpret their knowledge base. Much of this variation can be explained in terms of the different roles that professional associations have in the design of programmes at pre- or non-professional levels.[9]

The conclusion that I draw from this brief discussion of Moore's four propositions about knowledge is that they have to be developed further. One way of doing this is through the idea, implicit in each proposition, that knowledge is socially differentiated. The following section draws on the French philosopher Gaston Bachelard's historical epistemology to present a way of developing this idea.

The social differentiation of knowledge

The idea that there are real structured differences between types of knowledge that are not dependent on our perceptions – in particular between scientific and non-scientific knowledge – lies at the heart of the work of Gaston Bachelard, the French philosopher of science. In the United Kingdom his work has been largely associated with Louis Althusser's flawed attempt to construct a 'scientific' Marxism. However, and here I draw largely on Christopher Norris's account, this is to miss the broader importance of Bachelard's work. Norris (2000) points out, rightly I think, that Althusser, presumably for political reasons, misinterprets Bachelard and relied on 'a misplaced "scientific" rigour that seeks to emulate the physical sciences in fields where different criteria apply'.

This habit, Norris argues, gives rise to 'various kinds of false analogy and wire-drawn metaphors' which find no justification in Bachelard's own work. Furthermore, Bachelard's epistemology is more historically grounded than that of critical realists such as Bhaskar; it focuses on distinct episodes in the history of the physical sciences. For this reason it is more useful for clarifying what the 'differentiation of knowledge' might mean in sociological terms.

The following points are a necessarily over-simplified summary of the aspects of Bachelard's theory of knowledge which have particular relevance for the concerns of this chapter; they are drawn largely from Norris's discussions.[10]

Bachelard establishes a basis for distinguishing science from pre-science (or non-science) that has parallels with Lakatos's distinction between 'progressive' and 'degenerating' research programmes:

- He has a theory of how knowledge progresses from 'less efficient' to 'more efficient' concepts through the process of 'conceptual rectification and critique'.
- He provides examples from the history of science of how knowledge 'progresses' by tracing the discontinuous development of ideas such as the 'atom' from the Greeks 'atomism' to modern atomic theory. In each case he shows how ideas are transformed from being largely metaphorical into increasingly precise and testable 'scientific' concepts.
- He recognizes that a theory of knowledge must begin from 'the current best state of knowledge in the field concerned' – in other words where a discipline is currently at.
- He proposes a methodology for distinguishing between two kinds of historical enquiry which Norris argues are often confused in contemporary discussions: *histoire sanctionee* – the history of the growth of science (this focuses on those early steps, like Lavoisier's discovery of the role of oxygen in combustion, which led to further advances); and *histoire perimee* – the history of past scientific beliefs (those which were later rejected as leading nowhere). One of Bachelard's examples in this case was Priestley's attempt to explain combustion with the idea of phlogiston.
- His historical epistemology is underpinned by a trans-historical set of principles associated with rigour, clarity, conceptual precision and logical consistency.

None of these proposals can be easily applied to the social sciences[11] and I am not aware of any attempt by Bachelard to extend his theory beyond the physical sciences.[12] However his focus on the *historical* conditions for the growth of knowledge in any discipline does not imply that it must be restricted to the physical sciences or that the idea of a historical epistemology must take physics or any particular science as its model. Also for Bachelard, concepts are not just theoretical propositions; they are simultaneously embedded in technical and *pedagogic* activity – the material conditions for producing them. Thus he opens the possibility of a realist account of the differentiation and growth of knowledge and the role of educational institutions.

Approaches to the social differentiation of knowledge – Durkheim, Vygotsky and Bernstein

This section takes further the idea of knowledge differentiation by drawing briefly on the three theorists who focus specifically on the differentiation of educational knowledge – Durkheim, Vygotsky and Bernstein. Their analyses form the basis, I suggest, for a research programme into the differentiation of educational knowledge as the principles for a theory of the curriculum. The significance and range of work of the three theorists is only touched on briefly here. I have explored their ideas in more detail elsewhere (Young, 2007).

Durkheim

As a sociologist rather than a philosopher of science, Durkheim's theory of knowledge is broader than Bachelard's; he does not limit himself to the physical sciences and he does not differentiate between scientific knowledge and knowledge in any broader sense. The differences that he identifies between knowledge and experience can be traced back to his early rejection of Kant's transcendentalism and to the concepts – 'sacred' and 'profane' – that he developed in his studies of religion in primitive societies. Durkheim initially used the sacred/profane distinction to describe the separation of religion and everyday life that he found in primitive societies. However the 'sacred' and the 'profane' became, for Durkheim, a basic distinction at the heart of all societies, even those that have become largely secularized. He saw the distinction as a form of social organisation that was basic to science and intellectual thought; hence his reference to primitive religions as 'proto-sciences'. Without the conceptual and social moves from the everyday world of survival to the sacred world of totemic religion that those early societies made, Durkheim argued, no science and no knowledge, and indeed no society, would be possible.

Vygotsky

Entering adult life and beginning his short career at the start of the Soviet Revolution, Vygotsky inevitably focused on the immediate problems facing teachers in the new society. His primary concern was with how teachers could help students to develop the higher order concepts that they would not have access to in their everyday lives. Like Durkheim, his theory was about the differentiation of knowledge and he also relied on a binary distinction, between two kinds of concepts – the theoretical (or scientific) and the everyday. For Vygotsky, the task of the curriculum, and schooling more generally, was to provide students with access to theoretical concepts in all their different forms – from history and literature to the sciences and mathematics. Furthermore, he saw that access to higher order concepts was not a simple one-way process of transmission but a complex pedagogic process in which a learner's everyday concepts are extended and transformed by theoretical concepts. From the point of the role of knowledge in education, the implications of Vygotsky's ideas are most clearly expressed in the work of the Russian Vasily Davidoff and his ideas of 'kernel knowledge' and learning as moving beyond the abstract and gaining a grasp of the concrete 'real' nature of things.

Bernstein

Bernstein (1971, 2000)[13] took Durkheim's ideas of knowledge differentiation further in a number of important ways. Here I will only refer to three brief points which focus on the issue of knowledge differentiation:

- With his concepts of 'classification' and 'framing' Bernstein developed Durkheim's idea of boundaries as the key social category separating types of symbolic meanings. He used these concepts to show how boundaries in education play a major role in the development of learner and teacher identities.
- Bernstein distinguished two types of educational boundary that are crucial for any curriculum theory – those between knowledge domains and those between school and everyday knowledge. He analysed the implications of both these types of boundary being blurred or dissolved.
- Bernstein drew on Durkheim's concepts of the 'sacred' and the 'profane' and his argument that the 'sacred' represented a kind of 'proto-science' to develop a distinction between forms of the 'sacred' which he expressed as vertical and horizontal discourses. In his last work (Bernstein, 2000) he began to analyse the curriculum implications of these distinctions.

Forms of knowledge differentiation and the curriculum

In this section I want to comment briefly on *four* aspects of the social differentiation of knowledge that can be derived from the ideas of Durkheim, Vygotsky and Bernstein, and suggest that they could provide the basis for a theory of the curriculum that is based on the idea of the 'voice of knowledge'. Although each aspect has a distinct focus, there are overlaps between them and further conceptual clarification could no doubt reduce the number of types listed and define them more precisely.

The fundamental difference between knowledge and experience

Without this difference, which lies at the heart of Durkheim's social theory of knowledge, the idea of a curriculum is impossible. This has been demonstrated by the failed attempts of successive generations of progressive and radical educators to collapse the categories and construct an experience-based curriculum. The problems of the South African and Australian outcomes-based curricula, the English child-centred curriculum that followed Plowden and the more radical Queensland-based 'new basics curriculum' are among the many examples. Less publicised, but in social justice terms even more damaging, is the extent to which curricula based on the work experience of young people have been the basis of a wide range of vocational programmes which claim to offer educational possibilities to slow learners and those disaffected from schooling.

The conceptual separation of knowledge from experience was Durkheim's major point in his most explicitly philosophical book *Pragmatism and Sociology* (Durkheim, 1984). In that book he praised William James and the pragmatists for bringing philosophical questions about truth back to where he felt they should be located – in social life (or as he expressed it, in society) and not in academic philosophy. However, he criticized James and the pragmatists for having an undifferentiated concept of the social and society and therefore at least implicitly equating it with experience. For Durkheim, experience is a powerful force but inadequate as an epistemological principle and no basis for reliable knowledge or for the curriculum.

The differences between theoretical and everyday knowledge

This is a narrower and more concrete expression of the first difference. If these differences are dismissed or blurred, it becomes increasingly difficult to make reliable decisions about what to include and exclude in the curriculum, or indeed to say what formal education is for. There are two possible consequences of blurring the distinction between theoretical and everyday concepts. The first is that many kinds of knowledge are included in the curriculum, for broadly political reasons, which schools may not provide the conditions for acquiring – sex and moral education and employment-related skills are examples. The second consequence is that the contents that may be the condition for acquiring theoretical knowledge are excluded or replaced (as in the recent proposals for the secondary science curriculum in England). Thus, on the grounds of popular relevance or pupil interest, the opportunities that students have for acquiring systematic theoretical knowledge that cannot be acquired elsewhere are restricted.

Without a specification of the differences between theoretical and everyday concepts, as well as a focus on the relationships between them that go beyond the moral or political standpoints of those involved, curriculum decisions are inevitably reduced to politics.

The differences between knowledge domains

These differences refer to horizontal aspects of the intellectual division of labour in Durkheim's terms and what Bernstein describes as the classification of educational knowledge. A theory of knowledge differentiation presupposes that domain differences are not arbitrary but in some degree are the product of

Bachelard's historical processes of 'rectification and critique'. An understanding of the extent to which domain differences such as those between disciplines and subjects have an epistemological as opposed to a merely conventional basis is crucial to the analysis of the links between domain boundaries, learner identities, and learner progress, and to addressing the debate around multi-, trans- and inter-disciplinarity and the limits of modularization and student choice.

The differences between school and non-school knowledge

These differences follow from Vygotsky's distinction between theoretical and everyday concepts and my interpretation of Bernstein's concept of the framing of educational knowledge. However, the differences between school and non-school knowledge have a specific importance in that they indicate why it is important to distinguish between the *curriculum* – as the conditions for acquiring new knowledge – and *pedagogy* – which refers to the activities of teaching and learning involved in the process of acquisition. This is a distinction that both Durkheim and Bernstein were somewhat ambiguous about. Both, but explicitly Durkheim, relied on an over-deterministic transmission model of education which played down the active role of the learner in transmission and the extent to which the *recontextualisation* of school knowledge lies at the heart of pedagogy.[14] Vygotsky, on the other hand, was more sensitive to the complexity of pedagogic issues, but was less explicit about exactly what he meant by theoretical (or scientific) concepts. This maybe why the socio-cultural and socio-historical activity theories of learning which locate their origins in Vygotsky's work have largely neglected the role of knowledge in formal education. From the perspective being developed in this chapter, while pedagogy necessarily involves the teacher in taking account of the non-school knowledge that her/his students bring to school, the curriculum explicitly does not.

Conclusions

This chapter began by noting the emptying of the concept of knowledge in the increasingly globalised debates about education and the knowledge economy, and explored some of the implications of this trend in contemporary educational policy. In endeavouring to recapture knowledge as lying at the heart of the goals of all education, the idea of the 'voice of knowledge' does not divorce knowledge from knowers and hence from thinking and judgment. Rather it offers a counter to this divorce in much contemporary writing where thinking and learning are treated as if they were processes that can be conceptualised as educational goals independently of what the thinking and learning is about.

I have argued that the idea of the structured differentiation of knowledge is central to a more adequate conceptualisation of its role in education. The chapter focused primarily on the differentiation of school and non-school knowledge and discussed some of the dimensions of this differentiation and their educational significance. The growth of knowledge, whether in a subject like physics or history, or in an occupational field like engineering or financial management, and hence the opportunities for acquisition open to new learners whatever their age, will depend on the continued process of 'rectification and critique', to return to Bachelard's apt phrase, by the various specialists involved. Making this process explicit is the task of a realist sociology of knowledge in relation to the curriculum, if the 'voice of knowledge' is to shape educational policy and knowledge is not to continue to be an empty category. There is much to do.

Acknowledgements

I would like to thank Suzy Harris (Roehampton University) for her helpful comments on an earlier draft.

Notes

1 See: www.udir.no/Stottemeny/English/Curriculum-in-English/ (accessed 11 November 2011).
2 As in the case I recently came across of a lawyer whose new post was Head of Knowledge.
3 My account draws on Christopher Norris's (Norris, 2000, 2005) excellent accounts of Bachelard's ideas.
4 I am grateful to Professor Alison Wolf (Kings College, University of London) for pointing out to me the important role of Public Service Agreements and their potential influence on what counts as successful learning in school.
5 See: www.education.gov.uk/16to19/qualificationsandlearning/thediploma (accessed 11 November 2011).
6 I mention Norway for two reasons; one is that I have recently visited two Norwegian universities and the other because Norway has often been celebrated by English researchers as representing a model of strong educational policy making (Payne, 2002). My point is not to disagree with Payne but to suggest that this 'emptying of knowledge content' under the guise of promoting knowledge can be found even in a country as little prone to 'marketising' and 'individualising' tendencies as Norway.
7 Of course, knowledge is about power and 'the powerful' will always try to define what counts as knowledge. However it is not only about power; some types of knowledge *are* more reliable than others and we cannot afford to forget either aspect.
8 It is what I, and I imagine most teachers (and parents), want their students/children to acquire at school that they will be unlikely to be able to acquire at home.
9 One of the most successful programmes of vocational education in England (in terms of progression both to employment and to higher education and professional level programmes) is that developed by the Association of Accountancy Technicians (AAT). A major reason for this is the key role played by the professional association of Chartered Accountants (The Institute of Chartered Accountants in England and Wales) with which the AAT is associated.
10 A much more detailed account of Bachelard's epistemological theory is given by Mary Tiles (Tiles, 1984) and by Christina Chimisso (Chimisso, 2001) who locates her account in the context of Bachelard's work as a whole.
11 Althusser's failed attempt to apply Bachelard's proposals to Marxism as a theory of capitalism and his use of Bachelard's idea of an 'epistemological break' are an illustration of the difficulties.

12 George Canguilhem, who succeeded Bachelard at the Sorbonne, developed an influential historical epistemology with a focus on biology. However, I have not considered his work in this chapter.

13 I have only referred to two of Bernstein's many publications here.

14 Bernstein was the originator of the concept of 'recontextualisation'; however he was more concerned with its role in the structuring of pedagogic discourse than as a way of conceptualising pedagogy.

References

Bernstein, B. (1971) *Class, Codes and Control*, Volume 1, London: Routledge.

Bernstein, B. (2000) *Pedagogy, Symbolic Control and Identity*, London: Taylor and Francis.

Chimisso, C. (2001) *Gaston Bacelard: Critic of Science and the Imagination*, London: Routledge.

De Sousa Santos, B. (2001) 'Towards an epistemology of blindness', *European Journal of Social Theory*, 4(3): 251–279.

Durkheim, E. (1984) *Pragmatism and Sociology* (trans. J. Alcock), Cambridge: Cambridge University Press.

Karpov, Y.V. and Heywood, H.C. (1998) 'Two ways to elaborate Vygotsky's concept of mediation: Implications for instruction', *American Psychologist*, 53(1): 27–36.

Keen, A. (2007) *The Cult of the Amateur*, London: Nicholas Brealey Publishing.

Kronman, A. (2007) *Education's End: Why Our Colleges and Universities Have Given up on the Meaning of Life*, New Haven, CT: Yale University Press.

Moore, R. (2006) 'Going critical: The problems of problematising knowledge in educational studies', *Critical Education Studies*, 48(1): 25–41.

Moore, R. (2007) *The Sociology of Knowledge and Education*, London: Continuum Press.

Norris, C. (2000) *Deconstruction and the Unfinished Project of Modernity*, London: Routledge.

Norris, C. (2005) *Epistemology*, London: Continuum Publishing.

Payne, J. (2002) 'A tale of two curriculums', *Journal of Education and Work*, 15(2): 117–143.

Robertson, S. (2007) *Teachers Matter ... Don't They?*, Bristol: Centre for Globalisation, Education and Societies, University of Bristol.

Shapin, S. (1995) *The Social History of Truth*, Chicago, IL: Chicago University Press.

Tiles, M. (1984) *Bachelard: Science and Objectivity*, Cambridge: Cambridge University Press.

Young, M. (2007) *Bringing Knowledge Back In*, London: Routledge.

Young, M. (2009) 'What are schools for?', in Lauder, H., Porter, J. and Daniels, H. (eds) *Critical Perspectives on Education*, London: Routledge.

Young, M. and Muller, J. (2007) 'Truth and truthfulness in the sociology of educational knowledge', *Theory and Research in Education*, 5(2): 173–201.

Young, M. and Muller, J. (2009) *Three Scenarios for the Future: Lessons from the Sociology of Knowledge*, London: Knowledge Laboratory.

9 The problem with competency-based training

Leesa Wheelahan

Introduction

The aim of this chapter is to develop and extend a social realist critique of competency-based training (CBT). Its key argument is that knowledge must be placed at the centre of curriculum, and that because CBT does not do this, it excludes working-class students from access to powerful knowledge. Developing this argument reveals that constructivist critiques of CBT not only miss the point, they are part of the problem. The chapter argues that this is because the relationship between constructivism and instrumentalism structured the development of CBT in the vocational education and training (VET) sector in Australia, even though they are distinct theoretical approaches to curriculum. Constructivist discourses were appropriated and reworked through the prism of instrumentalism, thereby contributing to the justification and legitimation of CBT, but also to its continuing theorisation and development. The basis for the appropriation of constructivism by CBT is that both emphasise the contextual, situated and problem-oriented nature of knowledge creation and learning, and in so doing sacrifice the complexity and depth of theoretical knowledge in curriculum in favour of 'authentic' learning in the workplace. Consequently, in developing its critique of CBT and the instrumentalist learning theories that underpin it, constructivism evades the main problem, which is that theoretical knowledge must be placed at the centre of curriculum in all sectors of education, and that access to knowledge is the *raison d'être* of education (Young, 2008).

This is not just an esoteric argument; there are real practical consequences for students and society. CBT is hegemonic and pervasive in VET in Australia, perhaps to a greater extent than in many other countries. Australia has two sectors of tertiary education; a higher education (HE) sector and a VET sector. Training packages are the mandated form of publicly funded VET qualifications in Australia and they are based on CBT models of curriculum. All publicly funded VET qualifications must be based on training packages where they exist or on 'industry-specified' units of competency in their absence. Training packages are the equivalent of the British National Vocational Qualifications (NVQs). If CBT is structured so that students are not provided with access to theoretical knowledge, at least to the same level as those undertaking HE qualifications, then this represents a mechanism for social stratification, because VET in Australia is over-represented by students from lower socio-economic backgrounds, whereas HE is over-represented by students from high socio-economic backgrounds (Foley, 2007).

The argument in this chapter is developed through drawing on the sociology of Basil Bernstein and the philosophy of critical realism as complementary modes of analysis. While all social realists acknowledge their theoretical debt to Bernstein, not all draw on critical realism, so this chapter is part of a continuing discussion within social realism about the nature of knowledge and its place in the curriculum. However, this discussion proceeds on the basis of substantive agreement, which is that all students need to be provided with access to theoretical knowledge so that they can navigate the boundaries between theoretical and everyday knowledge and between different kinds of theoretical knowledge.

The first section draws on Bernstein and critical realism to analyse the nature of knowledge, the complexity of the social and natural worlds, the relationship between knowledge and the social and natural world, and the way in which the structures of knowledge are implicated in processes of knowledge production and acquisition. This framework is then used in the remainder of the chapter to critique CBT and to demonstrate the way in which constructivism aids and abets CBT because each has problematic ontological premises that are reflected in their theories of curriculum. It outlines the structure of CBT and how it denies students access to knowledge; the way in which CBT appropriates progressivism for its continued justification; the ontological premises of CBT that allow it do this; and the similarities and differences between CBT and constructivism. Both are critiqued for their focus on the contextual, and the implications for curriculum are considered.

The nature of knowledge

Basil Bernstein (2000) argued that fair access to theoretical knowledge was important for democracy because it is the means society uses to conduct its conversation about itself and about what it should be like. Society uses theoretical knowledge to imagine alternative futures through thinking the unthinkable and the not-yet-thought. This is why theoretical knowledge is socially powerful knowledge. Access to abstract theoretical knowledge is thus a question of distributional justice, and curriculum in *all* qualifications should be structured so that it provides students with this access.

Access to theoretical knowledge is becoming more important in work. Individuals need to draw on increasingly complex knowledge as a consequence of changes to society, work and technology. Young (2008, p.146) argues that while all jobs require context-specific knowledge, 'many jobs also require knowledge involving theoretical ideas shared by a "community of specialists"' located within the disciplines. Workers need to be able to use theoretical knowledge in different ways and in different contexts as their work grows in complexity and difficulty. This means that occupational progression is strongly related to educational progression, because education is the main way in which most people are provided with access to disciplinary knowledge. It also means that all qualifications should provide students with the disciplinary knowledge they need to study at a higher level within their field in addition to immediate occupational outcomes. VET qualifications do not do this because of their current exclusive focus on workplace-specific outcomes.

Critical realists argue that the (natural and social) world is complex and stratified. For example, Collier (1998, p.263) explains everything is governed by the law of physics; some, but not all things are governed by the laws of biology; and more recently, some but not all things are governed by the law of capitalist economics. In this instance, these different strata (and others not identified here) interact to make factory production possible. It is a *relational* philosophy because it examines the *interplay* between different objects and strata. A key premise is:

> that the world is characterised by emergence, that is situations in which the conjunction of two or more features or aspects gives rise to new phenomena, which have properties which are irreducible to those of their constituents, even though the latter are necessary for their existence.
>
> (Sayer, 2000, p.12)

For example, even though a society could not exist without people, society is more than the sum of its parts and it is not possible to add up all the individuals to understand the way society is structured and its dynamics, and the impact it in turn has on people.

It is necessary to identify *three* levels of reality in the social and natural worlds, and as will be demonstrated later, the central problem with both CBT and constructivism is that they fail to do so. The three levels are the real, actual and empirical.

The domain of the real consists of *underlying causal mechanisms*. An example of a causal mechanism in the social world is class, while gravity is an example in the natural world. Generative mechanisms interact in open systems, and this means that some cancel each other out, or change the way in which they act. Not everything that *could* happen *does* happen. For example, Sayer (1992, p.110) says that we do not need to explode neutron bombs to know their causal liabilities. Sayer (2000, p.11) explains that: 'Realists therefore seek to identify both necessity and possibility or potential in the world – what things must go together, and would could happen, given the nature of the objects.'

The interaction of generative mechanisms gives rise to *events*, which Bhaskar (1998a, p.41) describes as the domain of the actual, where things actually happen. Events are always co-determined by multiple stratified generative mechanisms, and as such, outcomes cannot be fully predicted in advance. Some events can be perceived while others cannot. The tree does indeed make a sound when it falls in the forest, even if there is no one to hear it. Whether or not we perceive events is an empirical question, one that is continually reshaped by science as we discover ways to empirically observe events that previously were only discernable through their effects. The third domain is the domain of the empirical, which 'is comprised only of experiences' (Collier, 1994, p.45). This means that it must have been generated in the domain of the real and taken place in the domain of the actual. This depth ontology allows us to see that the world is not reducible to what we experience or what happens, there is much that *could* happen and understanding this is necessary if we are to think the unthinkable and the not-yet-thought.

Even though knowledge is about objects it is not the same as those objects. There is no direct correspondence between objects and knowledge because knowledge is socially produced and mediated, and has its own conditions for its existence and causal properties. Bernstein's analysis adds depth to critical realism because he explores the causal properties of the *structures* of knowledge, and the implications for the way such knowledge is produced and acquired.

Bernstein (2000) argued that theoretical knowledge differs from everyday knowledge because each is embedded in a different system of meaning and each has a different structure. He characterised abstract theoretical knowledge as *vertical discourse*, and everyday or 'mundane' knowledge as *horizontal discourse*. Theoretical knowledge is general, principled knowledge. It is organised as a vertical discourse which is, to a greater or lesser extent, hierarchically structured. It consists of 'specialised symbolic structures of explicit knowledge' in which the integration of knowledge occurs through the integration of meanings and not through relevance to specific contexts (Bernstein, 2000, p.160). Students need access to the disciplinary system of meaning as a condition for using knowledge in contextually specific applications. For example, students need access to mathematics as a condition for understanding and applying particular formulas, and if they are to use these formulas in different contexts. In contrast, everyday knowledge is organised as a horizontal discourse, which consists of segmented knowledge structures. It is particularised knowledge, because its selection and usefulness is determined by the extent to which it is relevant in a particular context (Gamble, 2006). This is the tacit, context-dependent knowledge of the workplace. Bernstein (2000, p.157) explains that everyday knowledge is 'likely to be oral, local, context dependent and specific, tacit, multi-layered, and contradictory across but not within contexts'.

Theoretical knowledge organised through disciplinary frameworks is also strongly *classified* knowledge because the boundaries between it and everyday knowledge are clearly defined, and because each of the academic disciplines has a specialised language and strong boundaries that insulates it from other disciplines. In contrast, everyday knowledge is weakly classified because its contextual relevance is of primary importance. The way an academic discipline is structured has implications for the way in which it is translated for pedagogic transmission. Induction into a particular academic discipline requires induction into its system of meaning, which may have implications for the way knowledge is selected, sequenced, paced and evaluated. This is the 'how' of pedagogic practice, and Bernstein refers to this as the process of *framing*. The more hierarchical a body of knowledge (for example, physics) the more likely it is that pedagogy will need to be strongly sequenced because students need to understand what came before in order to understand what comes after (Muller, 2006).

Students need to be inducted into disciplinary systems of meaning as the basis of developing the 'recognition' rules they need to recognise the distinction between vertical and horizontal discourses, and between different types of vertical discourses so that they can, for example, distinguish between physics and chemistry, or micro-economics and sociology (Bernstein, 2000). In general, knowledge that is strongly classified into disciplinary frameworks provides students from disadvantaged backgrounds with more access to theoretical knowledge than weakly classified knowledge. Knowledge that is strongly classified and framed explicitly signals the boundaries between different areas of knowledge, and the way it is sequenced, paced and evaluated, whereas these relations are rendered opaque in knowledge that is weakly classified and framed. Consequently, collapsing the boundary between vertical and horizontal discourse is problematic because it denies students *epistemic* access to each kind of knowledge, and as a consequence, it denies students *social* access to this knowledge. This is the heart of the problem with both CBT and constructivism.

Structure of CBT and how it excludes access to knowledge

CBT excludes students from access to disciplinary knowledge because it only provides students with access to contextually specific applications of knowledge, and not the system of meaning in which it is embedded. Units of competency describe workplace tasks or roles. Competency is defined as the application of specified knowledge, skill and attitudes needed to undertake a work role or task to the required standard in the workplace (DEST, 2006, p.69). Units of competency include, among other things: elements of competency (that break down the unit of competency into demonstrable and assessable outcomes or actions); performance criteria that specify the required level of performance, required knowledge and skills; a range statement that describes the contexts and conditions in which the performance criteria apply; and evidence guides that describe the underpinning knowledge and skills that need to be demonstrated (assessed) to prove competence (DEST, 2006, p.117). The 'rules' surrounding training packages and units of competence are that while knowledge must be included, it should be in context, and should 'only be included if it refers to knowledge actually applied at work' (DEST, 2006, p.114). Furthermore, 'Units of competency that integrate knowledge into the overall performance specification of the unit and the assessment process advice *should fully include all relevant knowledge as it is applied in a work role*' (DEST, 2006, p.140, emphasis added).

This demonstrates that knowledge is included, but it is only contextually specific knowledge which has been delocated from the system of meaning in which it is embedded. It is only included if it is *directly* related to a work role. For example, 'Develop & update the legal knowledge required for business compliance' is a unit of competency in the Advanced Diploma of Hospitality Management, which, according to the unit descriptor, 'deals with the skills and knowledge required to ensure business compliance with legislation governing the tourism and hospitality industries' (CoA, 2002, p.477). This is quite different to the first year 'Business Law' subject in the Bachelor of Business (Hospitality Management) at the same university in Victoria which offers the aforementioned advanced diploma, which aims to 'provide students with an understanding and awareness of the basic principles of Contract Law, a familiarity with relevant case law and an introduction to the statutory provisions pertinent to the course'. It explains that the purpose is to help students 'develop an understanding of legal reasoning as it applies to the analysis of contractual relationships'.[1]

CBT translates knowledge from being general and principled knowledge to particularised knowledge, because its selection and usefulness is determined by the extent to which it is relevant in a particular context. Students thus have access to knowledge in its particularised form, but are not provided with the means to relate it to its general and principled structure and system of meaning.

Supporters of training packages argue that they merely specify the outcomes of learning and not the processes of learning, which means that 'providers' and teachers are free to develop a curriculum approach that most suits their 'clients'. For example, Schofield and McDonald (2004, p.2) say that: 'Consistent with their outcomes-based orientation, Training Packages are silent on how teachers and trainers should or could design the curriculum to achieve these outcomes.' However, the *Training Package Development Handbook* (DEST, 2006, p.126) says that: 'Performance criteria must be expressed precisely to enable appropriate training and assessment.' It is clear that training packages *do* shape teaching and learning, and that they constitute an important component of curriculum, because they specify *what* is to be taught and, in broad terms, *how* it should be assessed. The point of training packages was that they would reshape teaching and learning in VET so that it was more 'industry responsive'. Students are enrolled in, taught within the framework of, and assessed on the basis of, units of competency. This is curriculum by any other name.

CBT policy as pastiche – the ontology of CBT

The theoretical premise within instrumentalism that allows it to appropriate from constructivism is the way in which CBT divorces learning outcomes from processes of learning. Such appropriation is also possible because of theoretical commonalities between instrumentalism and constructivism.

CBT is a form of empirical realism based on atomism in ontology and epistemology, in which the 'real' consists of discrete, atomistic events that can be translated into unproblematic (empirical) descriptions of those events (Bhaskar, 1998a). This is expressed in units of competency, which are unproblematic descriptions of workplace roles or tasks. The ontology of CBT means that each of the constituent components of the model can be considered independently of the other and adjusted as appropriate to 'fix' deficiencies in the model. The model is then reassembled through an aggregative process rather than a relational one in which the constituent components are changed by their relationship to the whole and to each other.

For example, the design of units of competency has been augmented to accommodate concerns about, among other things, the inclusion of underpinning knowledge and to ensure that a broad range of contexts was specified in units of competency as insurance against overly narrow training (Rumsey, 2003, pp.13–15). However, the underlying definition of competency has not changed fundamentally in Australia since 1992, although the words may have slightly changed. The 'solution' to every perceived deficiency was to add required and optional components to the model and tight specifications for their inclusion.

This process of augmentation and aggregation makes it possible for supporters of training packages to distinguish between learning outcomes, curriculum, pedagogy and the resources used to support teaching and learning. If each is considered independently rather than relationally, then it is possible to invest each with differing content. In the case of CBT proselytisers, the outcomes of learning are held constant while other aspects are changed as needed. This is necessary because the underlying premise of CBT is that *employers* (or more charitably and inclusively, sometimes 'industry') should determine what is needed in the workplace. This is what an industry-led VET system is supposed to mean, with the result that *this* component of the model – industry specification of outcomes – is not negotiable.

The result is policy that uses as its justification and source of legitimation a pastiche of theories and approaches that draw from sometimes opposing theoretical premises, then blended through processes of recontextualisation so that constructivist theories of learning are mobilised to support human capital objectives, even though human capital theory is based on the self-maximising rational economic individual. Individualistic theories of learning styles (that ascribe learning styles as relatively fixed attributes of individuals) are unproblematically blended with theories that emphasise learning as a participative process (in which the construction of meaning is a shared process).[2] This process of selection, augmentation, blending and incorporation is achieved through the principles derived from the broader human capital policy context.

Why CBT can draw on constructivism in theorising

The relationship between instrumentalism and constructivism makes CBT possible not just at the level of its legitimation and justification, but also in its theorisation and development. Even though constructivists differ among themselves about the nature of contexts (Edwards and Miller, 2007), they share a common concern about context with instrumentalists, and with the contextual, situated and problem-oriented nature of knowledge creation and learning. Both constructivists and instrumentalists sacrifice the complexity and depth of knowledge (including vocational knowledge) in curriculum in favour of 'authentic' learning in the workplace. Both could agree with the statement that: 'Current thinking emphasises knowledge constructed as practical, interdisciplinary, informal, applied and contextual over knowledge constructed as theoretical, disciplinary, formal, foundational and generalisable' (Chappell *et al.*, 2003, p.7).

Because experience is the basis of knowledge, both minimise the differences between knowledge acquired at work and that acquired in education. This enables both to emphasise the commensurability of vertical and horizontal discourses rather than their differences, because each consists of experiences that form the basis of knowledge. Indeed, a stronger argument can be made; both privilege horizontal discourses over vertical discourses because of their emphasis on 'authentic' learning in the workplace and in sites other than the academy, because it is in the former that knowledge can be contextualised and applied. Knowledge is not valued *unless* it has application in the workplace or can be used to solve a problem, as in problem-based learning approaches to curriculum.

Where the existence and necessity of codified knowledge is admitted, both see it in instrumental terms and subordinate to 'authentic learning' rather than as systemised, structured bodies of knowledge. These structures have their own emergent properties that have pedagogic implications for the way students engage with this knowledge, and for its selection and sequencing. Consequently, both are unable to theorise the relationship between theoretical knowledge and knowledge acquired in the workplace. This is a problem because, as Young (2008, p.144) explains, it is 'the connections between the codified knowledge of the college-based curriculum and the tacit and often un-codifiable knowledge that is acquired in workplaces that is the basis for what is distinctive about vocational knowledge'. The boundaries between the two sites and the kinds of knowledge in each constitute the basis for navigating between the two, yet neither instrumentalism nor constructivism can adequately theorise this relationship because they collapse the distinction between the kinds of knowledge available in each.

Instrumentalism

Bernstein's insights allow us to see that in tying knowledge to workplace tasks and roles within units of competency, CBT fundamentally transforms the nature of knowledge by delocating it from the vertical discourse in which it is classified and relocating it into a horizontal and segmented knowledge structure. A focus on specific content does not provide students with the criteria needed to *select* the knowledge needed in new contexts. Content is disaggregated so that it consists of isolated 'bits' of knowledge. A focus on specific content for a specific context means that the meaning of that content is exhausted by the context. For example, apprentice motor mechanics will have difficulty understanding when and if they should use particular mathematical formulas in other contexts if they have been taught that this *particular* formula is used in a *particular* context. They will be able to relate the specific context and the specific formula, but will not have been provided with the tools to choose, select and apply other formulas within that context or a range of other contexts. Knowledge is not under their control.

Because CBT is based on descriptions of discrete atomistic events, it considers tasks and roles independently of their broader relationship to each other, the workplace or society more broadly, and this means that the same task or role can be identified in many workplaces. The task or role takes on universal properties because it is considered independently and non-relationally. It is the task or role that is unique even if it is applied over many contexts, and it is this that is translated into an unproblematic description within units of competency. There is a presumed 'correspondence' between the task or role that the unit of competency describes, so that the description results in objective statements that incorporate all aspects of the relevant task and role and associated skill. Assessment then becomes a straightforward matter of providing 'evidence' that the specified performance criteria have been met. That which can be specified and measured is measured, that which cannot be specified is not measured. The limits of the real thus become defined by the limits of language.[3] Units of competency are then added up, moved about, and reconfigured to make different qualifications through common core competencies (and employability skills). That is, the total equals the sum of the parts, and different sums (comprising many of the same elements) make different totals. This is the method that *aggregates*, and is less concerned with understanding the relationship between elements, and how these elements are transformed in the context of such a relationship.

In collapsing the domains of the real and actual into the empirical, CBT assumes that outcomes can be achieved by directly teaching to the outcomes, and in doing so ignores the complexity that is needed to create *capacity*, and this goes beyond the level of experience in the contextual and situated, while not ignoring the importance of such experience. Capacity implies the possibility of responding appropriately to that which has not yet happened, as well as that which has. Absences can be conceptualised and alternative realisations envisaged. However, envisaging alternative futures requires access to knowledge. In focusing on aggregations of specific skills, CBT limits the focus to what people have demonstrated they can do in one context, not what they know or could potentially do through creatively and innovatively considering how they can use what they know.

CBT's simplistic and atomistic notion of skill is what allows current state and Commonwealth government policy in Australia to insist that apprenticeships can be shortened. However, learning how to become a member of a trade, occupation or profession is not simply a matter of meeting all the specified learning outcomes, particularly when these are tied to specific tasks or roles. The holistic development of the person in the context of their profession is excluded, and this involves forming an identity as part of that profession. This cannot be easily codified as observable outcomes tied to specific skills. Bernstein (2000, p.59) explains that: 'This identity arises out of a particular social order, through relations which the identity enters into with other identities of reciprocal recognition, support, mutual legitimisation and finally through a negotiated collective purpose.' The emphasis on specific skills means that the importance and complexity of vocational knowledge recedes and becomes ephemeral, not only in the way in which knowledge is used to orient to work, but also in the role that knowledge plays in forming professional identities. Teaching and learning must engage the real and the actual and not just the empirical, because this is the only way to generate a varying and contextually sensitive performance in a variety of contexts, and to build capacity for dealing with the future.

By focusing on workplace roles and tasks rather than holistically preparing students for an occupation, CBT abstracts knowledge and skill from the bodies of those who must apply that knowledge and skill. *People* apply knowledge and skill, and education and training needs to address the enabling conditions that allow them to engage in knowledgeable and skilful work. One of the structuring mechanisms that shape particular workplace contexts is the broader knowledge and skills that workers bring with them as well as the way that they apply that knowledge and skill. This is why the aims of education and training should be to develop the knowledge, skills and capacities of workers and citizens in broad terms.

Constructivism

Constructivism is related to instrumentalism in two ways. The first is, as Moore (2007, p.35) explains, because each is committed to a foundationalist notion of truth and justified true belief, in which there is a correspondence between objects and our knowledge of those objects with the possibility of law-like statements about their operation. The difference is that whereas positivism thinks that access to such knowledge is possible, constructivism denies that it is so. Moore explains that for positivism '"things" give order to words' whereas for constructivism 'words give order to "things"' (2007, p.35). In constructivism, different words (and different meanings) consequently invest different kinds of order in things, none of which is more true than others because 'the ordering' of social reality is constructed through discourse and the meaning that actors invest in these creative acts.

The second way in which instrumentalism and constructivism are related is through their commitment to experience as the basis of knowledge. Unlike the empiricism (and positivism) of CBT, constructivists do not restrict themselves to the empirical *world*, while still privileging *experience* as the basis of knowledge. Constructivism's focus on contextualised social practices and processes of meaning-making means that the empirical world recedes in importance (where the existence of the empirical is admitted at all). Constructivists are generally not guilty of atomism in the same way as is empiricism, except as in some versions when considering the natural world (Bhaskar, 1998a). Constructivism shares with positivism a commitment to 'the use of the category of experience to define the world. This involves giving what is in effect a particular epistemological concept a general ontological function' (Bhaskar 1998a, 21). The limits of the world become identified with our knowledge of the world.

In focusing on the contextual, constructivism seeks to find the criteria of intelligibility within that context – the conditions *for* intelligibility are identical *with* the context, and the possibilities of the real are identified with the limits of experience of the context. This leads constructivists to a stronger emphasis on context than is the case with CBT. Learning outcomes are not (generally) divorced from processes of learning, because, according to Hager and Smith (2004, p.35), 'both the nature of work processes, as well as the standards that are applicable to those processes, are significantly shaped by contextual influences'. They explain that socio-cultural approaches focus 'on processes rather than entities or structures, and [stress] the inseparability of the individual and the social' (ibid., p.35). They argue that a focus on context leads to an integrated notion of competence, because knowledge, skills, abilities and attributes are not demonstrated atomistically, but through complex, intentional actions that simultaneously enact several competencies but which at the same time demonstrate situational understanding (ibid., p.37).

Situational understanding is thus contextualised and intersubjective, and this reduces all that is important to the intersubjective in ways that exclude the importance of (and reality of) theoretical knowledge. To insist on the externality and reality of knowledge is to be guilty of reification. The emphasis instead is placed on process and tacit knowledge and skill, and the way in which the social construction of both authorises a performance in one instance as skilled and in another as unskilled (and does not address the question of whether or not the performance really *is* skilled). The focus becomes the way in which meaning is constructed and in some versions of constructivism, truth defined intersubjectively in ways that exclude and include.

The problem with this analysis is that it only accounts for part of the context it seeks to describe, because it focuses on a discourse that is internal to itself and devoid of external referents. It focuses on the community of producers and how they *understand* what they are doing, and not on their actual practice – or *what* they are doing. Both aspects need to be analysed if the nature of practice is to be understood. As Moore (2006, p.123) explains: 'The fact that all human embeddedness, consciousness and action is, in the first instance, local does not mean that it is nothing *but* local.' In focusing on the contextual, constructivists must discount the way in which social and cultural structures provide the parameters for agential activity by setting the 'degrees of freedom' which facilitate or impede purposeful agential action, and the interplay between the social, material and natural worlds. The domain of the real is discounted, and only the actual and empirical admitted, because to admit that social and cultural structures exist independently of processes of instantiation by agents is to be once again guilty of the sin of reification.

Conclusion

CBT and constructivism both fail to identify that which *is* important about contexts, which is that students must be able to learn to distinguish theory and contexts if they are to recognise and determine contextually appropriate applications of that theory (Clarke and Winch, 2004, p.517). The capacity to recognise contexts and to appropriately apply theories cannot be solely learnt in the classroom, because students need to learn to relate the general to particular instances and different kinds of instances. This means that learning for the workplace must include learning *in* the workplace, but that learning cannot be limited *to* the workplace. The task of vocational pedagogy is to 'face both ways' to theory and the workplace as the basis for their integration in vocational practice (Barnett, 2006).

Bhaskar's (1998b, p.146) argument that 'no moment ever contains its own truth, or act its own criteria of intelligibility' has important implications for pedagogy. By seeking meaning within the contextual, constructivism and instrumentalism deny students access to the conditions of knowledge needed to understand the contextual. This is because the complexity contributing to the structuring of the contextual is denied, as is the means to access to the contextual by using the general to understand the particular. Not all knowledge that we need to use emerges from practice (Young, 2008), and we need the means to move beyond the contextual to access systems of knowledge and their generative principles. If the world is characterised by ontological depth, stratification, emergence and co-determination then students need to understand these processes, and not have their understanding restricted to the level of events or experiences.

Neither CBT nor constructivism can theorise the relationship between theoretical knowledge and workplace practice, and consequently for the complementary roles of educational institutions and the workplace and the kind of knowledge that is available in each. Blurring the distinctions between each results in segmental pedagogies, in which knowledge is decontextualised from the system of meaning in which it is embedded, and knowledge becomes tied to the contextual. Students do not have access to the criteria they need to select knowledge and use it in new and creative ways, and knowledge is not under their control.

While CBT has appropriated the language of progressivism and student-centredness from constructivism in legitimating and justifying itself, constructivism has aided and abetted in this process through the commitment it shares with CBT to the contextual and the experiential. The key criticism constructivism makes of CBT is the atomistic way in which the latter conceives of contexts and skills. However, the alternative offered by constructivism is to tie knowledge more tightly to the contextual and, as a consequence, constructivism is not able to mount a coherent critique of instrumentalism or CBT. This is because the most important feature of each approach is the privileging of horizontal discourse over vertical discourse. Consequently, both are complicit in locking VET students out of access to disciplinary knowledge.

Notes

1 Source: wcf.vu.edu.au/Handbook/DisplaySubjectDetails.cfm?SubjectID=32925 (accessed 20 June 2008).

2 See Smith and Blake (2005, pp.3–4) for a particularly illustrative example of this.
3 And instrumentalism shares this feature with constructivism, as illustrated in the next section.

References

Barnett, M. (2006) 'Vocational knowledge and vocational pedagogy', in Young, M. and Gamble, J. (eds) *Knowledge, Curriculum and Qualifications for South African Further Education*, Cape Town: Human Sciences Research Council, pp.143–157.

Bernstein, B. (2000) *Pedagogy, Symbolic Control and Identity*, 2nd ed., Oxford: Rowman & Littlefield.

Bhaskar, R. (1998a) 'Philosophy and scientific realism', in *Critical Realism: Essential Readings*, London: Routledge.

Bhaskar, R. (1998b) *The Possibility of Naturalism: A Philosophical Critique of the Contemporary Human Sciences*, 3rd ed., London: Routledge.

Chappell, C., Hawke, G., Rhodes, C. and Solomon, N. (2003) *High Level Review of Training Packages Phase 1 Report: An Analysis of the Current and Future Context in which Training Packages Will Need to Operate*, Brisbane: Australian National Training Authority.

Clarke, L. and Winch, C. (2004) 'Apprenticeship and applied theoretical knowledge', *Educational Philosophy and Theory*, 36(5): 509–521.

CoA (Commonwealth of Australia) (2002) *THT02 Tourism Training Package*, volume 2 of 5, Canberra: Department of Education, Science and Training.

Collier, A. (1994) *Critical Realism: An Introduction to Roy Bhaskar's Philosophy*, London: Verso.

Collier, A. (1998) 'Stratified explanation and Marx's conception of history', in Archer, M., Bhaskar, R., Collier, A., Lawson, T. and Norrie, A. (eds) *Critical Realism: Essential Readings*, London: Routledge, pp.258–281.

DEST (Department of Education Science and Training) (2006) *Training Package Development Handbook*, Canberra: DEST.

Edwards, R. and Miller, K. (2007) 'Putting the context into learning', *Pedagogy, Culture and Society*, 15(3): 263–274.

Foley, P. (2007) *The Socio-Economic Status of Vocational Education and Training Students in Australia*, Adelaide: National Centre for Vocational Education Research.

Gamble, J. (2006) 'Theory and practice in the vocational curriculum', in Young, M. and Gamble, J. (eds) *Knowledge, Curriculum and Qualifications for South African Further Education*, Cape Town: Human Sciences Research Council, pp.87–103.

Hager, P. and Smith, E. (2004) 'The inescapability of significant contextual learning in work performance', *London Review of Education*, 2(1): 33–46.

Moore, R. (2006) 'Hierarchical knowledge structure and the Canon: A preference for judgments', in Christie, F. and Martin, J.R. (eds) *Language, Knowledge and Pedagogy: Functional Linguistic and Sociological Perspectives*, London: Continuum Press, pp.109–130.

Moore, R. (2007) 'Going critical: The problem of problematising knowledge in education studies', *Critical Studies in Education*, 48(1): 25–41.

Muller, J. (2006) 'Differentiation and progression in the curriculum', in Young, M. and Gamble, J. (eds) *Knowledge, Curriculum and Qualifications for South African Further Education*, Cape Town: Human Sciences Research Council, pp.66–86.

Rumsey, D. (2003) *Think Piece on the Training Package Model*, Brisbane: Australian National Training Authority.

Sayer, A. (1992) *Method in Social Science: A Realist Approach*, 2nd ed., London: Routledge.

Sayer, A. (2000) *Realism and Social Science*, London: Sage.

Schofield, K. and McDonald, R. (2004) *High Level Review of Training Packages: Working Paper 7. Supporting Quality Teaching, Learning and Assessment*, Brisbane: Australian National Training Authority.

Smith, P. and Blake, D. (2005) *Facilitating Learning through Effective Teaching: At a Glance*, Adelaide: National Centre for Vocational Education Research.

Young, M. (2008) *Bringing Knowledge Back in: From Social Constructivism to Social Realism in the Sociology of Education*, London: Routledge.

Part III

Pedagogy, assessment, the demands of the knowledge economy and social justice?

10 Numbers in grids of intelligibility

Making sense of how educational truth is told

Thomas S. Popkewitz

In an important book about numbers and social affairs, Theodore Porter (1995) begins by asking: "How are we to account for the prestige and power of quantitative methods in the modern world? ... How is it that what was used for studying stars, molecules and cells would have attraction for human societies?" To consider these questions, Porter continues that only a small proportion of numbers or quantitative expressions have any pretence of describing laws of nature or "even of providing complete and accurate descriptions of the eternal world" (Porter, 1995, pp.viii–ix). Numbers, he argues, are parts of systems of communication whose technologies create distances from phenomena by appearing to summarize complex events and transactions. As the mechanical objectivity of numbers appears to follow a priori rules that project fairness and impartiality, numbers are seen as excluding judgment and mitigating subjectivity.

The importance of numbers to contemporary societies is easy to demonstrate, ironically, by citing numbers. One "fact" of numbers[1] is that measuring people and things absorbs 6 percent of the US gross national product (Porter, 1995, p.28). With current US educational reforms stressing the measurement of every child at almost every age to find and then eradicate the "achievement gaps," the percentage of gross national product spent on education has probably increased. But at a more general level, it is almost impossible to think about schooling without numbers: children's ages and school grades, the measuring of children's growth and development, achievement testing, league tables of schools, and identifying equity through statistical procedures about populational representation and success rates.

Porter continues that numbers are a technology of distance and used as a claim of objectivity instantiated by moral and political discourses. Any domain of quantified knowledge, he argues, is artificial through creating uniformity among different qualities of things (Porter, 1995, p.6). That uniformity gives social authority to the interrelation of science and policy.

This discussion extends and refocuses Porter's notion of the technologies of numbers to consider the politics of schooling. Ignored in most policy studies and research is the paradox of inscribing equivalency and comparability through numbers. The technologies of numbers are embodied in a grid of cultural practices that "act" on teachers' and children's lives in classrooms. To talk about "achievement" and the "achievement gap," shorthand for numerical differences between children, instantiates particular rules and standards of reason by which experiences are classified, problems located, and procedures given to order, classify, and divide. Exploring the "reason" through which numbers are made sensible and plausible puts focus on the processes of exclusion and abjection in the impulses to include.

The first section considers briefly the historical "making" of numbers as "social facts" inscribed as cultural practices that fabricate kinds of people for acting on others and for acting on one's self (Hacking, 1999). Fabrication has a double sense. It entails simultaneously practices of inventing fictions about people that respond to things of the world (such as adolescence as a human kind); and the making of that "kind" as theories, programs, and cultural narratives, producing people to navigate and order life itself. The second section examines two particular human kinds assembled through numbers to order who a child is and should be: a research report to identify characteristics of "the effective teacher" in instruction and the Organization of Economic Co-operation and Development (OECD) Program for International Student Assessment (PISA) international comparisons of children's curriculum knowledge report. Numbers in the making of human kinds as "actors" is pursued in the third section by historicizing the contemporary tropes of neo-liberalism and "markets." Fourth and finally, I bring the previous sections together to consider the limits of "reason" through numbers as they are deployed in contemporary reforms to define curriculum standards. I argue that the standards of schooling are not about the public statement of outcomes or performance indicators of assessment. The standards of curriculum are in the human kinds produced that exclude and abject in the name of democratic participation.

The discussion of numbers is about the "political" of schooling that is embodied in the systems of reason that order, classify and divide its objects – children and teachers, among others – as human kinds. The investigation is itself a political intervention[2] and a strategy of resistance against the commonsense of policy and research. It is to make fragile the seeming causality of contemporary life through naturalizing what is taken as given and inevitable; thus making possible alternatives other than those currently present (see, e.g. Foucault, 1991; Rancière, 2004). The concept of fabrication provides a way to rethink the political in social life and schooling without re-engaging the unfruitful divisions between text and context; subjective and the objective, discourses and context; or nominalism, relativism and social constructivism vs. realisms that dominate contemporary educational philosophy and social theory.

Numbers as fabricating kinds of people

I begin the inquiry into numbers through, first, considering numbers as an "actor" of change. Numbers order thought and action by visualizing "social facts" that in the nineteenth century were thought necessary for republican government and democracy. While later I raise questions about the limits of this assumption, the purpose of objectivizing and standardizing through numbers was to equalize processes and practices of new republican governments. That equalizing enabled the new systems of planning to tame the uncertainty associated with democratic life in the nineteenth century and to make the citizen necessary for the operation of government. The last part focuses on numbers as a clearing or cultural space through which kinds of people are fabricated. I use the notion of the adolescent to illustrate the making and enacting of a human kind. Throughout, numbers are seen as existing in a set of cultural practices that generate principles about *what is thought about, hoped for, and acted on.*

Faith in numbers and making an actor of change

Historically, belief in the truth-telling capacity of numbers to establish values about social and personal life has not always been the case. Prior to the eighteenth century, truth was expressed through the manners and rhetorical qualities that told of the gentleman (Poovey, 1998). Statistics was an official part of Swedish governance to register the reading ability of the population, but that register was individual and without the probability reasoning that appears in the nineteenth century. As a state function, considerable numerical information was collected by the British government in the first three-quarters of the eighteenth century. That data, however, was not collected in the context of coherent theory about statecraft (Poovey, 1998, p.214). Numbers as representative of observed particulars were devalued through the priority given to Newtonian universals and the invisible laws of nature.

Faith in numbers as a modern "fact" to be trusted arose with the emergence of commerce in double accounting procedures (Poovey, 1998). The innovation of double accounting entailed a ledger that recorded the money received and paid out, what is domesticated today as the checkbook's register. The double accounting procedures mutated in uneven ways into the sciences of political economy and moral philosophy from the 1790s. British theorists of wealth and society developed a mode of analysis that had no need for numerical data. Only in the political economic theory of Adam Smith, which I discuss later, did numbers appear as a strategy to actualize the philosophized fictions of markets as performative standards, instead of descriptions.

Numbers became visualized as a social fact in the service of democratic ideals during the nineteenth century. Numbers enabled the production of particular kinds of human kinds for government to act on and by which populations were to act as responsible and self-motivated citizens. To understand this quality of governing, we first need to consider numbers as defining a problem space for standardizing its subject and object to stabilize change and its agents. Numbers seemed technical, objective and calculable, and as embodying the idea of giving all equal chance and representation. They standardized the subject of measurement and the act of exchange so that they were no longer seen as dependent on the personalities or the statuses of those involved. The faith in numbers in social

affairs makes possible such notions as *transparency*[3] through which the performances and outcomes of schools, businesses and government become visible
through graphs and flow charts presented as statistical factors to measure change.

The apparently quantitative precision and specific delineations of social and
personal life lent authority to the new regimes of government. Modern nations
organized around the idea that the citizen would participate in the life of democracy. Yet the very regimes associated with democracy bring forth principles of
uncertainty. The future is tied to the wisdom and commitments to civic virtue
that reside in the action of the "demo." The trust in numbers for assessing and
planning affairs provided a technology of consensus and harmony in a world that
would appear, otherwise, as uncertain, ambiguous, and contentious. The use of
numbers and social science were to reduce uncertainty in processes of change
and continual assertions of crisis. Notions of decision-making, human interest,
and problem-solving ordered and regularized the processes of action through
numbers in a world where the future had no guarantees, only conditionalities.
Statistics in this historical context, to borrow from Hacking (1990), tamed
chance. It gave stability to things in flux, and inscribed an apparent consensus
that made things of the world seem amenable to control.[4]

The uniformity given by numbers brings unlike orders in social life into a system of magnitudes that regularize relations among social and psychological components (Rose, 1999, p.206). The regularizing of social and psychological
components circulates in the home through a variety of practices, such as the
nutrient charts on food packaging and the monthly budgeting of individuals
who compare income to expenditure. The mapping of boundaries and the internal characteristics of the spaces to be managed was a strategy to make judgments
outside of the subjective.

Before moving to numbers in fabricating human kinds in the next section,
three further comments are necessary. First, numbers historically become an
actor in processes of change. Their mechanical objectivity enters into and
becomes part of the action system of planning, assessing, and making of policy.
Second, the inscription of numbers in the systems of reason governing social life
was not the logical outcome of disciplinary knowledge; nor was it the result of an
evolutionary process from a single origin. Prior to the nineteenth century, statistics were concerned with individual phenomena. It was not until discoveries in
physics and the needs of statecraft to monitor large groups for taxes and disease
that statistical knowledge emerged through probability theories about large
groups (Desrosières, 1991).

Third, the hold of utopian dreams of administration through numbers was
continually fraught with multiple outcomes. For example, the system of house-
hold taxes in France that existed into the twentieth century counted the doors
and windows in a dwelling. To counter this system, peasants redesigned their
dwellings with as few openings as possible, which had a long-term effect on their
health. Mono-cropped scientific forestry developed from about 1765 to 1800 to
bring an administrative grid of straight rows of trees for more efficient growth;
such growth was stunted, however, by the second planting because the nutrients

produced with mixed growth were eliminated. And the rational planning of the city in the nineteenth century into grid-like streets created a particular spatial order that also produced concepts to respond to issues produced by that order, such as anonymity, alienation, and feeling of loss of community (Scott, 1998, p.58). The dark images of Expressionism in the 1920s and Fritz Lang's silent film *Metropolis* testify to this other side of life in the city as well.

Fabricating kinds of people

The objectivity of the descriptions lent to numbers obscures how such representations are *inscription devices*. Numbers constitute domains and render them stable forms that can be calculated, deliberated about, and acted on. While the numbers "act" as descriptions of real things of the world, they embody implicit choices about "what to measure, how to measure it, how often to measure it and how to present and interpret the results" (Rose, 1999, p. 199). The collection and aggregation of numbers participate in a "clearing" or space where thought and action can occur (ibid., p.212).

This clearing or space for thought and action is explored in this and the following section through the notion of the fabrication of human kinds made visible in school reform practices: research on the effective teacher, the international assessment of children in PISA, and the notion of markets. I focus on research here on the adolescent to initially explore the space or clearing for acting and reflection embodied through the making of human kinds. Adolescence as a fabrication has dual qualities. It was a fiction used in the child studies of G. Stanley Hall at the turn of the twentieth century. It was brought into the new scientific psychologies to think about the new populations of urban children entering school that older pedagogical forms were no longer considered appropriate (Popkewitz, 2008).[5] That fiction entered into schooling as categories of planning that designed programs and ordered the lives of children. Today, adolescence is not only a way of thinking about the child and organizing parenting, schooling, and medicine. Children "think" of themselves as having adolescent patterns of growth, development, emotion, and cognition. The classification and distinctions, however, are merely of psychology. Adolescence circulates in medicine, public discussions of morality about, for example, sexuality, crime prevention, and drug use that cross national boundaries (Petersson *et al.*, 2007).

As fabrication has a normative meaning about deception or lying, I want to reiterate that my use is as an analytic concept to pursue the governing of schooling. The concept is to think about the categories and distinctions of the child and teacher as simultaneous inventions that create maps for planning that respond to issues of the world; and *are* rules and standards to constitute what is thought about, hoped for, and done. To stay with the above example, the notion of adolescence is an assessment device that categorizes people which not only permits actions to change social conditions about. It enters and is part of a world through which society, its environment, and the people who become the agents of action are refashioned. The classifications enter into the ways people structure experience and think about what is practical and useful as they come to think of themselves and their choices within an apparatus created with the fictions (Hacking, 1986; Rose, 1999, p.203).

This double quality of fabrication is illustrated through focusing on the making of kinds of people. Adolescence, the gifted child, the child "at-risk" and the disadvantaged are kinds of people that are made up to respond to social commitments in liberal societies. But the categories are not merely labels assigned, ideas or "discourses" that are epiphenomena of something "real." Programs and research projects are devised to act on the child, with schemes for remediation and paths of rectification set up to remake the child who is recognized as different. The fictions that are made-up also make up! Modern statecraft and its deployment of numbers are not merely interpretative or descriptive. *Numbers simultaneously do something to us!*

Fabrications: "the effective teacher" and PISA

At this point I want to bring the argument about numbers and fabrication into two seemingly different reform practices. One is a research project to identify the *effective teacher* and the other is the PISA international comparative assessment of children's application of curriculum knowledge. Each entails numbers in creating a space of equivalence through which to judge, assess, and order practices that, in effect, make particular kinds of people. The measurement devices give magnitudes and correlations to particular abstractions (fictions) that work their way into the conduct of the world and have the potential to be materialized as what is taken as real in education.

The effective teacher: an abstraction in search of and being real

A recent article in a leading educational research journal focused on the methodological design for identifying "the effective teacher" who enables successful achievement of "all children" (Day *et al.*, 2008). The research links "value added" dimensions of the life of the teacher to make a more robust relation between the capabilities of the teacher and children's achievement results. The "effective teacher" is, I argue below, a particular human kind that becomes an actor of change. But that actor is not merely out there to be discovered by the researchers. The characteristics and capabilities of the effective teacher are created through research strategies concerned with empirically creating and correlating factors that can be administered through school reform.

The research assumes that the capacities of the teacher are part of a system of psychological and organizational qualities that enable success in school achievement. The system is described as an integrated "wholist, nuanced understanding of teachers' work and lives" (Day *et al.*, 2008; p.330) beyond achievement scores; hence "value added." The wholism is described, for example, as student motivation, school culture and leadership, the biography and career of the teacher, which combine to enable student attainment and achievement.

The abstraction of the effective teacher who produces high student achievement test scores is not something "there" to be touched and felt. It is an invention that is given magnitudes that fill-in what constitutes that abstraction, the "effective teacher", through thinking about life phases (ibid., tables 3 and 6). The life phases are "a value-added measure" that discursively positions a particular kind of teacher whose quantities and qualities are to be generated through the measurement practices. Later, this same use of an abstraction is explored through Adam Smith's "markets."

The research is described as innovative because of its use of a mixed-method approach. The mixed-methods approach is called "the third way" (to adopt a term used in political arenas) and describes the better of two different ideological worlds. The third way is the combining of quantitative and qualitative techniques to identify a more productive approach to improving the quality of instruction.

My concern here, however, is not with the internal adequacy of the techniques applied for measurement or the instrumentations applied in the "methods." The focus is on the inscription of numbers in a system of reason through which a particular space is cleared for reflection and action. That clearing is the human kind of "the effective teacher."

The effective teacher is made into an historical "fact" and agent who delivers on the calculated potential of the teacher. The language of certainty appears in this potential as a model of scientific rigor assigned to the right use of numbers: the materialization of the effective teacher is the "contextual value added using multilevel models" (ibid., p.334) that identifies differential qualities that relate "to sustaining commitment, (n=189, 61%) or sustaining commitment despite challenging circumstances (n=39, 13%)" (p.335).

The multiple methods of this "third way" appear as that of the objectivity and neutrality in the numbers. Yet the effective teacher and the mixed methods are not naturally there, but as the authors' state, tied to "high government priority in raising student attainment"; the measurements are combined with qualitative interviews.

Further, the classifications in which the numbers are placed give shape and fashion to a cultural thesis about who the teacher is and should be. The "added value" qualities of the life phases embody a mode of life that is defined as teachers' commitment, agency, life-work management, and well-being. Without going into the categories and how they embody assumptions and distinctions (what constitutes management and well-being?), the value–added measures are policing practices that inscribe a harmony and consensus about what is sensible as teaching. The subject, "The Effective Teacher," is made into an object where the abstraction is given magnitudes and correlations charted as the "Teacher Profession Life Trajectories" and correlated with children's achievement. The particular kind of human – the effective teacher – statistically joins the different factors that add "value" to efforts to improve achievement scores (ibid., tables 3 and 4; also figure 6).

This set of assumptions and procedures are taken for granted in research. My concern here is with the limits of that thinking through the making of human kinds. Before this is explored further, the human kind in OECD's PISA assessment is discussed.

International assessments and comparable human kinds

To this point, I have explored numbers in a grid of cultural practices that fabricates human kinds. One human kind was "the effective teacher." A different kind of human is embodied in international comparisons of students. While international comparisons would seem of a different order for thinking about schooling than research on effective teaching, they overlap by instantiating a way of telling the truth for political ends. Principles are generated about what is thought about, hoped for, and done. International comparisons of students are part of the new industry in the contemporary landscape of education. Among different international sites that order and differentiate the inputs and output performances of schooling are: OECD's Program for International Student Assessment (PISA); the Progress in International Reading Literacy Study (PIRLS) conducted by the International Association for the Evaluation of Educational Achievement (IEA); Trends in International Mathematics and Science Study (TIMMS); and the Adult Literacy and Lifeskills Survey (ALL) conducted by Statistics Canada.

PISA embodies a missionary theme about progress and creating a better life. For example, the program aims to provide an international comparison of students' use of knowledge that is not directed to achievement measures, as was the research on effective teaching (see Day *et al.*, 2008, table 4). The PISA testing of reading, mathematical and scientific literacy focuses on what is defined as the practical ability to apply skills in everyday life situations believed related to labor market core skills, such as literacy and mathematical ability. These skills are further related in the PISA summary to the capabilities and qualities of lifelong learning, a particular human kind that I will discuss briefly below. PISA documents relate its "practical knowledge" to its measurements of whether the child has "motivation to learn," "self-esteem," and learning strategies. These different capabilities embody particular modes of living embodied in the assessment process of PISA, inscribed as rules and standards of reflection and action.

My interest in PISA is to recognize that these curricular competences are not merely about what a child knows. They embody principles about modes of living. PISA's emphasis on psychological categories like "motivation to learn and learning", are not merely about the child's solving problems that will "open life opportunities" for children, as they suggest. The idea of motivation, as Danziger (1997) historically explicates, is to design the interior of the child's desire. Early psychology did not provide explanations of everyday conduct. It was not until the emergence of mass schooling that an interest emerged about removing children's "fatigue" in learning through calculating and influencing the children's will, motives, interests, needs and desire. This treatment of inner "thought," daily life and experience were objects of administration. Motivation became a key player in this administration; it is neither disinterested, impartial nor existing objectively outside of the historical grid through which it is given intelligibility.

The historical configurations that order and classify the psychologies of reflection and action are scaffolded into the very definitions of reform to the present. Today, motivation is articulated and given nuance through notions of self-esteem and efficacy in social and educational planning. When examining the criteria of scientific competences important to PISA, the competences in international school literature are measured through psychologies of the child. The categories have less to do with what constitutes science and more with cultural theses about modes of living. Curriculum learning and motivation relate individual capacities and dispositions to national values about citizenship (McEneaney, 2003).

Further, the principles of "practical knowledge" assume that what is translated and transported into schooling is a reliable, objective representation of disciplinary fields in the school curriculum. The pedagogical principles classify and order what constitutes disciplinary knowledge, how that knowledge is made knowable, and how it is to be acted on: the distinctions through which difference and diversity are made recognizable have little to do with disciplines.

The procedures of classification and ordering are an alchemy through which academic practices (performed in labs, university science buildings, historical societies, etc.) are translated and transformed into the school curriculum (theories of learning, age and grade organizations of children, didactic practices, among others). The practices of translation are never just a copy of the original. The tools of translation provide rules and standards for recognition and enactment (participatory structures) that give school subjects their identities as objects as well as the conditions of their operation in schooling.

School subjects are ordered through psychological "eyes" that generate specific rules and standards about what is known and its conditions of participation. The psychological concepts of motivation, problem-solving and "lifelong learner" order and classify what constitutes teaching school subjects as well as the child. The principles generated in curriculum, I have argued elsewhere, have little relation to the patterns of interaction and communication of the academic fields (Popkewitz, 2004, 2008). The translation tools of curriculum are cultural theses about who the child is and should be. Learning more "content" knowledge, then, is never just that. It embodies learning how to see, think, act, and feel.

The alchemy of disciplinary knowledge in school subjects assumed in PISA has a double quality. If I use science "literacy" examined internationally (McEneaney, 2003), there is a dramatic shift to emphasize greater participation and increased personal relevance and emotional accessibility in the science curriculum. That participation, however, links the child's "expertise" in solving problems to the iconic stature of professional knowledge. Children's participation and problem-solving are organized to learn the majesty of the procedures, styles of argument, and symbolic systems that assert the truthfulness of the expertise of science. Yet the conclusions of academic expertise are located outside the bounds of children's questioning and problem-solving.

PISA assessment of students' performance and data collected on the student, family and institutional factors that explain differences in performances embodies a particular cultural thesis about modes of living. The different categories for organizing what children learn, their attitudes, and how they reason to solve problems in the curriculum are related to the notion of lifelong learning. These performance criteria define the child as a particular human kind. A cultural thesis forms about modes of life. The indicators are to create "the development of future scientific personnel" and embody principles that are not merely about learning science or literacy. They are about how a citizen is to live, through embodying abilities to participate in society, and in the labour market, through the manner in which students demonstrate the science competencies that "will enable them to participate actively in life situations related to science and technology" (OECD, 2007, p.3). The human kind entails a permanent condition of making choices with limited resources, with the only thing that is not a choice being making choices (Popkewitz, 2008)!

The measurements of PISA and "the effective teacher" do not act directly on people but act on the principles generated, or as clearing spaces where "freedom" realizes its potential. Simons and Masschelein (2008) argue that this new individuality entails the shift from earlier notions of emancipation to empowerment in which individual life becomes a continual learning process. Individuality is in learning as the capacity for appropriations that engage the uncertainties of the present. Virtue is managing effectively the limits and opportunities of the environment through steering one's performances in a continual feedback loop of self-assessment. The measurements provide constant performance indicators in a continual process of locating one's self in the world that are analogous to global positioning systems (Simons and Masschelein, 2008). PISA globally positions the child and nation through identifying highest overall performing countries, with Korea, for example, above and the USA below average. Moving around in environmental feedback loops functions as a permanent "global positioning" that provides the criteria to judge someone and one's self in the choices that are made for seeking to be permanently 'empowered'" (Simons and Masschelein, 2008).

The technologies of comparing through numbers are navigational tools that bring into view a universe of capabilities to place the child, ordered through standardized properties that enable comparisons (Lindblad, 2008). The quality indicators are about particular kinds of people in which the comparative equivalences through numbers classify practical abilities and everyday life situations. The assessing of students' performance and collecting of data on the student, family and institutional factors overlap with differences explained in measures of performances in educational policy and practice.

Europe is a discourse and program being transformed through new reterritorialization and scaling of the relation of individuality, the city, state and the EU within processes of globalization (Brenner, 1999). The numbers become an actor as it drives policy through inscribing a seeming naturalness to reflection and action in different national settings (Nóvoa, 2002). The research and assessments create new senses of collective belonging and "homes" through the creation of spaces of equivalences. The comparative measurements of PISA and "the effective teacher" become tools for building a new European space of competitiveness and cohesion. The tools are embodied in establishing equivalences in categories and distinctions related to children's achievement that establish "standards" across nation spaces (Grek, 2009; also see Delanty, 1995; Stråth, 2002). PISA becomes part of the space in which European education is to become a "world best" system through the production and use of data that is to signify successful competition and high quality and standards through measureable outcomes. Grek *et al.*, for example, trace how the production of data acts as it circulates through different institutions, such as the OECD, and makes new actors that cross border positions as "International Comparisons Programmes Managers" (Grek *et al.*, 2009, p.15). The numbers form a space of governance through the standardization and technologies that transform cognitive schemes of statistics and scientific thinking into spaces of equivalences. Policy and research are classificatory schemes that become a practical category, but now internally focused in a manner that has resonance with Europe's former "civilizing missions" of colonialization. There is a shift in governance from institutional indicators and audit and performance-monitoring to governance that mixes technical components of measuring and procedures with principles that order the capacities and qualities of individuality (Lascoumes and Le Galès, 2007).

Markets as desired world filled in with numbers

The comparison and creation of equivalent spaces explored above embody principles of life as "systems" that bring human kinds strategically into being. This was given focus in the effective teacher research through the expression of "wholeness" and in PISA through its concern with relating practical knowledge to labor skills. The notion of system circulates in current US reforms, for example, through the use of terms like "systemic school reform", which seek to link various elements of administration, curriculum, teaching, and evaluation into a seamless and comprehensive approach to school change. Less apparent in discussions of school standards and assessment about instruction is so-called "backward design", where researchers start with performance outcomes desired and work backward to design curriculum and organizational patterns to produce that outcome. This section focuses on the notion of system as given expression in contemporary education policy and reform research and debates about neoliberalism and markets.[6] The exploration of systems in policy and research debates about neoliberalism and markets is considered historically through numbers that become "actors" acting on contemporary debates.

Systems in contemporary social theory have linguistic and social structural qualities. Linguistically, language can be thought of as embodying structures or systems through which its parts congeal into a whole, organized by a grammar and syntax. Language (discourse) is a system whose principles enable what is said to be understood across particular localities and spaces through its rules and standards of ordering and classifying phenomena. It is this use of system that directs this study of the reason of schooling. My interest is to explore the principles of *social* systems in theory and policy studies through which numbers are embedded.

Assumed (but not spoken) in the PISA and the effective teacher research are conceptions of social systems.

The notion of systems in the merging of numbers to make human kinds is embodied in the notion of the market that appears in the late eighteenth century and again in today's debates about neoliberalism.

British theorists of wealth, society and political economy deployed systems to realize a desired world which the philosopher hoped for, but not necessarily through numbers, until the work of Adam Smith. If I again draw on Poovey (1998), the notion of system was embodied in the work of David Hume, Scottish Enlightenment philosopher concerned with the explanation of phenomena through natural causes and laws.[7] Hume wanted to construct a bridge over the gap between the written records of the past and the unrecorded origins of society, which otherwise was only divinely given and belonged only to Providence (Poovey, 1998, p.215). Hume's naturalist philosophy, Poovey argues, was not interested in empirically exploring the effects of that system through its vestiges of providentialism (ibid., p.264). Hume and other political economists prior to Adam Smith saw notions of equity and equivalence between objects that were less questions of knowledge than of justice with respect to the law governing market exchange. The questions of "the definition and equivalence of goods were posed in cases where *conflict* arose, and judges had to decide if an item was of satisfactory *quality*" (Desrosières, 1991, p.199, italics in original). Numbers did not play a part in deciding justice and equity.

The idea of system in social theory was used by Scottish Enlightenment historians and experimental moral philosophers to "see", calculate and administer things of the world. With the founding of the discipline of economics, theories of wealth and political economy brought numbers into the particular register of equity and equivalence that placed value on numbers. Smith's *Wealth of Nation* (1776), in contrast to Hume, wanted to probe the effects of the metaphor of system to see how the theoretical entities of philosophy could actually work by measuring and quantifying things such as rents and profits as well as wages influenced by commodity prices (Poovey, 1998, p.237).

The new sciences of society and wealth drew on conjectural history to describe the origins of modern society and how it went from uncivilized to civilized. The sciences would "solve" the problem of studying the particulars observed so as to standardize in a manner that could be projected into a resemblance of the future. The philosophical operations of abstracting and generalizing markets re-inscribed conjectural history into the philosopher's hope that its knowledge would lead to action and "if the action was diligently pursued, it could actualize the future of which the philosopher was the first to dream. The idea of what counted inaugurated a future that the philosopher had already imagined and the task of philosophy as an actor of change" (Poovey, 1998, p.273).

The heart of Smith's moral economy, the "market system" created a new role for numerical representation as descriptors of the products (actual and theoretical) created by institutions. By privileging the abstraction of "markets", Smith (borrowing from the conjectural historians) could include phenomena constructing the aggregate and register the significance of these phenomena which could only be known in retrospect and discounting what diverged from type so as to describe "nature" (Poovey, 1998, p.226).

Smith was not interested in calculations about particulars that were considered as doubtful and speculative. He sought theories that generalized, and thus particular numbers were not important. The system to which numbers were applied "embodied [Smith's] *a priori* assumptions about what the market system *should be*" (Poovey, 1998, p.216, italics in origin). Numbers did not exist that were tied to the abstraction of markets, so Smith set up ways of measuring and calculating as if they did exist, to say something about wealth and governing (Poovey, 1998, pp.240–241).

Markets became an historical agent of "human nature," a philosophical universal that could be named and quantify the effects of the abstraction (Poovey, 1998, p.247). Smith posited the notion of markets as an agent through which the causes of increase in national wealth would be increased through "the invisible hand" of human motives and competition. He viewed the precondition for the existence of a central market as not only the existence and the uniqueness of a system of prices, in general mentioned, but also, more often forgotten, the existence and uniqueness of a system of *goods*, subject to a common definition.

The significance of Smith's science of society and wealth was that it was possible to trace the movement from systemic philosophy claims about the universal (human nature) to descriptions of abstractions (the market system) to the quantification of the effects or products of these abstractions (labor, national prosperity) as "social facts" that enable comparisons (Poovey, 1998, p.237). Numbers with magnitudes was to make visible what counted, that is, the self-regulating market system. The numbers would provide useful information about how the system worked. To do that was to assume a consensus about what the truth of numbers rested on (Poovey, 1998, p.243). The seemingly practical question of markets was a theoretical question bound to cultural and social practices that would make the theoretical abstraction significant.

The appeal of Smith's science of wealth was that its epistemological entities appealed to government officials to consolidate and theorize government's relations with its subjects at home and abroad for a number of reasons. Political economic facts were to be understood as impartial, transparent, and methodologically rigorous. Further, abstractions like the market system set limits to the kinds of legislative interference, yet enabled mandates for the implementation and enforcement of other kinds of laws and policies (Poovey, 1998, p.217). Numbers increasingly came to be seen as a mode of representation less imbued with providential overtones or theoretical prejudices; and appealed to the British government as not being supported by God (Poovey, 1998, p.265).

Markets, as the applications of numbers, could create facts about human kinds. Smith provided a new basis for linking the theories about subjectivity with apologies for liberal governmentality (Poovey, 1998, p.217). The "invisible hand" of wealth and society is the formation of value and the circulation of visible wealth, and a form of "evidence" presupposes the connection between individual pursuit of profit and the growth of collective wealth; and shows the incompatibility between optimal development of economic process and the maximization of governmental procedures (Foucault, 2004/2008, p.321).

The notion of markets created a particular kind of human in the theory of wealth and society. The epistemological implications of the historical schema is that it focused on the intersection of subjectivity and sociality, giving importance to domesticity, manners, women, and also in considering commercial society as "the most sophisticated incarnation of human sociality through which the human mind would be collectively revealed." The abstraction performed as a cultural thesis that enabled "second order abstractions such as labor and happiness that was no longer a universal claim" but a "non-rhetorical (nonsuasive) place for a kind of representation that described what *could be* as if this potential was simply waiting to materialize" (Poovey, 1998, p.248, italics in original). The market that Smith theorized was to order relations between the self-love and the division of labor in a system in which there is sympathy found that is common to all human beings. This enabled the codification of political economy (Poovey, 1998, p.239). And thus was born the notion of banning government interference in the domain that was seen as essentially self-governing, as it realized something greater than the will of any parties or individuals (Poovey, 1998, p.227).

The market in contemporary discussions is in a different grid of practices from which the wealth of nations was given intelligibility. Contemporary German and American variations of neoliberalism are not a limiting of the state but the state as a founding element (Foucault, 2004/2008). Whereas in Europe debates of liberalism and neoliberalism were about the rule of law, the debate in the USA was about liberalism, and interventionist policies of the state were considered as non-liberal. Neoliberalism and its critiques, Foucault argues, embody similar rules and standards of reason that focus on tests of government actions, validity, fruitfulness, and was wasteful of expenditures (Foucault, 2004/2008, p.246).

Neoliberalism is a method of thought, a grid of economic and sociological analysis and an imagination, and a method of governing that is different from classical liberalism (ibid., p.218). It moved into non-economic phenomena through its recasting of labor as a variable of time into the specifics and objects of labor as a consequence of substitutable choices that relate to the scarce means of allocating for competing ends. Behavior rather than process is important as there is a focus on activity. Labor is capital tied to the individual and the worker is a machine of capital/ability. The individual is *Homo oeconomics* but not in its classical meaning as the partner of exchange and theory of utility (ibid., p.225). The individual has become an individual entrepreneur that has its own capital, and the producer of its own satisfaction, where innovation and self-improvement becomes an ethical-economic and psychological quality (ibid., pp.229–311). There is, if I return to the earlier discussion of the lifelong learner, a homology between the subjectivity embodied in PISA and the *Homo oeconomics* of neoliberalism.

Further, and important to contemporary policy debates, the notion of *market* is neither a consequence nor the development of markets. Through Smith's use of numbers as 'abstract spaces' about markets and neoliberalism, it is possible to think about how numbers are fabrications that are simultaneously fictions and material: made up inscriptions that are acted upon by techniques of social life and "utilized as the basis of organization architecture and divisions of managerial responsibility, and utilized as a grid to realize the real in the form in which it may be thought" (Rose, 1999, p.213). Markets today are no longer the fictions of Adam Smith but "real" in contemporary policy and critical analyses related to defining reform through the calling of neoliberalism.

Numbers, the democratic citizen, and the clearing of spaces in school standards

> Would it not be a great satisfaction to the king to know at a designated moment every year the number of his subjects, in total and by region, with all the resources, wealth & poverty of each place; [the number] of his nobility and ecclesiastics of all kinds, of men of the robe, of Catholics and of those of the other religion, all separated according to the place of their residence? … Would it not be a useful and necessary pleasure for him to be able, in his own office, to review in an hour's time the present and the past condition of a great realm of which he is the head, and be able himself to know with certitude in what consists his grandeur, his wealth, and his strengths?
>
> (Marquis de Vauban, proposing an annual census to
> Louis XIV in 1686, cited in Scott, 1998, p.11)

I start with this quote by the Marquis de Vauban in 1698 to make the final link between numbers, making human kinds, and governing. The discussion of PISA and the science of wealth and society, for example, continually brought to the fore the conduct of the citizen through the fabrication of human kinds. This section focuses on standards in school reforms as a method of governing, through which numbers are assembled and connected to produce human kinds. My argument about standards for teaching and curriculum in schooling, however, is not about the publically expressed outcomes or performances. The standards of assessment embody cultural theses about who the child is and should be, and who is *not* that child. The production of human kinds in schools entails a simultaneous process of exclusion and abjection embodied in the impulse for inclusion.

Standards in contemporary US reforms are linked to assessment criteria. The reform emphasis on school standards is to create alignments between assessment and educational aims and curriculum. It is expressed in a popular strategy mentioned earlier of "backward instructional design." The problem of teaching is first to decide on the appropriate measureable instructional outcomes. Instructional design works backward from that criterion to design teaching to best achieve the outcomes. The reasoning is almost commonsensical: what is assessed should make visible what schools are to teach (curriculum standards) and thus whether schools are doing what they should be doing.

Historically, educational standards and their links to numbers are related to the formation of the modern state in the eighteenth and nineteenth centuries and the new requirements of government. The philosophers of pre-revolutionary France viewed standard measurements as enabling the state to be "revenue-rich, militarily potent, and easily administered" (Scott, 1998, p.32). Standards were invented to the capacity for direct knowledge to what was previously opaque about the territories and populations in the realm. The arbitrary measures of anthropomorphic origin (e.g. the foot) were revisioned into standardization measures that were interconvertible (Porter, 1995, p.23). The state needed to know who fell under its domain to provide less variable and systematic tax systems, but people had no last names to be put into the census and tracked. Measurement was almost random, because each local area had its own system of measurement (*a hand, a foot, cartload, basketful, handful, within earshot*) that prevented any central administration (Scott, 1998).

In place of measurements tied to things, like the sundial tied to nature's uneven temporal dimensions, the centralizing state and large-scale economic institutions regulated time as a social phenomenon. The reliable means of enumerating populations, numbers to gauge the wealth, and creation of maps of land resources and settlements were produced to intervene and regulate the people of a realm. Economy of markets, length, weights, volume were socially ordered to administratively respond to the needs of church and state in paying taxes, reporting for military service (calendar), or the timing for observing religious days (Porter, 1995, p.23).

The production of standards was important to Enlightenment notions of the state that used "reason" to promote equality and freedom. The academicians of pre-revolutionary France, for example, saw the standardized measurements of the metric system as important for creating an equal citizen. The French philosophers prior to the French Revolution argued that there could be no equality with unequal measures and sought to standardize through the metric system. Here, we can return to an earlier discussion about numbers as placed "in service of the democratic ideal." If the citizen did not have equal rights in relation to measurements, then it was assumed that the citizen might also have unequal rights in law. Thus the Encyclopedists writing immediately prior to the French Revolution saw the inconsistency among measurements, institutions, inheritance laws, taxation, and market regulations as the greatest obstacle to making a single people (Scott, 1998, p.32).

Standards and numbers to create the equal citizen were produced in a different grid of practices related to American Progressive education at the turn of the twentieth century. It was linked to the emergence of the modern "planning" or welfare state and the social sciences in the problem of making the citizen who embodied principles that ordered "reason." Notions of child development, cognition, and learning installed standards that had a double quality. The theories were to make the child legible, easily administrable, and equal. The standards of development and learning to order thought, the mind, and the social interactions of children were also brought into daily life through the practices of pedagogy in the name of the freedom of the future citizen (Popkewitz, 2001).

The notion of equality embodied a double gesture of hope in the future and fear of those who were dangers and dangerous populations to that future. The hopes and fears were instantiated in Edward L. Thorndike's Connectionist psychologies and psychometrics through establishing standards about who the child was and should be (Popkewitz, 2008). The psychology assembled the more general cultural premise discussed earlier about the self-motivated and self-responsible individual whose participation was necessary for the functioning of the republic. That notion of the individual in Thorndike's psychology embodied a continuum of value about human kind created through equivalences and difference. The aim of schooling for Thorndike was to provide for freedom through making individuals "captains of [their] own souls" and their minds and "spirit" entrusted to the future as "noble and trustful" (Thorndike and Woodworth, 1901/1962, p.46). The hope simultaneously generated fears about threats to the future through a comparative mode of thought that circulated in the science of pedagogy. Thorndike wrote that the "only cure" for the nation's ills was for education to "prevent each new generation from stagnating in brutish ignorance, folly and pain" (Thorndike, 1912/1962, pp.142–143). The hope of freedom and happiness, Enlightenment cosmopolitan values about individuality, lay in the science that found the "facts and laws" that decrease discomfort by satisfying the "urge for children [to study] those subjects by ... which they may get health, escape poverty, enjoy their leisure hours, and otherwise have more of what a decent, but not very idealist, person wants" (Thorndike, 1912/1962, pp.142–143).

Ignorance and moral disorder were placed into psychological registers of schooling. Education "as a whole should make human beings wish each other well, should increase the sum of human energy and happiness and decrease the sum of discomfort of the human beings that are or will be, and should foster the higher, impersonal pleasures" (Thorndike and Woodworth, 1901/1962, p.46). "[F]ostering the higher, impersonal pleasures" was a narrative of moral order that eliminated or reduced those conditions that prevent progress through "the still appalling sum of error, injustice, misery and stupidity" (Thorndike, 1912/ 1962, p.72).

The double gestures of hope and fear circulate in contemporary standards and assessment through which numbers are articulated. The differentiation and division are embodied in the call for equity that ensures that "every child matters," "all children learn," and, in the USA, "no child left behind." At one level, the phrase that "all children will learn" is an expression of obligation and commitment towards an inclusive society. The gesture of hope to put all children on an equal footing overlaps with fears of children whose characteristics are different and thus embody a threat to the moral unity of the whole – populations designated as ethnic urban populations and immigrants at the turn of the twenty-first century. The phrase *all children*, a cultural territory of inclusion, assumes a unity of the whole from which difference is enacted. The *all* is an erasure of differences and politics of difference.

When school standard documents and research to create more effective teaching for "the child left behind" are examined, the texts are not about all children but the child who does not fit into that space and whose characteristics and qualities are feared as dangers and dangerous. The process is one of abjection, the placing of the child in unlivable spaces. These spaces embody fears of social-cultural disintegration and moral disorganization. The child is a particular human kind with psychological disabilities of low self-esteem and poor self-concept that overlap with social characteristics of the dysfunctional family – juvenile delinquency, poverty, "at-risk," and the urban child.[8]

Further, the very principles generated to fulfill the commitment to the equality of "all children" insert inequality as equality. Ironically, policy and research start with the assumption of inequality even as the goal is equality. But as Rancière (2004) has argued, the very commitment that begins with inequality to achieve equality that potentially compensates by devising well placed strategies, actually (re)envisions equality as inequality. The comparative inscription of difference to address the fundamental wrong produces the precondition of difference, and re-inscribes divisions that are to be erased at every step by the philosophy and social scientist as the shepherd. Rancière argues that this epistemological position embodies a fear of democracy itself.

Some concluding comments: critical inquiry and the problem of change

My focus on historical numbers assembled in a system of reason was to make visible that numbers and issues of assessment are not merely those of quantification. Numbers are inscribed in a grid of practices that perform as "social facts" and as actors. This was explored through different sites of educational policy and research: the notion of markets in the sciences of wealth in the nineteenth century, the effective teacher and the students in PISA measurements as "having practical knowledge". This way of interpreting numbers was also explored through talk about curriculum standards as not merely about what is given value in school learning. Each measurement device constitutes domains rendered as stable, representable forms that can be calculated, deliberated about, and acted on. Numbers are brought into programs of schooling and theories of teaching that perform as "actor" that order what is thought about, hoped for, and acted on.

The focus on numbers as an "actor" was located in the idea of fabrication and the making of human kinds. In part, the two nuances of fabrication – as fiction and as making – were explored to consider the issue of exclusion, abjection, and inclusion as part of the same phenomenon. The comparativeness brings into focus particular qualities of the "reason" and rationality that appear with European Enlightenment cosmopolitan notions about the emancipatory hope of future and fears of groups and qualities of individuals who threaten that promise of progress (Popkewitz, 2008). I raise this here to suggest that the problem of studies of policy and research is not merely correcting false ideological positions in relation to commitments but to give attention to the limits of a system of reason of contemporary educational reforms and reform-oriented research.

The fabrication of human kinds engages a way of considering the *political* of schooling that is rarely considered in policy studies, school research about social exclusion, and even less in defining issues of measurement and assessment. The latter is frequently expressed as the question of whose knowledge is represented in testing or how that knowledge is biased. While the general question of what knowledge gets sanctified in social institutions is important, that question, by itself, is not sufficient. It is important to consider, I have argued, the principles that historically order, classify, and differentiate what is "seen," thought about, and acted on so as to constitute the subject. The principles of reflection and action are not just there as part of the nature of phenomena but formed through the historically inscribed rules and standards that differentiate, distinguish, and divide what is constituted as sensible/not sensible as thought and action. At this point, I want to move the focus to the epistemological ordering of social theory. One central set of categories relate to a series of oppositions, such as experience or lived experience, and useful knowledge versus theory; subjective versus the objective and material. Fabrication, as an epistemological concept, is a strategy to think about how such opposites are not separate but intertwined. This strategy challenges a long standing strand in the social sciences that places knowledge within a realist philosophy, and which posits the theories and concepts of research as an epiphenomenon to the materiality of social life. Harvey argues, somewhat paradoxically, for a phenomenological realist in human geography that worries about abstract discourses that are not grounded (connected) to "material circumstances of a lived geography" (Harvey, 2000, p.544).[9] That connection of theories to the "tangible" and the material (read as "real") is, recalling Rancière's discussion of the political and the fear of democracy, to enable geographers to lead the way to "remake the world in emancipatory and practical ways" (ibid., p.560).

To take as natural the "lived experiences" of geography or the populational categories of "voice" in contemporary reforms imposes distinctions and divisions as questions about bias or the phenomenological/structural concern of "whose knowledge." This naturalized the very categories, subjects and rules of reason through which comparativeness of human kinds are produced. Unexamined are the cultural practices that order and produce how judgments are made, conclusions drawn, rectification proposed, and the fields of existence made manageable and predictable in school reform. As Joan Scott (1991) argued, experience is itself a theoretical concept and not merely there to be recouped by the researcher.

If we think about the political in this manner, as it produced a way of telling the truth, it is possible to approach the contemporary trope of reform and research about producing *useful* knowledge. The idea of being "useful" entails implicitly, if not explicitly, the notion of system and its assumption of consensus and harmony. The providential of nineteenth-century philosophy is (re)visioned, preserved and assembled in different configurations. Poovey argues that the sciences of political economy overlap with moral philosophy in the late 1790s and 1830s to provide performative standards in social affairs (Poovey, 1998, pp.269–278). The consensus and harmony of the system given through the inscription of notions of markets, for example, polices the present system through the rules and standards of "reason" applied. The very framework of the contemporaneous society which needs to be problematized becomes the terrain in which debate and change are modeled.

The argument should not be read as a modern (or even post-modern) Luddite fearful of numbers. Nor should it be read as moral relativism. Philosophically, relativism is situated and assumes that there is an objective reality that language can theoretically represent faithfully. This discussion, as expressed in the notion of fabrication, rejects this philosophical genre and its dichotomy of nominalism and objectivism for what it elides. My argument has been to address how particular notions of objectivity come into being that recognize different standards of objectivity exist in the sciences about how to get at the truth (Hacking, 1992).[10]

So it is possibly the appropriate time to ask or question the question of many policy studies: Who says that discourse is only about discourse?

At the outset of this chapter, I suggested that the focus on "the reason" of schooling is to rethink theories of change, resistance, and the principles of democracy embodied in contemporary scholarship that uses numbers. The strategy is one of a cautious optimism. To make the naturalness of the present as strange and contingent is a political strategy of change or reform; to make detectable the internments and enclosures of the commonsense of schooling is to make them contestable and thus about change itself. Critical thought is directed to "what is accepted as authority through a critique of the conditions of what is known, what must be done, what may be hoped" (Foucault, 1984, p.38). Agency is in the testing of the limits of making visible the particular dogma of the present through a resistance to what seems inevitable and necessary by "modifying the rules of the game, up to a certain point" (Foucault, 1984, p.48). The tracing of epistemological shifts in the cultural theses of schooling provides a tactic by which we may challenge the habitual ways of working and thinking in school reform, teacher education, and the sciences of education.

Notes

1 The quotes around "fact" is to historicize what is constituted as real as its relation to numbers is not just there in the world to recoup or as a testimony to what is discovered. What constitutes facts entails complex assemblages and connections of cultural and social practices that enable truth to be told in the way that it is is told. While there may be technical accuracy given by the numbers, my concern is with the reason governing what is said and done.

2 I am using political in a double sense: to work against the grain of the commonsense of working by making visible its rules and standards of thought and action.

3 The word "transparent" in contemporary policy and research in the United States conjures images of distancing, impartiality and the mechanical objectivity of numbers. My dropping of the word in this text is mostly to express my wonderment about the facile quality of its public uses to talk about accountability as if to signal that policy and research will enable a "seeing" through all impediments in order to make visible the real. I would have thought that this chimera was long ago laid to rest by, among others, the Spanish philosopher José Ortega y Gasset when he spoke about history as a system of ideas. My guess is that the hubris of

the researcher and the policy maker who speaks about transparency is resistant to such arguments.

4 The term "statistics" as a numerical expression of human activity did not emerge from the English context of quantification but from eighteenth-century German related to "cameral statistics" as a science of the description of the State in its most varied aspects. Later and through successive (re)visioning of the word, "statistics" separates the political management of people from the scientific management of things and the autonomy of statistics as a field of knowledge. For example, statistics was a literary term in the eighteenth century, the numerical part of the description of the state in the nineteenth century, and by the twentieth century was tied to mathematical techniques for numerical analysis of data of whatever type (Desrosières, 1991, p.200).

5 Adolescence was a word that existed prior to Hall but brought into the realm of the new sciences of psychology to provide a particular rationalizing and classifying of stages of childhood.

6 I realize the irony of examining systems as a concept deployed through numbers and talking about systems of reason. My excuse is actually twofold. First, the notion of systems of reason is concerned with the principles that historically order "thought" rather than analytical and ahistorical abstractions about the constitution of social and individual life. Second, the attempt to give coherence to different things that do not necessarily seem related requires, at least at the surface level, applying some resets to relations or notion of system.

7 The Scottish Enlightenment philosophers, as David Hamilton (1989) explores, were influential in the development of modern schooling and its notions of "knowledge" in curriculum theory.

8 An ethnographic study of urban education teacher education reforms (Popkewitz, 1998) illustrates the constituting of standards through the making of difference.

9 Harvey, in positing differentiating abstract discourses from something that is not connected to lived experience, is in fact (my realism) engaging in a discourse that by its very existence acts as (again, my realism) abstracted from "lived experience" through the gaze of geography that de facto is given as outside of history – or at least someone else's lived experience. His argument, I think, would benefit philosophically and theoretically from recognizing the limits of the categorization of difference and identity that he imposes.

10 Hacking discusses these styles of reason or thought, focusing on the conditions through which different sciences and mathematics pursue truth and establish what is objective knowledge without reverting to constructivism or realism.

References

Brenner, N. (1999) "Globalisation as reterritorialisation: The re-scaling of urban governance in the European Union," *Urban Studies*, 36(3): 431–451.

Danziger, K. (1997) *Naming the Mind: How Psychology Found its Language*, London: Sage.

Day, C., Sammons, P., and Gu, Q. (2008) "Combining qualitative and quantitative methodologies in research on teachers' lives, work, and effectiveness: From integration to synergy," *Educational Researcher*, 37(6): 330–342.

Delanty, G. (1995) *Inventing Europe: Idea, Identity, Reality*, London: Macmillan.

Desrosières, A. (1991) "How to make things which hold together: Social science, statistics, and the state," in Wagner, P., Wittock, B., and Whitley, R. (eds) *Discourses on Society: The Shaping of the Social Science Disciplines*, Dordrecht: Kluwer Academic Publishers, pp.195–218.

Foucault, M. (1984) "What is the enlightenment? Was ist Auflärlung?" in Rabinow, P. (ed.) *The Foucault Reader*, New York: Pantheon Books, pp.32–51.

Foucault, M. (1991) "Governmentality," in Burchell, G., Gordon, C., and Miller, P. (eds) *The Foucault Effect: Studies in Governmentality*, Chicago, IL: University of Chicago Press, pp.87–104.

Foucault, M. (2004/2008) *The Birth of Biopolitics: Lectures at the Collège de France 1978–1979*, (ed. Michel Senellart, trans. Burchell, G.), New York: PalgraveMacmillan.

Grek, S. (2009) "Governing by numbers: The PISA effect in Europe," *Journal of Education Policy*, 24(1): 23–37.

Grek, S., Lawn, M., Lingard, B., Ozga, J., Rinne, R., Segerholm, C., and Simola, H. (2009) "National policy brokering and the construction of the European Education Space in England, Sweden, Finland and Scotland," *Comparative Education*, 45: 5–21.

Hacking, I. (1986) "Making up people," in Heller, T.C., Sosna, M., and Wellbery, D.E. (eds) *Reconstructing Individualism: Autonomy, Individuality, and the Self in Western Thought*, Stanford, CA: Stanford University Press, pp.222–236, 347–348.

Hacking, I. (1990) *The Taming of Chance*, Cambridge, MA: Cambridge University Press.

Hacking, I. (1992) "'Style' for historians and philosophers," *Studies in the History and Philosophy of Science*, 23(1): 1–20.

Hacking, I. (1999) *The Social Construction of What?* Cambridge, MA: Harvard University Press.

Hamilton, D. (1989) *Towards a Theory of Schooling*, London: Falmer Press.

Harvey, D. (2000) "Cosmopolitanism and the banality of geographical evils," *Public Culture*, 12(2): 529–564.

Lascoumes, L., and Le Galès, P. (2007) "Understanding public policy through its instruments: From the nature of instruments to the sociology of public policy instrumentation," *Governance*, 20: 1–21.

Lindblad, S. (2008) "Navigating in the field of university positioning: On international ranking lists, quality indicators, and higher education governing," *European Educational Research Journal*, 7(4): 438–450.

McEneaney, E. (2003) "The worldwide cachet of scientific literacy," *Comparative Education Review*, 47(2): 217–237.

Nóvoa, A. (2002) "Ways of thinking about education in Europe," in Nóvoa, A., and Lawn, M. (eds) *Fabricating Europe: The Formation of an Education Space*, Dordrecht: Kluwer Academic Publishers, pp.131–162.

OECD (2007) *Executive Summary: PISA 2006: Science Competencies for Tomorrow's World*, Paris: OECD, The Programme for International Student Assessment (PISA).

Petersson, K., Olsson, U., and Popkewitz, T. (2007) "Nostalgia, the future, and the past as pedagogical technologies," *Discourse: Studies in the Cultural Politics of Education*, 28(1): 49–67.

Poovey, M. (1998) *A History of the Modern Fact: Problems of Knowledge in the Sciences of Wealth and Society*, Chicago, IL: University of Chicago Press.

Popkewitz, T. (1998) *Struggling for the Soul: The Politics of Education and the Construction of the Teacher*, New York: Teachers College Press.

Popkewitz, T. (2001) "Rethinking the political: Reconstituting national imaginaries and producing difference in the practices of schooling," *International Journal of Inclusion*, 5(2/3): 179–207.

Popkewitz, T. (2004) "The alchemy of the mathematics curriculum: Inscriptions and the fabrication of the child," *American Educational Journal*, 41(4): 3–34.

Popkewitz, T. (2008) *Cosmopolitanism and the Age of School Reform: Science, Education, and Making Society by Making the Child*, New York: Routledge.

Porter, T. (1995) *Trust in Numbers: The Pursuit of Objectivity in Science and Public Life*, Princeton, NJ: Princeton University Press.

Rancière, J. (2004) "The Politics of Aesthetics." Available at http:/theater.kein.org/node/99.

Rose, N. (1999) *Powers of Freedom: Reframing Political Thought*, Cambridge, MA: Cambridge University Press.

Scott, J. (1991) "The evidence of experience," *Critical Inquiry*, 17: 773–797.

Scott, J. (1998) *Seeing Like a State: How Certain Schemes to Improve the Human Condition Have Failed*, New Haven, CT: Yale University.

Simons, M., and Masschelein, J. (2008) "From schools to learning environments: The dark side of being exceptional," *Journal of Philosophy of Education*, 42(3–4): 687–704.

Stråth, B. (2002) "Introduction: The national meanings of Europe," in Malmborg, M.A., and Stråth, B. (eds) *The Meaning of Europe: Variety and Contention Within and Among Nations*, Oxford: Berg, pp.1–26.

Thorndike, E.L. (1912/1962) "Education: A first book," in Joncich, G.M. (ed.) *Psychology and the Science of Education. Selected Writings of Edward L. Thorndike*, New York: Bureau of Publications, Teachers College, Columbia University, pp. 69–83, 141–147.

Thorndike, E.L., and Woodworth, R.S. (1901/1962) "Education as science," in Joncich, G.M. (ed.) *Psychology and the Science of Education: Selected Writings of Edward L. Thorndike*, New York: Bureau of Publications, Teachers College, Columbia University, pp.48–69.

11 Assessing educational reform

Accountability, standards and the utility of qualifications

Harry Torrance

Introduction

Changes in assessment policy and practice have been used to drive changes in the education system in England for more than 20 years. Other countries have engaged in similar debates and actions, notably the United States with advocacy of 'Measurement Driven Instruction' (Popham, 1987) and the No Child Left Behind legislation of 2001 (NCLB, 2001), but only in England has the focus on assessment been so relentless across the compulsory school system as a whole.

The arguments in favour of using assessment to change teaching essentially fall into two distinct, but nevertheless related, categories. One argument derives from educational issues and values; the other is much more oriented towards accountability and the use of political pressure to bring about change.

The educational arguments revolve around the role that assessment plays in determining the curriculum, using the so-called 'backwash' effect of assessment in a positive way; as Resnick and Resnick have put it: 'You get what you assess; you don't get what you don't assess; you should build assessment towards what you want ... to teach ...' (Resnick and Resnick, 1992, p.59).

This is very much the thinking that influenced the 'Measurement-Driven Instruction' movement in the USA in the late 1980s and 1990s. Put desired objectives into testing programmes and teachers will teach those desired objectives (Airasian, 1988; Popham, 1987). Thus, the intention is to use changes in assessment directly to influence curriculum content and the process of teaching and learning. More recently such arguments have developed to incorporate the notion of a 'standards-based curriculum', whereby standards are set in terms of curriculum content and achievement levels and tests are aligned with the curriculum to measure whether and to what extent such standards have been achieved.

A rather more complex interpretation of the same broad insight focuses much more at classroom level. Thus, it is also recognised that routine, informal assessment can play a key role in underpinning or undermining the quality of teaching and learning in the classroom. How teachers assess students' work, what sorts of positive or negative feedback is given, and whether or not advice on how to improve is provided can make a great deal of difference to what is learned and how it is learned. This is the thinking which underlies the 'formative assessment' movement in England (Black and Wiliam, 1998; Torrance and Pryor, 1998) though it has also been acknowledged as potentially important for developments in the USA and elsewhere (Shepard, 2000; Carless *et al.*, 2006).

The accountability arguments are much simpler and more clear-cut. Here the claim is that education systems in general, schools in particular, must have their efficiency and effectiveness measured by the outcomes produced. Expected standards of achievement must be prescribed and tests regularly employed to identify whether or not these expectations have been met. In publicly maintained school systems such prescription is controlled by government and the quality of teaching and learning in the classroom is assumed to rise if results improve. Essentially, testing is a used as a 'lever' to effect the system *qua* system; the detail at classroom level is assumed to look after itself. If results are improving, the quality of students' educational experience and achievement is assumed to be improving. However, just as with 'measurement-driven instruction' or a 'standards-based curriculum', it is crucial to the logic and practice of such an accountability system that the tests employed do indeed validly sample the curriculum, and reliably measure student achievement. The tests must be valid indicators of quality across the system as a whole otherwise they may 'drive' the system in the wrong direction.

In England, we are very much dealing with this politically driven, accountability-oriented analysis of the nature of the problem of 'educational standards' and what to do about them; though some elements of the arguments about standards-based instruction and formative assessment, or 'assessment for learning' as it is now more commonly known, also feature in debate. In this respect it is interesting to note that change in the education system is unlikely to occur just as a result of compliance with government pressure and legislation. In the systemic social and institutional 'space' of education, educational arguments are likely to be deployed in policy debates in order to increase the rhetorical and symbolic legitimacy of policy and mobilise action at local level.

Policy development in England

The explicit use of assessment to drive educational change in England dates back to the introduction of a single system of secondary school examinations, the General Certificate of Secondary Education (GCSE), for 16 year olds (the minimum school leaving age), by the then Conservative government of Margaret Thatcher in 1986 (with the first new exams taken in 1988). In the 1960s and 1970s England operated with two parallel secondary school examination systems: 'GCE O-level'[1] for those students considered to be in the top 20 per cent of the ability range; and 'CSE'[2] for those considered to be in the next 40 per cent of the ability range. The 'bottom 40 per cent' were not considered capable of taking examinations at all. Selection of the 'top 20 per cent' for entry to grammar schools was based on the '11 + intelligence test' and, overall, such a selective system derived from very outdated notions of innate ability, and more specifically the 'normal distribution' of ability in a population (Torrance, 1981). Selection started to be phased out following the election of a Labour government in 1964, but the process was highly contentious and took place over a long period. The creation of a single system of examining, GCSE, to match the aspirations of a still developing comprehensive secondary school system might be said to mark the point at which governments in England fully began to buy into human capital theory and treat education as an investment in the population as a whole, rather than as a way to select a social and economic elite. Of course education, and particularly assessment, still does play a major role in selecting and legitimating the selection of a social and economic elite, but it is at least now arguable that this outcome is an unintended effect of policy, rather than an overt intention.

One effect of selectivity was that, precisely because it was not thought appropriate for all children to take secondary school examinations, there was no overall data in the system about how well schools were doing and what standards were being attained across the system as a whole. Moreover the selection test for secondary school allocation (the 11 +) could only provide evidence that 80 per cent of pupils 'failed' their 11 + and therefore 'failed' primary education. Also, as this exam was being phased out with the introduction of comprehensive secondary schools, it looked as though there would be no data whatsoever on the output of primary schools.

The Labour government of the 1970s launched the Assessment of Performance Unit (APU) to try to provide evidence of standards achieved. This employed a sampling approach, testing a 2 per cent sample of 11 years olds and 15 year olds in English, Maths, Science and Modern Languages. Many interesting assessment methods were developed and materials produced, some of which eventually found their way into GCSE courses and even the National Curriculum. But the APU did not provide unequivocal and easily usable evidence about national standards; nor, because of its sampling strategy, could it reach into and influence every classroom. First GCSE (1986), then the National Curriculum and National Testing (1988), were introduced in order to control directly what was taught and how it was taught, and to measure whether or not it was being taught effectively. The APU was closed down by the Conservative government with the introduction of National Testing, since it was considered unnecessary. This means that there has been no independent research-based check on whether or not standards have risen over time, unlike in the United States which has monitored national standards for more than 30 years via the sampling procedures of the National Assessment of Educational Progress (NAEP).

There has been extensive detailed argument about the scale and scope of the National Curriculum and Testing system and many modifications have been put in place since 1988 (cf. Daugherty, 1995; Torrance, 1995, 2003). However, the issue of educational accountability has remained the key policy problem for over 20 years now and the development of a standards-based, test-driven education system has remained the key policy solution up to the present. While endless tinkering has taken place, it is puzzlingly difficult to find a single, coherent, integrated statement of education policy for the twenty-first century in England. Continuity with the 1988 National Curriculum and Testing regime is completely taken for granted, and elements of policy have been built up, layer by layer, in successive attempts by both Conservative and Labour governments to try finally to realise the vision of a national curriculum and testing system and render it operational. Indeed in his foreword to a recent Education White Paper 'Higher Standards, Better Schools for All' (DfES, 2005), the then Prime Minister Tony Blair rehearsed and claimed the history for himself, with the Conservatives conveniently omitted from the narrative:

> In the 1960s and 1970s ... there were simply not enough pressures in the system to raise standards. Lord Callaghan recognised this as Prime Minister in 1976 when he urged a National Curriculum. When it was introduced in the late eighties it was accompanied by greater accountability through national testing. ... After 1997 this government extended such accountability, with literacy and numeracy reforms and targets to encourage improvements ...
>
> (DfES, 2005, pp.1–2)

The National Curriculum was originally introduced in nine subjects with National Testing proposed in every subject at ages 7, 11, 14 and 16. This was abandoned as the logistical implications became clear, and testing focused on English and Maths at age 7 (the end of 'Key Stage 1'); and English, Maths and Science (re-designated 'core' subjects) at ages 11 and 14 (end of 'Key Stage 2' and 'Key Stage 3'). GCSE was retained to assess standards at age 16 + and to provide single subject qualifications for students at the end of the compulsory phase of schooling. More recently, in response to almost constant criticism of the testing of very young children, elements of this testing regime have been relaxed at Key Stage 1. Since September 2004 teachers have only had to report results based on 'teacher assessment' at Key Stage 1. Subsequently, National Testing has also been abandoned at Key Stage 3. The system is 'withering on the vine' but government commitment to a centrally controlled National Curriculum and Assessment system remains.

Thus 'assessment policy' for the compulsory maintained school system now comprises:

- a 'core' National Curriculum of English, Maths and Science with additional 'Foundation' and 'Entitlement' subjects;
- national teacher assessment of the whole cohort in English, Maths and Science at age 7;
- national testing of the whole cohort in English, Maths and Science at age 11; and GCSE at age 16;
- national and local target setting (at school level and student level) for levels of attainment to be achieved, with emphasis on constant improvement;

- publishing of results in public performance tables (i.e. league tables of schools and local authorities);
- inspection of schools by the Office for Standards in Education (OfSTED) and publication of reports, with a particular emphasis on results obtained and trends in results over time;
- 'naming and shaming' of so-called 'failing schools' with threat of closure if improvement (as reported by OfSTED) is not evident within a year.

Are standards rising?

The increasingly feverish activity of both Conservative and Labour governments, and the continuing cross-party agreement on testing at ages 11 and 16, indicates that educational standards are still considered to be a political issue about which 'something must be done', or at least be seen to be done. National test scores have risen since national testing was first introduced but have plateaued since around 2000 and, insofar as they indicate anything meaningful about educational standards, this suggests that progress has stalled, or appears to have stalled. The problem for government derives precisely from the acceptance of the basic analysis that a National Curriculum and Testing system is a good idea. It is an idea which is twenty years old and new policy initiatives have tinkered and intensified pressure at the margins (e.g. the National Literacy and Numeracy Strategies, DfES, 2006); however, new policies have not, as yet, taken the system in a different direction. Furthermore, figures indicate that tests scores have risen progressively over many years, irrespective of which government is in power or which specific curriculum interventions have been pursued, though, as noted above, they have levelled off since 2000 (Table 11.1; Figures 11.1 and 11.2).

Not every year's results are recorded here; rather sufficient years are recorded to indicate trends over time along with key dates at which government has variously used and dropped indicators of progress.

Progress since 1997 was the measure routinely deployed by the New Labour government at national level. At first sight such progress seems significant. But closer scrutiny indicates significant improvements in results prior to 1997. Thus, for example, in the two years after National Testing was first introduced at Key Stage 2 under a Conservative government (1995–1997) results improved by 15 percentage points in English and 17 percentage points in Maths. In the *ten* years after 1997, results improved by 16 percentage points in English and 14 percentage points in Maths (1997–2006), with most of this improvement being achieved by 2000. The plateau effect since 2000 has continued through to the most recent results available.

Results for GCSE are even more instructive. They have been rising steadily since the exam was first introduced in 1988 and indeed were rising prior to its introduction. In the mid-1970s, when only the 'top 20 per cent' of students were thought capable of passing O-level, the percentage of students passing at least 5 O-levels or their equivalent under the previous dual system was 22.6 per cent.[3] By 1988, the first year of GCSE results, this had risen to 29.9 per cent. By the

Table 11.1 Percentage of pupils gaining national curriculum assessment level 2 or above at age 7 and level 4 or above at age 11

| | Age 7 | | Age 11 | | |
	English %	Maths %	English %	Maths %	Science %
1992[a]	77	78			
1995	76	78	48	44	
1996	80	80	58	54	62
1997[b]	81/80	83	63	61	69
2000	81/84	90	75	72	85
2002	84/82	90	75	73	86
2005[c]	85/82	91	79	75	86
2007	84/80	90	80	77	88
2008	85/80	90	81	78	88
2009	84/81	89	80	78	88

Source: http://www.dcsf.gov.uk/rsgateway/

Notes
a 1992 first 'full run' of Key Stage 1 tests; 1995 first 'full run' of Key Stage 2 English and Maths; 1996 first 'full run' of Key Stage 2 Science.
b New Labour government elected. Key Stage 1 English results now being reported separately in terms of attainment targets (81% gained level 2 in Reading, 80% in Writing). Such details had been available previously but results were routinely reported as 'whole subject' levels. The 'Writing' score is averaged across the writing test and the spelling test. The scores are averaged in Figure 11.1.
c Key Stage 1 tests now conducted as 'teacher assessment' so no longer directly comparable with previous results at Key Stage 1, though interestingly, teacher assessment does not seem to diverge from the established trend in test results.

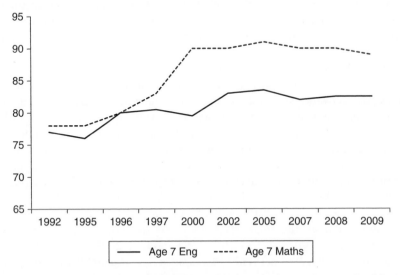

Figure 11.1 Percentage of pupils gaining national curriculum assessment level 2 or above at age 7 (Key Stage 1).

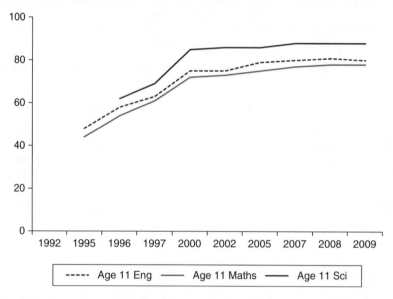

Figure 11.2   Percentage of pupils gaining national curriculum assessment level 4 or above at age 11 (Key Stage 2).

mid-1990s this had risen further to 43.5 per cent and the most recent results for 2009 indicate that almost 70 per cent of students now pass 5 or more GCSEs at grades A*–C. That is, 70 per cent of the school population now achieve what 30 years ago it was thought only the 'top 20 per cent' could achieve. Furthermore, taking the full range of grades into account (A*–G), as an indicator of the numbers of students gaining at least some benefit from their secondary education, almost 60 per cent gained at least 5 A*–G grades in 1975, while 92 per cent achieved 5 A*–G grades in 2009 (Table 11.2 and Figure 11.3).

So from the published statistics in the public domain there is no evidence of scores going down or standards getting worse; quite the reverse, pass rates have been steadily improving over many years. A key debating point, however, is that some critics and commentators argue that the standard expected of students is lower – i.e. that passing is easier than hitherto, a point to which we will return.

Overall pass rates also conceal other issues. Within these general trends different sub-groups perform better than others. Thus for example 87.5 per cent of candidates of Chinese origin gained at least 5 A*–Cs in 2009 (*n*=2,275), while only 67 per cent of candidates of Black African and Caribbean origin did so (*n*=23,609), though this itself represents a very significant improvement from the 35 per cent recorded in the early 2000s (Torrance, 2005).[4] Of candidates of White British origin 69.8 per cent passed at least 5 A*–Cs in 2009 (*n*=461,445), but a recent Joseph Rowntree-sponsored study indicates that poor working-class white boys do worst of all (Cassen and Kingdon, 2007). Clearly these figures

Table 11.2 Percentage of pupils gaining O-level/CSE/GCSE equivalents[a] 1975–2009

	5 or more A*–C %	5 or more A*–G %
1975	22.6	58.6
1980	24.0	69.0
1988	29.9	74.7
1990	34.5	80.3
1995	43.5	85.7
1997	45.1	86.4
2000	49.2	88.9
2005	55.7	88.9
2007	62.0	90.9
2008	64.3	91.3
2009	69.8	92.0

Source: Torrance, 2003 and http://www.dcsf.gov.uk/rsgateway/

Note
a For details of calculating equivalence between O-level, CSE and GCSE see Torrance, 2003.

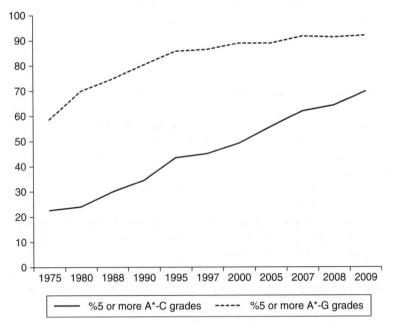

Figure 11.3 Percentage of pupils gaining O-level/CSE/GCSE equivalents 1975–2009.

raise major political and educational issues, but for the purposes of the present discussion about testing and standards, the key point is that overall pass rates have been rising for more than 30 years.

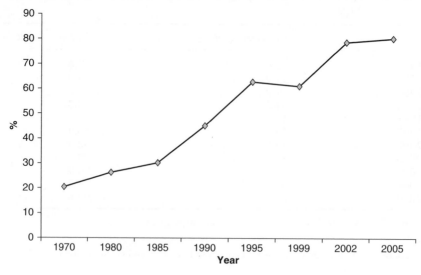

Figure 11.4   Percentage of cohort (18 year olds) obtaining a Baccalaureate (France).
Source: http://www.inca.org.uk/1383.html#6.4.9%20Output%20statistics

Interestingly enough, this long-term trend is not restricted to England. Pass rates in the French Baccalaureate examination have been rising similarly (Figure 11.4).

A recent review of such trends across Europe also indicates that the number of students completing upper secondary education has risen over time. Of those aged between 25 and 29 in 1999 83 per cent had completed upper secondary education compared to 74 per cent aged 50 to 64.[5] What exactly is the explanation for this international trend is difficult to discern. Some element of a genuine rise in standards is likely to be present, driven by better socio-economic conditions of students, higher expectations of educational outcomes by students, parents and teachers, and better teaching. This is probably combined with and compounded by an increasingly more focused concentration on passing exams, by teachers ('teaching to the test') and students (extrinsic motivation), because of the perceived importance of educational success in institutional accountability and individual life chances.

Problems of National Curriculum and Testing

The evidence in England suggests that 'teaching to the test' is the most likely recent explanation for rising scores which tail off as teachers and students come to be about as efficient as they can be at scoring well on the tests within a regime of coaching and practice. Many research studies have reported an increasing focus on test preparation, particularly in the final year of primary school prior to the tests being taken (cf. McNess *et al.*, 2001; Hall *et al.*, 2004; Wyse and Torrance, 2009) but also at GCSE (e.g. Gillborn and Youdell, 2006).

However it is not only independent research studies which highlight such problems. School inspectors who routinely visit schools on a regular basis have reported on a narrowing of the curriculum and summaries of their inspection findings have been included in the annual reports from OfSTED. For example, a recent report by the current Chief HMI Christine Gilbert states:

> In many [primary] schools the focus of the teaching of English is on those parts of the curriculum on which there are likely to be questions in national tests ...History and, more so, geography continued to be marginalized. ... In [secondary] schools ... the experience of English had become narrower ... as teachers focused on tests and examinations. ... There was a similar tension in mathematics ....
>
> (OfSTED, 2006, pp.52–56)

Comparable evidence can also be identified internationally. Klein *et al.* (2000), Linn (2000) and Shepard (1990) report similar findings from previous studies of test-based reform in the USA and the same issues are now beginning to emerge from studies of No Child Left Behind. State level NCLB test scores are rising (CEP, 2007), but equally 'Administrators and teachers have made a concerted effort to align curriculum and instruction with state academic standards and assessments' (CEP, 2006, p.1). A recently completed study by Rand Education funded by the US National Science Foundation noted that: 'changes included a narrowing of the curriculum and instruction toward tested topics and even toward certain problems styles or formats. Teachers also reported focusing more on students near the proficient cut-score ...' (Hamilton *et al.*, 2007, Summary: p.xix). This is exactly the sort of practice that is also reported in England at the D/C borderline in GCSE – 'triage' as Gillborn and Youdell (2006) have termed it.

So rising test scores do not necessarily provide unequivocal evidence of rising educational standards, and indeed rising scores might actually mask falling standards as students are exposed to a much restricted curriculum. However, successive governments, and particularly the New Labour governments of 1997 onwards, seem to have taken an almost actuarial view of the role of rising pass rates. Examination success is correlated with social and economic success, so, the thinking seems to be, maximise exam passes, especially for previously disadvantaged groups, and social and economic mobility will necessarily improve, irrespective of the educational experience of the students or the quality of the outcomes achieved.

All of which is not to say that there is no validity or potential benefit in using tests. Good quality outcome measures are important if we can produce them. Equally the results that we currently have in the public domain are all that we have got within and across systems, and as such should be treated as potentially useful, if fallible, sources of evidence (cf. Torrance, 2006). The problem, of course, is that these sources of evidence are not treated as fallible in the context of current policy imperatives. There are many weaknesses and cautionary riders to be considered which do not appear to trouble policymakers. Furthermore the use of a narrow range of tests actually seems to be impacting very negatively on the educational experience of even successful students, let alone unsuccessful ones. Successive research studies over 40 years have indicated that the vitality of teacher–student relationships and the quality of teacher–student interaction are the most important factors in improving student learning experiences and raising attainment (Jackson, 1968; Mehan, 1979; Galton *et al.*, 1980; 1999; Mercer, 1995). Yet this is precisely what is threatened by an over-concentration on testing.

In focusing on standards and accountability, the government seems to have lost sight of the curriculum and the nature of individual achievement – of what it is that standards are supposed to embody in terms of the knowledge, skills, attitudes and competences that we might expect of young people leaving school in the twenty-first century.

It is almost as if the 'unit of analysis' for policymaking, so to speak, has shifted from the curriculum and the building blocks of individual student learning and achievement, to the overall output of the system. Individual achievement and, more particularly, the content and quality of that achievement – the traditional focus of assessment – has been ignored, or at least taken for granted, as policy has focused on raising test scores across the system as a whole.

Nor is this simply a matter of updating curriculum content. Plenty of updating activity can be identified in successive revisions to the National Curriculum; for example the introduction and modification of Curriculum 2000, and the more recent development of 14-19 Diplomas. But these developments continue to be undertaken within the taken-for-granted framework of output targets and accountability pressure. They continue to be *ad hoc* modifications within a basic policy problematic, rather than representing a major re-think of policy. The research evidence is clear about the narrowing of the school curriculum and there is an increasing perception in higher education and among employers that despite rising test scores, the skills and capacities of school leavers and job applicants are not improving. Coaching for tests is producing learners who are too dependent on support to operate effectively in other more challenging environments (Hayward and McNicholl, 2007; Torrance, 2007).

Scale and scope

Another significant problem with any national testing system is the sheer scale and cost, both financial and human, in terms of motivation and morale, coupled with the threat to quality control when there is insufficient time and resource dedicated to the piloting, marking and moderation of results. Certainly in England we are now operating a system which involves tens of millions of tests

Table 11.3 Total numbers of candidates in 2006 tests[a]

Key Stage 1	559,778
Key Stage 2	578,328
Key Stage 3	607,072
Key Stage 4 (GCSE)	594,135
Total	2,339,313

Source: http://www.dfes.gov.uk/rsgateway/

Note

a 2006 represents the 'high water mark' of the National Testing system. It is the last full set of data involving large scale tests at all four age groups: Key Stage 1 changed with effect from 2005, when teacher assessment was instituted, but teachers still largely used centrally produced tests and results were still reported for Key Stage 1 as if they were test results; then Key Stage 3 testing was dropped from 2009 after significant problems with lost papers and scripts returned unmarked in 2008; whole cohort testing of Key Stage 2 Science was dropped in 2010 and replaced by testing of a sample of schools and students.

being written and administered and marked every year. A recent Qualification and Curriculum Authority's (QCA) 'Fact Sheet' on the examination system tells us that 1.5 million students took examinations in the summer of 2007 (qca.org .uk/1158_2175.html). The fact sheet does not tell us exactly which exams this figure includes but we must presume it is GCSE, A/S-level and A-level since the age cohort is 500,000 + and including all key stage tests would push the figure up to 3 million plus. We are also told that 5,000 separate exam papers were set with 25 million examination scripts and coursework assignments being marked. Over 5.8 million GCSE results were issued (i.e. individual grades for each subject taken by each candidate). National Testing probably doubles these totals.

Table 11.3 indicates the total number of candidates entered for national tests and GCSE in 2006. These figures should then be multiplied by at least 5 for each key stage cohort to include separate papers for English (usually x2) and Maths (usually x2) and by at least 10 at Key Stage 4 to cover multiple GCSE subjects and papers; thus the total number of scripts to administer in the compulsory system will be a minimum of 15 million. Add in A/S and A-level and the total will easily top 30 million.

Globalising educational management

So what is going on here? How is it that a commitment to testing outweighs the negative impact that testing has on the system under consideration? We seem to be faced with an international convergence in the use of testing in evaluation and accountability, with both international studies such as TIMSS[6] and PISA,[7] and national systems of testing, treating a small range of quite narrow measures as proxies for the quality of the system as a whole. This seems to be linked to the economic pressure exerted on governments by globalisation. Education policies over the last 25 years have been increasingly linked to and justified by the need to constantly improve educational standards in order to improve the economic competitiveness of nation states. As a recent White Paper on School Choice in England put it:

> Standards must keep rising in the globalised world in which we now live ... given the scale of the global economic challenge we face there is no other choice .... We cannot content ourselves with a schools system which, while much improved, is not universally good.
>
> (DfES, 2005, pp.7 and 20)

The question remains however, given these pressures, why the focus on testing? Part of the explanation seems to lie in the scepticism of government about the negative impact of testing and particularly a sense that the short-term harm that testing *might* do to individual schools and children is nevertheless still outweighed by the longer term control that testing affords system management and development. System control outweighs the nebulous benefits of trying to improve quality by other means. Tests and testing allows governments to exert direct pressure on schools and classrooms and they are unlikely to relinquish them lightly. The recent abandonment of testing at Key Stage 3 (age 14) in England has come only after the complete shambles of the 2008 testing programme with mislaid papers, unmarked papers and so forth.

Tests and testing also seem to promise a tangible return on relatively low and predictable levels of expenditure when compared with other tools which might raise standards, such as increased in-service training and/or lower student–teacher ratios. In this respect it is worth noting that the commitment to test-based evaluation and accountability not only spans continents but also persists across administrations. New Labour continued with and in some key respects intensified the previous Conservative government's commitment to a National Curriculum and Testing system. The Republican Bush administration introduced NCLB following the Democratic Clinton Educate America Act. NCLB attracted wide bi-partisan support and even though this diminished over time (Dillon, 2007) testing remains at the heart of the Obama 'Race to the top' programme.[8] So the use of testing is not peculiar to England or New Labour and the national testing system continues under the new Conservative controlled coalition government, though the focus on test-based accountability is more intense in England than in other countries of the United Kingdom.

The issue seems to revolve around risk management and governance. Large sums of public money are invested in education systems and the pressure of economic globalisation is intense, or at least is perceived to be intense. To maintain legitimacy governments have to at least *be seen* to be doing something in response to concerns about economic competitiveness and educational standards, and testing programmes and test scores are certainly visible. The urge for managerial control, in the face of global uncertainties, seems to outweigh the 'collateral damage' of testing.

Equally, the very act of testing, in the context of system-wide monitoring and accountability, both assumes and at one and the same time creates the managerial 'right-to-test', the 'right-to-manage' the system. It is almost as if democratic governments now conceive of their role as more corporate than representative, managing systems *qua* systems irrespective of the impact of particular technologies of control on that system, or indeed on individual citizens. Citizens are treated as conscripts in the constant struggle for national economic supremacy. Rather than acting on our behalf, governments now expect us to help them in their struggle with globalisation. To reiterate a point made earlier, it seems as if the key focus for policy is the system as a whole, rather than the quality and content of individual achievement.

Developing educational quality

The problem remains, however, that narrow test-driven accountability systems are unlikely to produce flexible and creative workers for the so-called 'knowledge economy', far less contribute to more general deliberation about the curriculum and the democratic purposes and organisation of schooling. Moreover, the government in England must address the 'plateau effect'. Some new spin of the policy wheel is required if the government's own rhetoric about raising standards is to continue to be credible. There is a large minority of students, usually located in poor communities, who are still not benefiting from even the apparently inflated test scores which are currently being produced (20–30 per cent at age 11 and 16; Figures 11.2 and 11.3). It is becoming apparent that a one-size-fits-all 'standards agenda' in educational policymaking has run its course and that what is needed is a new focus on curriculum content and responsiveness: on the production of diverse experiences of learning in and for an uncertain world. Understanding and addressing issues of poverty and the disputability of knowledge and values is a key issue for education, as is the development of creativity and self-confidence in the community at large, particularly those most marginalized at the present time. There is a pressing need for schools and the communities they serve to act more in tandem, for schools and educational policymakers to identify the potential strengths of their communities and to better understand how to support student learning in interaction *with* schooling, rather than force it to accord with institutionalized learning *through* schooling.

This provides a challenge to policy and an opportunity for research. The government in England has acknowledged some criticisms to some extent by, for example, the recent abandonment of testing at age 14, and by introducing specific programmes to reinstate and support 'creativity' in the school curriculum, particularly the primary school curriculum (Hall and Thomson, 2007). These efforts have been rather piecemeal and tokenistic to date. Nevertheless they indicate an uncertainty that simply teaching and testing Maths, Science and English will indeed produce the creative talent that a knowledge economy needs.

Policy options for the future

There are no simple or straightforward policy options with respect to assessment and testing. Assessment intersects with every aspect of an educational system:

- at the level of the individual student and teacher and their various experiences (positive or negative) of the assessment process and its outcomes;
- at the level of the school or similar educational institution and how it is organized and held to account; and
- at the level of the educational and social system with respect to what knowledge is endorsed and which people are legitimately accredited for future economic and social leadership.

Governments in England over the last 20 years or so seem to have only partially appreciated this, assuming that 'standards' can be measured without the process of measurement impacting on and, in key respects, distorting the system as a whole. Similarly, because educational achievement is correlated with social and economic well-being, the efforts of post-1997 Labour governments seem to have concentrated on pushing as many children as possible through as many examinations as possible. Policymakers seem to have assumed a causal relationship but one which operates in the opposite direction to that which most research would suggest – i.e. that educational achievement determines wealth, rather than wealth determining educational achievement. This causal assumption seems to have been conceived of as part of a systemic drive for social inclusion and improving social mobility, without reflecting on the restricted educational experience it creates for even high achieving students, let alone the 30 per cent who still do not attain at least 5 A*–C grades at GCSE.

An alternative vision of 'you get what you assess' would operate at classroom level, supporting curriculum development and underpinning high quality teaching by the development and use of high quality assessment tasks which could help to structure and focus classroom activities. This is the 'formative assessment' version of the vision, starting from broad curriculum goals, focusing on clear objectives and assessment criteria, high quality tasks, and good use of criteria-related formative feedback to students on what they have achieved and how they might improve. Again, recent policy has made some gestures towards this prompted by the lobbying of the Assessment Reform Group (2002). 'Assessment for Learning' for example is a significant part of the rhetoric of the revised National Strategies for primary schools. However, in a context which is still dominated by testing and targets, an alternative vision of formative assessment is unlikely to gain much of a foothold in everyday teaching practices.

The key policy problem is that assessment will *always* impact on teaching and learning; the key issue is to try to accentuate the positive impact and diminish the negative impact as far as possible. It is clear that the greater the scope and scale of the testing system, the simpler and more focused the tests will become. For the last 15 years *all* students have been tested at *four* ages/stages, totalling 2.4 million candidates per year. Not many high quality, expansive and challenging tasks will be produced or used in such circumstances – the scale of the enterprise is just too vast; and in fact, of course, the system collapsed under its own weight when in 2008 the company which was sub-contracted to set and mark the tests (ETS) mislaid and did not mark large numbers of papers (see Baird and Lee-Kelley, 2009 for a detailed account of the pressures of examination development).

If accountability is seen to be the main purpose of the exercise then quality of teaching and student experience will be subjugated to this purpose. Thus, given the overwhelming need to refocus attention on curriculum content and quality of learning rather than attainment of tests scores, and insofar as we might construe formative assessment as more positive than negative, the key implications of what we now know about National Testing for future policy would seem to be:

- The greater the scale and scope of the testing system, the simpler the tests will be.
- The more individual student achievement is tied to system accountability the more accountability measures will dominate student experience.
- Therefore:
  - restrict testing to a politically necessary minimum;
  - attend to monitoring standards by use of small national samples;
  - reintegrate discussion of curriculum development and assessment;
  - put resources and support into re-thinking curriculum goals for the twenty-first century and developing item banks of high quality assessment tasks that underpin and reinforce these goals, for teachers to use as appropriate, plus in-service training for formative assessment.

Central control of the curriculum and of testing may have been a short-term solution to perceived problems of teaching quality and student achievement, but it will always threaten long-term systemic sustainability, professional development and capacity building. Now is definitely the time to reinvest in local developments at local level, especially with respect to classroom level assessment skills and understandings, and to re-build the communities of practice within which judgments about standards are made and ultimately reside.

The government has made a start by restricting testing to teacher assessment at Key Stage 1 and abandoning testing at Key Stage 3. This will allow more time and resources to be devoted to developing better quality assessment tasks and teacher assessment at Key Stage 2; with the development of better quality materials and more in-service opportunities focused on the other foundation subjects, beyond English, Maths and Science. In due course an alternative model of test development and use should be produced, involving:

- central development of an item-bank of challenging assessment tasks encapsulating meaningful and challenging curricular objectives, to test performance more validly and underpin high quality teaching;
- to be used by teachers to structure their own classroom work towards the end of each Key Stage and inform their teaching more generally;
- with provision of in-service support to administer and mark tasks in similar fashion, organised collaboratively in local consortia, and leading to further

development of assessment criteria and local and possibly national items (i.e. teachers would be able to both draw from and add to the national resource and reconnect with their disciplinary communities of practice);

• further in-service support, again organised via local consortia, to analyse patterns of pupil responses and particularly common errors and misconceptions.

In this way assessment could be modified to address the continuing political agenda while contributing to, rather than detracting from, the quality of teaching.

Inspection too, should focus far more on the quality of classroom interaction, far less on 'leadership', 'management', 'targets' and all the other currently fashionable mantras of so-called school effectiveness. Indeed inspection reports which focused on the quality of classroom interaction could be fed into local consortium discussions of assessment tasks and how best to use them.

What is required is an understanding that, ultimately, quality provision, of teaching, learning and assessment, must be developed by local groups of teachers discussing the nature of what they do and how they do it, just as student learning is produced out of the interactions which they have with teachers and peers. This process can be supported by centrally produced materials and structured by engagement with local authorities, governing bodies, parent groups and parents' evenings to discuss the progress of individual children. The possibilities for making local discussions of assessment processes as rigorous as possible are many. But the space must first be made available for them to begin to occur so that assessment is oriented towards the development of understanding, rather than the achievement of compliance.

Notes

1 General Certificate of Education – Ordinary Level; GCE Advanced Level was and still is taken at around 18 + to qualify for entry to university.
2 Certificate of Secondary Education.
3 That is, the equivalent of 5 GCSEs at grades A*–C: the top GCSE grades of A*–C are officially accepted as the equivalent of the old O-level passes; the percentage of students gaining at least 5 A*–Cs is the officially and commonly accepted measure of a good secondary education; the percentage of students gaining at least 5 A*–Gs (the full range of grades) is the officially and commonly accepted measure of a minimally satisfactory secondary education.
4 See: www.dcsf.gov.uk/rsgateway/.
5 See: www.inca.org.uk/1434.html#6.4.9%20Output%20statistics.
6 TIMSS – Trends in International Maths & Science Study administered from Boston College, USA.
7 PISA – Programme for International Student Assessment administered by the Organisation for Economic Co-operation and Development, Paris.
8 See: www2.ed.gov/programs/racetothetop/index.html.

References

Airasian, P. (1988) 'Measurement-driven instruction: A closer look', *Educational Measurement: Issues and Practice*, 7(4): 6–11.

Assessment Reform Group (2002) *Assessment for Learning: 10 Principles*, see: http://arg.educ.cam.ac.uk/CIE3.pdf.

Baird, J. and Lee-Kelley, L. (2009) 'The dearth of managerialism in implementation of national examinations policy', *Journal of Educational Policy*, 24(1): 55–81.

Black, P. and Wiliam, D. (1998) 'Assessment and classroom learning', *Assessment in Education*, 5(1): 7–74

Carless, D., Joughin, G., Liu, N.-F. and Associates (2006) *How Assessment Supports Learning*, Hong Kong: Hong Kong University Press.

Cassen, R. and Kingdon, G. (2007) *Tackling Low Educational Achievement*, York: Joseph Rowntree Foundation.

Centre on Education Policy (2006) *From the Capital to the Classroom: Year 4 of the No Child Left Behind Act: Summary and Recommendations*, see: www.cep-dc.org/.

Centre on Education Policy (2007) *Has Student Achievement Increased Since No Child Left Behind?* see: www.cep-dc.org/.

Daugherty R. (1995) *National Curriculum Assessment: A Review of Policy 1987–1994*, London: Falmer Press.

Department for Education and Skills (2005) *Higher Standards, Better Schools for All*, see: www.dfes.gov.uk/publications/schoolswhitepaper/index.shtml.

Department for Education and Skills (2006) *Primary and Secondary National Strategies* London, DfES; see: www.standards.dfes.gov.uk/.

Dillon, S. (2007) 'Battle grows over renewing landmark education law', *New York Times* 7 April 2007: www.nytimes.com/2007/04/07/education/07child.html (accessed 25 August 2011).

Galton, M., Simon, B. and Croll, P. (1980) *Inside the Primary Classroom*, London: Routledge and Kegan Paul.

Galton, M., Hargreaves, L., Comber, C. and Wall, D. (1999) *Inside the Primary Classroom: 20 Years on*, London: Routledge.

Gillborn, D. and Youdell, D. (2006) 'Educational triage and the D-to-C conversion: Suitable case for treatment?' in Lauder, H., Brown, P., and Dillabough, J.-A. and Halsey, A.H. (eds) *Education, Globalisation and Social Change*, Oxford: Oxford University Press.

Hall, C. and Thomson, P. (2007) 'Creative partnerships? Cultural policy and inclusive arts practice in one primary school', *British Educational Research Journal*, 33(3): 315–330.

Hall, K., Collins, J., Benjamin, S., Nind, M. and Sheehy, K. (2004) 'SATurated models of pupildom: Assessment and inclusion/exclusion', *British Educational Research Journal*, 30(6): 801–817.

Hamilton, L., Stecher, B., Marsh, J., Sloan McCombs, J., Robyn, A., Russell, J., Naftel, S. and Barney, H. (2007) *Standards-Based Accountability Under No Child Left Behind*, Santa Monica, CA: Rand Education.

Hayward, G. and McNicholl, J. (2007) 'Modular mayhem? A case study of the development of the A level science curriculum in England', *Assessment in Education*, 14(3): 335–351.

Jackson, P. (1968) *Life in Classrooms*, New York: Holt Reinhart and Winston.

Klein, S., Hamilton, L., McCaffrey, D. and Stecher, B. (2000) 'What do test scores in Texas tell us?' *Education Policy Analysis Archives*, 8(49); see: http://epaa.asu.edu/epaa/v8n49.

Linn, R. (2000) 'Assessments and accountability', *Educational Researcher*, 23(9): 4–14.

McNess, E., Triggs, P., Broadfoot, P., Osborn, M. and Pollard, A. (2001) 'The changing nature of assessment in English primary schools: Findings from the PACE Project 1989–1997', *Education 3–13*, 29(3): 9–16.

Mehan, H. (1979) *Learning Lessons: Social Organization in the Classroom*, Cambridge, MA: Harvard University Press.

Mercer, N. (1995) *The Guided Construction of Knowledge*, Clevedon: Multi-Lingual Matters.

No Child Left Behind Act (2001) *Public Law 107-110* see: www.ed.gov/nclb/land ing.jhtml and http://en.wikipedia.org/wiki/No_Child_Left_Behind.

Office for Standards in Education (2006) *The Annual Report of Her Majesty's Chief Inspector of Schools 2005/06* London: OfSTED; see: www.ofsted.gov.uk.

Popham, J. (1987) 'The merits of measurement-driven instruction', *Phi Delta Kappan*, 68: 679–682.

Resnick, L. and Resnick, D. (1992) 'Assessing the thinking curriculum', in Gifford, B. and O'Connor, M. (eds) *Future Assessments: Changing Views of Aptitude, Achievement and Instruction*, Boston, MA: Kluwer.

Shepard, L. (1990) 'Inflated test score gains: Is the problem old norms or teaching to the test?' *Educational Measurement: Issues and Practice*, 9(3): 15–22.

Shepard, L. (2000) 'The role of assessment in a learning culture', *Educational Researcher*, 29(7): 4–14.

Torrance, H. (1981) 'The origins and development of mental testing in England and the United States', *British Journal of Sociology of Education*, 2(1): 45–59.

Torrance, H. (ed.) (1995) *Evaluating Authentic Assessment: Issues, problems and future possibilities*, Buckingham: Open University Press.

Torrance, H. (2003) 'Assessment of the National Curriculum in England', in Kellaghan, T. and Stufflebeam, D. (eds) *International Handbook of Educational Evaluation*, Dordrecht: Kluwer.

Torrance, H. (2005) 'Testing times for black achievement – some observations from England', paper presented to Symposium 'Leaving No Child Behind: How Federal Education Agencies are Addressing Achievement Gaps for Linguistic and Racial/ Ethnic Groups' American Educational Research Association Annual Conference, Montreal, 11–15 April.

Torrance, H. (2006) 'Globalising empiricism: What, if anything, can be learned from international comparisons of educational achievement?' in Lauder, H., Brown, P., Dillabough, J.-A. and Halsey, A.H. (eds) *Education, Globalisation and Social Change*, Oxford: Oxford University Press.

Torrance, H. (2007) 'Assessment *as* learning? How the use of explicit learning objectives, assessment criteria and feedback in post-secondary education and training can come to dominate learning', *Assessment in Education*, 14(3): 281–294.

Torrance, H. and Pryor, J. (1998) *Investigating Formative Assessment: Teaching Learning and Assessment in the Classroom*, Buckingham: Open University Press.

Wyse D. and Torrance H. (2009) 'The development and consequences of national curriculum assessment for primary education in England', *Educational Research*, 51(2): 213–238.

12 School and pupils' work

Bernard Charlot
(Translated by Thomas Kundert)

When my French children got back from school, in the 1980s, I asked them: 'Did you work hard at school?' Today, when my Brazilian children get home I ask a different question: 'Did you study hard at school?' This change is connected to my research and reflections about school, but is also linked to the differences between the French and Portuguese language. In French one says that pupils *work* at school. In Portuguese, at least in Brazil, one does not say pupils work, but rather they *study* at school. Likewise, in Portuguese one says that the teacher *teaches* and the pupil *learns*. In French one can say that the teacher *teaches* or that he *learns*, in other words, the teacher learns (teaches)[1] things to pupils, who have to learn these things. A third difference I believe is also interesting. In Portuguese the pupil *accompanies* the teacher, or the lesson. In French the pupil *follows* the teacher, or the lesson. These are implicitly two completely different models. The French model calls *work* what the pupil does at school, but, in fact, highlights the teacher's activity: the teacher 'teaches' things to the pupil, who should 'follow' them. The implicit Portuguese model, or at least the Brazilian model, does not call the pupil's activity *work*, but emphasises its specificity: the teacher teaches, the pupil learns; these are two activities that cannot be confused.

These differences lead me to two questions. The main one concerns the activity of the pupil: What is the nature and the specificity of the pupil's activity at school? The second question is less important, but is also relevant: Does this activity merit the label of *work*?

The question of the pupil's activity: a theoretical and epistemological debate

What is at stake in the debate about the pupil's activity is whether it is merely a reflection of their social class position or whether it is a specific activity, which produces effects, changes, and should be considered an essential aspect of what is happening in the school. The debate covers the question of the differences between pupils coming from various social classes, but also includes the question of gender.

The question of activity in sociology of the positions and dispositions in the 60s, 70s and 80s of the twentieth century, the way school was thought out was heavily influenced by the sociology of reproduction, especially that of Bourdieu, i.e. a sociology of positions and dispositions. Even today explanations remain pressing about the difficulties of pupils at school owing to factors such as the family and social background of the children. It is therefore worth reflecting on the place this sociology attributes to the pupils' activity. In this model, what is important is the social position of the pupils, defined based on their father's occupation, and not their own activity. The position of the pupils starting school (*in*) and their position leaving it (*out*) are analysed. Both are compared and the conclusion is that the school contributes towards social reproduction. From this point of view, what happens inside school does not produce anything new. This approach, of course, serves to undermine or lessen the value of the pupil's activity; it is not necessary to analyse it in detail.

However, a distinction should be made between the sociologies of reproduction developed by Baudelot and Establet and by Bowles and Gintis, in which the activity is almost not mentioned, and Bourdieu's more interesting sociology (Baudelot and Establet, 1971; Bowles and Gintis, 1976; Bourdieu, 1998; Bourdieu and Passeron, 1992). Bourdieu raises the question of what the pupil does in the school. He does not analyse, therefore, the activity itself, but rather the resources, i.e. the *dispositions* that back them up. These dispositions depend on the social position of the pupil. It is the dispositions that are important and not the way the activity itself is carried out. They appear in theory as cultural capital and *habitus.*

In Bourdieu's conceptual system, society is made up of a set of fields. In these fields there are battles: all parties try to preserve, and if possible improve, their position. To do so, they use the resources that are within their reach. These resources derive from their social position. In each field the battles for power depend, before all else, on the resources available to each person: their *capital.* In the cultural field (school, press, arts, etc.) the cultural capital prevails, which comprises a set of knowledge and relations with culture and language. Those who have more cultural capital can develop more effective strategies in this field to improve their position; in the cultural field these are strategies of *distinction* (Bourdieu, 2007). Hence, according to Bourdieu's theory, there is space for the battles, but the development and outcome of these battles depend on the resources backing them up, i.e. at the end of the day they depend on the social position of the person who acts: the principle of intelligibility of the activity is not the activity itself, but the social structure of the capital invested in the activity. Therefore, Bourdieu does not talk about *actors*, but instead he talks about social *agents.*

The concept of *habitus* clarifies the difference between the actor and the agent. The *habitus* is a set of psychic dispositions, which are durable and transposable, which have been socially structured and which function as the structural principles of the practices and the representations (Bourdieu, 1989). To understand an activity one has to understand why the individual acts, and how he/she acts. Hence, one has to know his/her ideas, expectations, tastes, etc., in other words, the psychic dispositions of the person. This means that to understand an activity or a practice one has to analyse the *habitus*, the system of psychic dispositions that it is based on. And to know the *habitus*, one has to analyse the social conditions in which it was built. As such, what enables a practice to be explained are the social conditions that construct the *habitus*. Therefore, in the final analysis, the social position is the principle of the intelligibility of the activity. The social positions are *reproduced* from one generation to the next, at least in terms of probabilities: the conditions in which a child is brought up socially mould his/her psyche, and this leads to the representations and practices that reproduce the social structure of origin. A person who acts is the *agent* of the social structures, given that these are reproduced through mediation of her/his *habitus*, s/he is not an *actor* who, in line with his/her situation, will react against the social order of things.

In line with this sociological model, what happens in the school depends essentially on the cultural capital and the pupils' *habitus*. Those who have the psychic dispositions and cultural capital necessary for school will become successful pupils, whereas those who do not are destined to fail. The concepts of activity or school work do not comply with any important function in the explicative system.

Meanwhile, the question of the activity is not completely absent from Bourdieu's system, as mentioned above. But it is a form of *practical sense*, as Bourdieu says: rarely does the *habitus* function in social situations that are exactly the same as those that structured it, and therefore, a constant adaptation has to be made, carried out through practical sense. Most of the time, this adaptation does not bring problems, as there are a lot of similarities between the conditions in which the *habitus* was built and those in which it later has to function. However, late on Bourdieu became sensitive to the non-coinciding phases, which are increasingly common in a modern society engaged in rapid change, between the essential psychic dispositions of individuals (their *habitus*) and the social situations in which they live today. These non-coinciding phases do not, however, lead Bourdieu to show more interest for the current activity of the individuals, the transformation of the *habitus*, or the construction of new cultural resources. They lead him to highlight the suffering produced by this disorder, contributing to the 'misery of the world' (Bourdieu, 2003).

Are we condemned to eternal reproduction? Bourdieu leaves the door open, which allows one to surmise that, despite everything, the individual Bourdieu himself engaged in determined fashion in the social battles of the 1990s. The past and the future are articulated in the *habitus*, the key to reproduction. Therefore, to break the reproduction, disconnect the future from the past and as such change society, one has to change the *habitus*. As such, becoming aware of the sociological conscience is the essential condition of change: the world can be changed by people who understand that their representations and practices have been socially conditioned, and in grasping this, can free themselves from this conditioning. Becoming aware is the necessary condition of social transformation, as in the thinking of Paulo Freire (Freire, 1976, 1983). However, while according to Paulo Freire, becoming aware may be the effect of training, in Bourdieu's opinion this cannot occur in school, as this is where the ruling classes exercise their symbolic violence and their 'cultural tyranny'. Awareness can only be produced in social struggles. Therefore, activity is the principle of transformation, but we are talking about activity carried out in the social struggles and not the activity of the teacher and pupil in the classroom. Indeed, Bourdieu shows no interest regarding school activity, what happens in the classroom, but instead he is interested in the social functions of the school and the process of social reproduction that takes place through it.

Analysis of the implicit nature of the activity according to Bourdieu's sociology and similar studies

When Bourdieu focuses on school activity he highlights the implicit nature of this activity, in detriment, again, to its actual undertaking. Bernstein had already pointed out the difference between the elaborated code (explicit) and the restricted code (full of implicitness), and the existence, in school, of a hidden curriculum (Bernstein, 1996). Going down the same path, Bourdieu argues that the true criteria of assessment of the pupils' activity are, for the most part, implicit. Implicitly, the school requires a certain kind of relationship with culture and language, and in its assessments of the pupil it is this relationship that the school assesses. In other words, the school does not teach what it assesses. Pupils who have already constructed this relationship in their family can achieve academic success and those who have not will fail. This relationship is socially constructed, but it is implicit, and therefore hidden; it is considered a fact of nature: it is the 'good pupil' who is naturally intelligent. The teachers themselves, as Bourdieu points out, value the talented pupil, who seems to achieve success without trying, and looks down on the pupil who works hard to meet the requirements of the school, considering them 'too scholarly'. In other words, and however paradoxical it seems, it is the school that does not value the school work.

Taking into account these analyses, one can distinguish what the school activity seems to be and what it actually is in truth. Apparently, it is an educational activity supplied to all the pupils. It is, in fact, through this façade that the real activity functions and remains implicit: academically and socially legitimising the power of the dominating classes. Hence, in this perspective, the sociological work does not aim to analyse the development of the activity itself, but to unveil its implicit facets.

One can therefore understand why, for many years, people talked about school and the social inequality of school without analysing in depth what was happening in the classrooms. The diagnosis was made before opening the classroom door: in it a vast process of illusion and deception took place, and it was not worth concerning oneself with the details. On this subject there are some very significant lines at the end of the book entitled *Reproduction in Education* (1992), in which Bourdieu and Passeron put forward the hypothesis of a rational pedagogy, which would make the implicit facets of the school explicit, and in doing so would allow success to be achieved by the youths coming from the dominated classes. They immediately throw out this hypothesis: why would the ruling classes implement pedagogy in school that would allow everyone to succeed, when the current pedagogy only benefits their children? No doubts are left: in this sociological model the democratisation of the school depends on the social struggles that must be fought outside school and not on an internal transformation of the school practices.

Today, a large proportion of the researchers who investigate social inequality at school take an interest in the school activity itself. Unveiling the implicit facets of the activity remains the overriding approach in another area: gender studies. To highlight the hidden masculine values that permeate the school environment, the textbooks, the behaviours of male and female teachers and the assessment practices, etc., are researched into. These implicit facets have been identified by multiple research projects and are undeniable. Nevertheless, the gender studies neglect, and generally silence, one very important fact: in several countries it is proven that girls are much more academically successful than boys. How can this happen in a school whose values are implicitly masculine?

Very often the gender studies ignore this question with the following argument: girls are more academically successful at school, but they cannot make the most of their qualifications in the job market. This reasoning highlights that women are always victims, including when they seem to have an advantage over men, but it does not answer the question. Schools have no responsibility with regard to what happens in the job market and the paradox remains: at a school permeated by masculine values, it is females who obtain more success. By failing to take this fact into account the research slides into a victimisation discourse.

Adriana Marrero, a Uruguayan sociologist, has worked on this issue (Marrero, 2007). She explains that, as well as the implicit masculine values, at school there is also an explicit discourse, which must be taken into consideration. What does this explicit discourse say? It asserts that school success does not depend on the sex or social category of the pupils and anybody can be successful at school, provided they study. The time has also arrived to hear the explicit discourse of the school. Of course, it does not annul the implicit masculine values, but it produces mobilisation effects. If a girl hears that she can be as good as a boy, the girl will commit herself at school and feel motivated to study. This mobilisation is mobilisation of what? It is mobilisation of the female pupil's activity.

At the end of the day, no matter how masculine the school's values are, there are not many places where a girl can hear this message: that she can surpass men. The school is one of the few places that explicitly champions equality between the sexes and which paves the way for women to outdo men – which, indeed, they do. Of course, this is partially deception, an illusion, given that the masculine values seep through the school. One knows, however, that this illusion has a social reality. Sociology calls it a *self-fulfilling prophecy*, whereby a conviction that is objectively wrong ends up generating what was predicted. One can consider the academic success of girls, and also of pupils coming from the popular classes, a self-fulfilling prophecy: in stating that anybody can be successful, the school creates the conditions for anybody to be, although this demands a greater personal investment if you are a girl or from the popular classes.

The research on the school should take into account, at the same time, its implicit values and its explicit principles. In paying attention to the latter, one is faced with the question of the pupils' mobilisation in their studies, and hence the pupil's activity. It is therefore necessary to build a model of analysis and not the sociology of reproduction – without, in so doing, forgetting the social and gender inequalities.

Why does the question of the pupil's activity have to be raised?

The sociology of education managed to surpass the reproduction and victimisation discourse when it paid attention to the resistance of the pupils. The book by Paul Willis, *Learning to Labour* (1991), played an important role, showing that the young English working class do not value school, and therefore contribute to the social reproduction through it. In effect, this resistance of the pupils to school regulations confirms that the dominated classes do not accept the processes of domination passively. The author who best developed this idea was Michel de Certeau, in particular in his book *The Art of Practice*, the first volume of *The Practice of Everyday Life* (1996). He highlighted that the dominated try to subvert the ruling order to gain some advantage. For example, they know that to receive social benefits they have to have the appearance of being a 'good poor person'. Those who are dominated cannot implement *strategies*, as they do not have control over their time and the domination of the means that allow them to achieve their ends. Meanwhile, this does not make them remain passive. They use *tactics* to take advantage of the situations that crop up, and as such 'invent their everyday life' through a permanent social 'bricolage'. To sum up, no matter how dominated one is, a human being remains a subject, he/she acts and his/her activity has effects.

This is a fundamental departure from the sociology of reproduction and victimisation, and it brings to the forefront the question of activity. It is worth pointing out that this approach fits perfectly into the Marxist tradition: Marxism is a theory of the class struggle, i.e. activity in conflict; it is not a theory of reproduction of the social positions, or at least not only this. Marxism is a theory of the *praxis*: in transforming the world, man transforms himself. The human being occupies a position in the world, but based on that position he acts on the world. The pupils' activity in the classroom and outside it is as important as their social or sexual category to understand what is happening in the school.

Therefore, one has to outline an activity. Alexis Leontiev, a collaborator of Vygotsky's, explains that an activity is a series of actions and operations, with a motive and an objective (Leontiev, 1984). Why is this done? It is the motive. What do I do it for? To achieve an objective. How can this objective be achieved? By carrying out actions, which require operations. An activity has an effectiveness and a meaning. It is effective when the operations lead to the objective aimed for. The meaning of the activity, according to Leontiev, depends on the relationship between the motive and the objective. When they coincide, it is a real activity; if not, it is merely an action. We use an example proposed by Leontiev himself. If I am reading a book to prepare for an exam, it is an action, not an activity: the motive (the exam) does not coincide with the objective of the action (getting to know the content of the book). If I am reading the book because I am interested in its content (motive), then it is an activity. This distinction between action and activity is interesting as it highlights the gap between the results of an action and its real motive. To analyse an activity, including that of the pupil, one has to be interested in the meaning of the activity and its efficacy.

Why and towards what aim does a pupil study? In my opinion this is the basic question, including when you research into the question of social inequalities or gender at school. At the end of the day, when pupils fail, it is not directly caused by their social condition, although this may also influence the teacher's assessment; it is, before all else, because they did not study enough. Why did they not study enough? This question takes us to the meaning that the pupils attribute to their studies. To understand this meaning, one has to take into account the social position and gender of the pupils, which has a large bearing on their relationship with knowledge and with school. My research into this relationship focuses on three connected questions. For a pupil, especially one from a popular class background, what does going to school mean? For him/her what is the meaning of studying, or refusing to study? What is the point of learning and understanding, either at school or outside school? (Charlot, 1999, 2000, 2005a; Charlot *et al.*, 1992.)

It is a question, essentially, of researching the pupils' mobilisation in their study. I avoid talking about *motivation*, preferring to use the word *mobilisation*. In effect, 'motivating the pupils' often consists of inventing a trick so that they study subjects they are not in the least interested in. Paying attention to the mobilisation of the pupils leads one to question the internal engine of study; in other words, what is it that makes pupils invest in their studies? Someone can be motivated from the outside, but one mobilises oneself from the inside. In raising the question of mobilisation, one comes across the issue of desire, and straight away the sub-conscious, and in a more general way, the psychoanalytical theory – which Vygostky and Leontiev dismiss (Charlot, 2005b).

The question of meaning can be looked at from another angle, directly linked to the teaching experience. Nobody learns without implementing intellectual activity; in other words, whoever does not study does not learn. Straight away the question of 'motive' arises concerning this investment in the activity, to use the words of Leontiev. What is the meaning of this activity for the pupil? When there is no meaning, there is no activity: nobody does anything without a motive. But the most common situation in school is for the pupil to act for a motive not related to the knowledge itself. In the most extreme case, one can cite a French adolescent who one day said: 'at school I like everything, apart from the lessons and the teachers'. The more common case is for pupils to study to get a good grade or a mobile phone promised by their father. In the ideal case, pupils study because they are interested in the content being studied. Of course, the efficacy of the study is not the same in all these cases. Leontiev would say that only the latter is an activity, while the other examples are actions whereby there is a gap between the motive and the objective.

Learning requires an intellectual activity. An individual only engages in an activity that has a meaning for him/her. When this meaning is some distance from the desired result of the action of studying, this engagement is fragile. In contrast, when the motive and the objective of the activity coincide, the latter is carried out with a lot of meaning, and pleasure is gleaned in undertaking it, even more so in achieving the objective. Activity, meaning, pleasure: these are the terms of the pedagogical equation that has to be solved.

The issue of social and gender inequality at school has not been neglected. It is integrated into a broader perspective than merely reproduction, victimisation, and unilateral action of the ruling classes: what is the meaning of school, school activity, knowledge, learning when one belongs to a social class or gender that is dominated? This meaning is constructed outside school, but is also heavily influenced by what happens inside the school. The pupils are not the same at school: on this point, the sociology of reproduction is right and its findings remain important. But taking into consideration the issue of school activity, which it ignores, it is possible to dismiss the sociological determinism, and therefore understand how it is possible that pupils from the popular classes are successful at school, despite all the likelihood of the opposite being the case, and how it is possible that girls are more successful than boys in a school that is permeated with masculine values.

However, in analysing the pupil's activity it is not sufficient to raise the question of its meaning; one also has to pay attention to its efficacy. This is what we shall now do.

School activity from the perspective of the school and the pupils

The pupil who does not study will fail, but also the pupil who carries out an activity at school other than that which characterises the school will fail.

What is the specificity of school activity?

Answering this question in depth requires a precise and long analysis, for which there is insufficient room here. Therefore, I will directly present some conclusions, considered as affirmations to be discussed (Charlot, 1999, 2000; Charlot *et al.*, 1992).

School is a place where the world is treated as an object and not as an environment, a place of experience. At times, this object of thought has a referent outside school, in the environment of the pupil's life. But in this case the relationship with the object of thought should be different to the relationship with the referent. The Lisbon that the geography teacher talks about should not be confused with the Lisbon in which the pupils live. To a certain extent, it is the same city, but their relationship with it is not the same in the two cases: the latter is a place of experience, the former an object of thought. When the pupils do not manage to make the difference between the two and relate to the former as if it was the latter, they will have problems at school. For example, the teacher asks what the functions of the city of Lisbon are, which requires the city to be thought of in its role as the capital, and the pupils respond narrating how they, their parents and their friends live in the city.

Very often, the object of thought of the school does not have a referent in the environment of the pupil's life. It belongs to a specific world, constructed by science and by the school. The basic arithmetic operations have some referents in social practices outside school, where the pupils count, add, multiply, but these referents are rare when the pupil moves on to algebra: who, in his lifetime, has to solve second-degree equations? The notion of weight has a referent in the everyday world, but the atom does not. Controlling the relationship between the object of thought and its referents in life's environment, and introducing the pupil to intellectual worlds made up of objects whose meaning does not derive from a relationship with the real world as it is experienced is, under two correlated forms, the overriding problem of the school pedagogy.

As such, we have to rethink the question of the connection between the pupils' family background and what is taught in school. Very often an attempt is made to solve school failure by linking everything to the pupil's daily life. This connection, however, can constitute both a support and an obstacle at the same time. It is a support because it gives meaning to what the school teaches. It is an obstacle when it hides the specific meaning of the school activity. Therefore, Vergnaud showed how the family representation of subtraction prevents its mathematical understanding (Vergnaud, 2005). José leaves home with thirty euros and loses ten euros: how many euros will he return home with? The pupil solves this problem without difficulty because the meanings 'lose' and 'subtract' converge. Now, José leaves home with thirty euros, earns money and comes back home with fifty euros: how much did he earn? To solve the problem the pupils have to do a subtraction, which they do not find logical, given that José earned money. One can give lots of examples in which the reference to the everyday world creates a difficulty for the pupil (Silva, 2004, 2009). One can also evoke the notion of Bachelard's epistemological obstacle and the ideas of Vygostsky, stating that there is a difference in nature between common knowledge and scientific or school knowledge (Bachelard, 1996; Vygotsky, 1987). What is important is that the teaching has meaning, not whether or not it is linked to the pupil's family world; this option represents only one possible solution, in certain cases, and can be dangerous or impossible in others.

To relate to the world as an object of thought, the distancing/objectivation and systematisation processes are fundamental. The distancing enables the pupils to leave the subjective world of their emotions, feelings, experience and view the world as an object to be thought out. Distancing and objectivation cannot be separated and occur in a single process: the Self constitutes an epistemic Self, different from the empirical Self, in the process through which the world is placed as an object of thought. This process of distancing/objectivation is only possible thanks to language; only through language can objects of thought exist and can a rational subject think them (Vygotsky, 1987). If in school language rules, it is because this enables objects of thought to be constructed which are different from the objects of experience, which is the specificity of the school.

Systematisation is a complementary process of distancing/objectivation. It is possible to constitute objects of thought without linking them in a system, but this is always the horizon of thought, given that a concept is defined as the set of relations that it maintains with other concepts and not by a direct connection with a referent. Systematisation enables construction of the subjects (mathematics, physics, history, etc.) and it is not by chance that the interdisciplinary project is always on a collision course with the problem of systematisation. Both in Vygotsky and in Piaget, the question of systematisation is fundamental. According to Vygotsky, there are three differences between everyday knowledge and scientific knowledge: the latter is conscious, voluntary and systematised differently to the former (Vygotsky, 1987). In Piaget's opinion one gets to the end of the construction of intellectual operations when one can think in systems, in other words, when the real is the undertaking of a possibility of the system (Inhelder and Piaget, 1976; Piaget, 2008).

Distancing, objectivation, systematisation, in other words, inseparable constitution of the Self as the epistemic Self and the world as the object of thought, define the specificity of the school activity. This definition is valid for the essential subjects (mathematics, history, Portuguese, etc.), but also for the subjects that occupy the body or the Arts. There is a difference between street conflict, with kicks and cuffs, and the sporting battle at school. The battle has rules, regulations, which may be spoken or explicitly outlined, while the conflict is an experience of life without words (apart from swear words). Likewise, there is a difference between a pretty picture drawn by an infant school pupil and a Picasso picture: a difference in technique, construction, incorporation or ostensive refusal of rules.

There is a specificity of the school activity. It requires certain relationships with the world, with others and with oneself, with language and with time, which define a certain relationship with knowledge and with the school (Charlot, 2000, 2005a). These relations are not socially neutral, given that they start to be constructed within the middle classes, who value language, while the relationship with the world of the popular classes is a different one. Therefore, it is not surprising that the children of the popular classes have more difficulties at school than middle-class children.

Meanwhile, this specific school activity is not a 'cultural tyranny', a simple reflection of the rules of the ruling classes, as argued by Bourdieu and Passeron (1992). It has an educational value, an anthropological value, as a specific and extremely elaborate form of relating to the world. One has to avoid making mistakes. The first mistake: considering this activity as a simple imposition of the ruling class, forgetting its educational value. The second, symmetrical, mistake: considering that only this activity has value. There are other ways to learn, other valuable ways to relate to the world, to others, to oneself, other activities that are worth being carried out and perfected in a human lifetime. On this matter we should reflect on the fact that today school has invaded the lives of the young and tends to make other forms of relating to the world impossible.

Can school activity be considered a job?

The answer to this question depends, obviously, on how one defines what a 'job' is.

From three points of view school activity can be considered a job. It demands effort and expends energy. It functions under conditions of time, space, material and is assessed. Finally, it takes place in a social background. Therefore, it presents certain characteristics of work. Indeed, at least in France, young children, especially in infant education, make a point of saying that at school *they work*. Having a social and serious activity outside home, like their parents, is proof that you are now a 'grown-up'. However, there are fundamental differences between the pupil's activity and work outside school. Alain's philosophy makes the distinction between the pupil and the apprentice. The latter may not waste material nor time, because material and time are money. Hence, he cannot take a 'trial and error' attitude, and as such is not in a good position to think. In contrast, the pupil can test, try, fail, start again, and do so without losing money: in doing so he gains learning (Alain, 1969).

From the Marxist point of view, work is also distinguished from school activity. In effect, school work does not lead to a profit, at least not to an immediate and direct one; it produces learning. The pupils do not receive a salary; they gain knowledge, skills, grades, qualifications.

So at the end of the day, is school activity a job or not? One can say that the pupils 'work' (between quotation marks), doing a specific task which is to study. Meanwhile, the pupils themselves are less and less aware of the specificity of the school activity. As we shall see, they tend to consider it as work imposed on the young by adults.

When school activity deteriorates into transferred work

Nowadays, school is increasingly seldom viewed as a place of learning and thinking and it is thought of more as a route to a job. This relationship with knowledge and with school is reflected in the words of parents, in the discourse of politicians, in newspaper articles, in the marketing of private schools, and it is therefore unsurprising that it has become the dominant thinking also among pupils.

My research into the relationship with knowledge has highlighted that many pupils go to school to pass the year, and obtain their diploma in order to subsequently get a good job later on. This is a realistic position, of course, but the problem is that more and more pupils attend school solely for this reason (and, of course, to see their friends). School as a place of knowledge and education is being superseded by school as a promise of insertion into the job market. I have heard the young ask: 'teachers receive a salary, so why don't we?' In their logic this is a legitimate question: school is the start of the professional career, and hence the pupils should receive a small salary.

Furthermore, for a lot of pupils, in Brazil as well as in France, the active person in the teaching–learning act is not the pupil – it is the teacher. What does studying mean, for Brazilian children in the fourth series (fifth year)? It is doing what the teacher says to do. It is listening to her, without messing about, playing, quarrelling (Ireland *et al.*, 2007). Pupils who go to school and pay attention to what the teacher says are complying with their duty as a pupil. What happens next depends on the teacher. If she explains well, the pupil will learn and get a good grade. The logical conclusion is as follows: a bad grade is unfair when the pupils listened to the teacher. If they did not understand anything, it is because the teacher did not explain properly and it is the teacher who should get a bad grade.

Following this logic, the idea of the pupil's intellectual activity disappears. The school becomes a place where tasks have to be completed. Why? Because the teacher said so and whoever disobeys her will not pass the year and will not get a good job later. According to Leontiev, as we have seen, one can only talk about activity when the motive and the objective coincide: one studies to appropriate knowledge. In the thinking that is becoming dominant, pupils study (when they study ...) to get good grades, pass the year, get into university, get a good job: the motive and the objective do not coincide. Therefore, there is no activity. As such, what is the meaning of what the pupils do in school? Leontiev would answer that it is a question of actions. We can also say that it is a job: a transferred job. The pupils have to expend energy to comply with the rules and earn good grades, but they are misappropriated and misappropriate themselves to do so. When school activity loses its specificity, all that is left is transferred work, both that of the pupil and that of the teacher. And it is this work, we have to admit, that is annoying and very boring.

We should reflect on this. To what extent can our schools induce the pupils to carry out intellectual activity, to immerse themselves in new worlds, to build other ways of relating to the world? To what extent, in contrast, do they put the emphasis on standardised tasks and compliance with regulations? Here is part of the answer: when pupils arrive late at school, they are immediately sent to a staff member's office to justify their lateness, and as such they miss a little more of the lesson. Satisfying the needs of the institution is more important than learning ...

Note

1   In French the same word is used for the verbs learn and teach: *apprendre*.

References

Alain (1969) *Propos sur l'éducation*, Paris: PUF.
Bachelard, Gaston (1996) *A formação do espírito científico*, Rio de Janeiro: Contraponto.
Baudelot, Christian and Establet, Roger (1971) *L'école capitaliste en France*, Paris: Maspero.
Bernstein, Basil (1996) *A estruturação do discurso pedagógico: classe, código, controle*, Petrópolis: Vozes.
Bourdieu, Pierre (1989) *O poder simbólico*, Lisbon: Difel.
Bourdieu, Pierre (1998) *Escritos de Educação*, Petrópolis: Vozes.
Bourdieu, Pierre (2003) *A Miséria do Mundo*, Petrópolis: Vozes.

Bourdieu, Pierre (2007) *A Distinção: crítica social do julgamento*, Porto Alegre: Editora Zouk.

Bourdieu, Pierre and Passeron, Jean-Claude (1992) *A reprodução*, Rio de Janeiro: Francisco Alves.

Bowles, Samuel and Gintis, Herbert (1976) *Schooling in Capitalist America*, New York: Basic Books.

Certeau, Michel de (1996) *Invenção do Cotidiano: 1 Artes de Fazer*, Petrópolis: Vozes.

Charlot, Bernard (1999) *Le rapport au savoir en milieu populaire. Une recherche dans les lycées professionnels de banlieue*, Paris: Anthropos.

Charlot, Bernard (2000) *Da Relação com o saber. Elementos para uma teoria*, Porto Alegre: ARTMED.

Charlot, Bernard (2005a) *Relação com o saber, Formação dos professores e globalização: questões para a educação hoje*, Porto Alegre: ARTMED.

Charlot, Bernard (2005b) 'O sociólogo, o psicanalista e o professor', in Leny Magalhães Mrech (org.), *O impacto da Psicanálise na Educação*, São Paulo: Avercamp Editora, pp.33–55.

Charlot, Bernard, Bautier, Élisabeth and Rochex, Jean-Yves (1992) *École et savoir dans les banlieues ... et ailleurs*, Paris: Armand Colin.

Freire, Paulo (1976) *Educação como Prática da Liberdade*, Rio de Janeiro: Paz e Terra.

Freire, Paulo (1983) *Pedagogia do oprimido*, Rio de Janeiro: Paz e Terra.

Inhelder, Bärbel and Piaget, Jean (1976) *Da Lógica da Criança à Lógica do Adolescente*, São Paulo: Pioneira.

Ireland, Vera Ester *et al.* (2007) *Re-Pensando a Escola: um estudo sobre os desafios de aprender, ler e escrever*, Brasília: UNESCO e INEP.

Leontiev, Alexis N. (1984) *Activité, Conscience, Personnalité*, Moscow: Ed. Du progres.

Marrero, Adriana (2007) 'Hermione en Hogwarts, o sobre el éxito escolar de las niñas', in Adriana Marrero (org.), *Educación y Modernidad, Hoy*, Montevideo: Ediciones de la Banda Oriental, pp.203–245.

Piaget, Jean (2008) *Psicologia e Pedagogia*, Rio de Janeiro: Editora Forense Universitária.

Silva, Veleida Anahi da (2004) *Savoirs quotidiens et savoirs scientifiques: l'élève entre deux mondes*, Paris: Anthropos.

Silva, Veleida Anahi da (2009) *Por que e para que aprender a matemática?* São Paulo: Cortez.

Vergnaud, Gérard (2005) 'Prefácio', in Maria Lucia Faria Moro and Maria Tereza Carneiro Soares (orgs.), *Desenhos, palavras e números: as marcas da matemática na escola*, Curitiba: Editora da UFPR.

Vygotsky, Lev (1987) *Sémionovitch. Pensamento e linguagem*, São Paulo: Martins Fontes.

Willis, Paul (1991) *Aprendendo a ser Trabalhador: escola, resistência e reprodução social*, Porto Alegre: Artes Médicas.

13 Social class and school knowledge

Revisiting the sociology and politics of the curriculum in the 21st century

Geoff Whitty

Introduction

One of the things that is clear from international studies of educational achievement is that, while the best performers in English schools attain as well as those anywhere in the world, there is an unusually long tail of underperformance and this is concentrated among children from socially disadvantaged backgrounds – largely from working-class and certain minority ethnic communities (Hansen and Vignoles, 2005; Cassen and Kingdon, 2007).

At a rhetorical level at least, a key policy priority in the last two terms of the New Labour government in England was to 'narrow the gap' between the educational outcomes of those from more and less advantaged backgrounds (Whitty, 2002, 2008). The two drivers underpinning this aim were achieving increased competitiveness in a global marketplace and enhancing social justice. As Prime Minister Gordon Brown stated in the introduction to a White Paper on social mobility:

> If Britain can seize the opportunities of this new global age, our future is full of potential. Our country will be richer in the years to come. But the ultimate prize will be greater still: the opportunity to create not just a richer country, but a fairer society. This is the modern definition of social justice: not just social protection but real opportunity for everyone to make the most of their potential in a Britain where what counts is not where you come from but what you aspire to become, a Britain where everyone should be able to say that their destiny is not written for them, but written by them.
>
> (HM Government, 2009, p.1)

Working-class failure in English schools

This is not, however, an entirely new concern. From the 1950s onwards, British sociology of education, as well as much education policy rhetoric, has had a central focus on the failure of working-class children in English schools (Whitty, 1985). Until the 1980s, the focus of sociology of education was often to understand how aspects of working-class culture on the one hand and school culture on the other, and the interactions between them, produced working-class failure in school (see, for example, Craft, 1970). In recent years, sociologists have tended to approach the issue more indirectly (or relationally) through attempts to understand how education policy and practice, whatever its claims, has consistently favoured middle-class children (for example, Ball, 2003; Power *et al.*, 2003; Reay, 2006, 2008).

In practice, for electoral reasons, New Labour seemed reluctant to remove middle-class privilege in education, despite its apparent interest in benefiting the disadvantaged (Whitty, 2009). Labour's record on this front has allowed the Conservative party to claim that their own policies will do more to help the disadvantaged. In a lecture in 2008, the then shadow Secretary of State for Children, Schools and Families, Michael Gove cited the Italian Marxist Antonio Gramsci to support his view that educational methods which call themselves progressive are actually regressive in social terms. More specifically, he suggested that Labour's reforms to the secondary school curriculum in England have had this effect:

> And also with the abandonment of subject disciplines, the poorer lose out again. As the *Times Educational Supplement* reported this week those comprehensive schools which have most enthusiastically abandoned specific subject teaching for a more flexible, porous, curriculum, have seen their standards and performance drop. Richer parents who can afford it access specific subject teaching earlier rather than later with the most successful prep schools introducing discrete subjects taught by subject specialists before pupils go on to secondary education.
>
> (Gove, 2008)

Interestingly, the sociology of education has itself, very recently, gone back to the 'knowledge question' in exploring the basis of middle-class success and working-class failure. In particular, Michael F.D. Young has raised the question of whether subject-based curricula favour middle-class children or, conversely, whether project or theme-based curricula, which were once thought to suit working-class children better, are actually even more socially regressive. Indeed, Young's recent book, *Bringing Knowledge Back In* (Young, 2008a), is a critique of progressivism and constructivism in which he stresses the distinctiveness of the sort of disciplined knowledge acquired in school and states that this 'powerful' knowledge is especially important for working-class children who do not have access to it at home.

As he put it in an interview in the RSA Journal:

> the knowledge issue is both an epistemological issue and a social justice issue, because those kids who don't get to university often don't get access to what I call powerful knowledge and they are the people who need it most, because they're going to find life really tough without it.
>
> (quoted in RSA Journal, 2008, para. 6)

On this basis we would need to ensure that any weakening of the boundaries between school subjects and between the school curriculum and everyday life, a key feature of initiatives designed to appeal to working-class pupils and engage them more in learning, does not have the unintended consequence of denying disadvantaged groups access to this 'powerful' knowledge.

Young considers that the distinctive role of schools is to transmit knowledge. While his earlier work explored who decides what counts as knowledge and who has access to it ('knowledge of the powerful' to use Young's term), he now goes on to consider what knowledge should be transmitted in schools, especially to socially disadvantaged pupils. He argues that schools need to focus on 'powerful knowledge' as this is the knowledge needed to progress in the world but also that least likely to be discovered outside of school for those from disadvantaged backgrounds (Young, 2009).

He is therefore critical of certain new secondary school curricula, which seek to introduce more project and theme-based teaching, in so far as they do not give pupils sufficient access to structured subject knowledge:

> The curriculum has to take account of the everyday local knowledge that pupils bring to school, but such knowledge can never be the basis for the curriculum. The structure of local knowledge is designed to relate to the particular; it cannot provide the basis for any generalisable principles. To provide access to such principles is a major reason why all countries have schools.
>
> (Young, 2009, p.16)

Interestingly, he resorts to Basil Bernstein (Young 2008a, p.220), in support of his case. I too take the view that Bernstein deserves revisiting by British sociologists of education. I believe his work can help us understand the interaction between home and school and point us towards solutions to the endemic underachievement of working-class children in English schools. Before examining the work of Bernstein in more detail, I will outline some recent developments in curriculum policy in England and Northern Ireland, which seem to me to demand analysis in these terms.

Recent changes to secondary school curricula

In response to criticisms of subject-based curricula in general and the English National Curriculum in particular, there have recently been various attempts to design curricula in ways that, among other things, enable teachers to make more meaningful links between school knowledge and pupils' everyday lives. In some ways these go back to the sort of work some of us were involved in during the 1970s and 1980s prior to the introduction of the National Curriculum, as outlined above. This work, much of it in the field of integrated humanities (see Gleeson and Whitty, 1976; Whitty and Kirton, 1995), was strongly influenced by the 'new sociology of education'.

Recent changes to the National Curriculum for secondary school pupils in England exhibit some similarities to those earlier innovations.[1] The new secondary curriculum, developed by the Qualifications and Curriculum Authority (QCA) and phased in from September 2008, aims to:

- provide a better fit between the curriculum and the Every Child Matters outcomes;[2]
- cut back on the amount of compulsory subject content to give teachers more time and space to support personalised learning;
- develop a stronger focus on the development of personal attributes and practical life skills.

(QCA, 2009a)

The new curriculum is intended to enable young people to become:

- *successful learners* who enjoy learning, make progress and achieve;
- *confident individuals* who are able to live safe, healthy and fulfilling lives;
- *responsible citizens* who make a positive contribution to society.

(QCA, 2009b)

While pupils will still be taught subject knowledge, the new curriculum seeks to balance this with the key concepts and processes which underlie the discipline of each subject and the development of skills for life and work. The functional skills of English, mathematics and ICT are embedded in the new programmes of study. Personal, learning and thinking skills are also part of the new curriculum.[3]

While individual subjects remain important, greater emphasis, than hitherto, is placed on cross-curricular linkages. Schools are provided with a list of non-statutory 'cross-curriculum dimensions', which they are encouraged to use in order to enhance the 'relevance and authenticity' of education (QCA, 2009c).[4] It is these cross-curriculum dimensions that are particularly relevant to this chapter.

These sorts of changes have been taken rather further in the Northern Ireland curriculum. Developed by the Northern Ireland Council for the Curriculum, Examinations and Assessment (CCEA), this more explicitly encourages teachers to move beyond their subject emphases and make meaningful links across subjects and with pupils' own experiences. Changes in place since 2007 mean that the statutory curriculum is now organised in terms of 'Areas of Learning'. While subjects are retained, these are set out as 'strands' within these broader Areas of Learning and share common curriculum objectives.

The overall aim of this new Northern Ireland curriculum is 'to empower young people to achieve their potential and to make informed and responsible decisions through their lives' and it therefore seeks to provide learning opportunities for each young person to develop as: 'an individual; a contributor to society; a contributor to the economy and the environment' (CCEA, 2007, p.3).

Not surprisingly, at the heart of the curriculum lies an explicit emphasis on the development of skills and capabilities. These skills are embedded within the curriculum at each Key Stage and pupils are to be given opportunities to develop and demonstrate these skills in all areas of the curriculum. To assist with this, the content requirements for each strand have been reduced dramatically.

Rather than move away entirely from subjects – which, on the basis of the New Basics experience in Queensland,[5] was considered too radical at this time – Northern Ireland has chosen to offer guidance which encourages teachers and schools to progressively enhance connections across the Areas of Learning to a degree which suits their stage of development.

Beyond official curriculum agencies, such as QCA and CCEA, various other organisations have put forward a range of aims- or skills-based approaches to the curriculum. One example is the Opening Minds project led by the Royal Society for the Encouragement of Arts, Manufactures and Commerce (RSA), which is organised in terms of broad areas of capability, rather than individual subjects, and emphasises 'the ability to understand and to do, rather than just the transmission of knowledge' (RSA, 2009).

Six secondary schools were originally involved in piloting the Opening Minds framework – all comprehensives in a range of settings and circumstances. Their Opening Minds provision involved cross-curricular modular courses, group work, project work, skills development, self-evaluation and the use of, for example, peer mediation. As a result of such provision the schools have reported improvements in: pupils' transition from primary to secondary school; pupil performance (including in conventional tests); pupil behaviour and motivation; teacher morale; and co-operation between pupils and between pupils and teachers (BBC Online, 2003). This approach is becoming increasingly significant with over 200 schools now using Opening Minds, and in September 2008 the first school based entirely around Opening Minds principles – the RSA academy – opened.

The Association of Teachers and Lecturers (ATL) has put forward a similar curriculum framework based around seven skills (ATL, 2006, p.3),[6] while the National Endowment for Science, Technology and the Arts (NESTA) has called for a national curriculum which develops the wider skills needed to stimulate innovation. These skills include the flexibility, resourcefulness and capacity to seek out and learn new competencies as changes in the working environment demand. They are underpinned by self-belief, self-awareness, the ability to collaborate effectively and an informed attitude to risk-taking (NESTA, 2008).

Knowledge versus skills or knowledge and skills?

Two key features of all these reforms are that they are 'aims-based' and that they give at least as much emphasis to skills as to subject content. Part of this shift towards more use of competency or skills-based curricula has been due to a perceived change in the skills, knowledge and dispositions needed for success in modern societies and a globalised economy. For John White, if the aim is to produce certain kinds of people, he says we have to work out what kinds of learning best prepare children to acquire the appropriate qualities. Given the sorts of aims likely to be appropriate to twenty-first century societies, he sees themes, project work, interdisciplinary work and class outings as likely to be at least as important as subjects as vehicles for realising such a curriculum. He is not advocating a retreat from knowledge as part of the curriculum, though skills and personal qualities are equally important. But, while knowledge acquisition is an important aspect of schooling, not all valuable knowledge falls within traditional subjects. He also points out that 'discrete subjects are not the only ways of generating intellectual pleasure' (White, 2005, p.1). This again is reminiscent of the arguments used to champion integrated humanities. For the purpose of monitoring pupil progress, White advocates teacher assessment and records of achievement in place of impersonal national tests and, in terms of school performance, he argues for school inspections in place of quantified performance data (White, 2005, 2006).

As White points out, knowledge is not the same thing as school subjects and school subjects are not the same thing as academic disciplines. Yet there is often a slippage of terminology, so that it is difficult to know what exactly is being talked about and what distinctions are being made. Futurelab is a not-for-profit organisation advocating the use of new technologies in educational innovation. Its submission to the CSF Select Committee inquiry into the National Curriculum makes some useful distinctions but also suggests how a recognition of the importance of received knowledge and pupil involvement in constructing their own curriculum might be reconciled:

> While it is obvious that all students require familiarity with the conventions of distinct disciplines, this does not militate against the idea that schools may then take responsibility for defining aspects of the content and knowledge which their students will investigate. In line with this, the national curriculum should set out a broad set of entitlements for all children, with responsibility for defining the content, processes and outcomes deferred to teachers and schools. A ... truly personalised approach to the curriculum would regard children as taking some of the responsibility for defining what and how they learn through constructive conversations with teachers. The 'subjects' of the curriculum may be seen as perspectives that can be used by teachers to respond to children's needs, interests, and experience.
>
> (Futurelab, 2008)

This notion of subjects as resources for learning was again very similar to the argument put forward for a meaningful and critical approach to integrated humanities (see Gleeson and Whitty, 1976; Whitty, 1985). The Northern Ireland curriculum is even more ambivalent about the role of school subjects in the curriculum, but retains them on the grounds that there is likely to be too much resistance to abandoning them at this time.

How then can this emphasis on disciplines be reconciled with the need to arouse the interest and curiosity of pupils? As we have seen, Young acknowledges the everyday knowledge which young people bring to the classroom, but emphasises the importance of 'context-independent' knowledge and the role of schools in enabling access to this 'powerful knowledge' (Young, 2009). One way forward may be to develop insights from Bernstein's theoretical framework.

Revisiting Bernstein

It is contended here that Bernstein's work in the sociology of education can help us understand the interaction between home and school and point us towards solutions to the endemic underachievement of working-class children in schools. The remainder of this chapter will revisit some of the central concepts in Bernstein's work to consider why it has proved so difficult for working-class children to succeed, particularly in English schools, and to demonstrate the power of his concepts to clarify issues in relation to the curriculum, especially those concerning the possibilities and problems of current attempts at curricular reform.

The two concepts at the root of Bernstein's analysis, and the ones which will inform this discussion, are those of classification and framing, introduced by Bernstein (1971) and refined in later publications (Bernstein, 1977, 1990).[7] Classification reflects the distribution of power and the principles by which boundaries are established between categories. Strong classification is underpinned by the rule that 'things must be kept apart'. Weak classification is underpinned by the rule that 'things must be brought together'. Framing, on the other hand, reflects the distribution of control over communication. Strong framing is where the transmitter has explicit control over the communication; weak framing gives the acquirer more apparent control over the communication. While Bernstein noted that boundary strength could be used to explore relations between categories more generally, his most productive use of the notion was in relation to school subjects and their links to learner identities.

The traditional model of secondary education in England entailed strong classification and strong framing. This is sometimes seen as the best model for all pupils and even as particularly important for disadvantaged pupils as it seeks to 'insulate' the school against non-school influences. However, it seems unlikely that just giving working-class pupils more of the very kinds of activities at which they are failing is likely to work, though this seems to be the solution offered by Gove (2008) and other Conservative politicians. As Bernstein argues, it is strong classification and framing which gives the middle class its advantages in the first place. Because middle-class children have been prepared from an early age to distinguish the difference between home and school they are more likely to understand what the school context demands of them. Unless disadvantaged pupils understand this they will always be at least one step behind. Simply increasing the frequency and intensity of conventional educational activities is hardly going to transform failure into success.

By contrast, there have been a variety of so-called 'compensatory education' strategies over the years which seek to address educational disadvantage through weakening classification and/or framing, e.g. by weakening the strength of classification between school and non-school knowledge and weakening the framing of the relationship between the teacher and the parent or child. If maintaining or strengthening the classification and framing between home and school is likely to do little to reduce educational disadvantage, then it might be argued that breaking down these barriers and building more inclusive relations can only prefigure a greater mutual understanding.

Bernstein, in his own comments on compensatory education, certainly argues that 'the contents of the learning in school' should be drawn much more from the child's experience in his family and community (Bernstein, 1971, p.192), though it is unclear what elements of the 'content', as opposed to the pedagogy, he envisages being so derived. However, the idea that simply weakening boundaries will of itself make a significant difference is both empirically and theoretically difficult to sustain. The equivalent valuing of different cultures which was called for in Keddie's (1973) critique of the 'myth of cultural deprivation', another key text of the relativist phase of the new sociology of education of the early 1970s, now seems strangely naïve and misguided. And although Bernstein might have argued for teachers forging greater connections between school knowledge and everyday knowledge, he was surely not arguing for a collapsing of the distinction. Certainly his later work on knowledge structures (Bernstein, 1996) would have questioned both the possibility and the desirability of doing this. Even in an early article (Bernstein, 1970), he argued that education must involve the introduction of children to the universalistic meanings of public forms of thought. This would seem to offer support for Michael Young's recent emphasis on the importance of extending the learning of disadvantaged pupils into abstract knowledge that goes beyond the local and the experiential (Young, 2008a).

Some recent educational initiatives, of the more therapeutic variety (such as parenting skill programmes and activity-based, team-building group work for poor attenders) entail weak classification and strong framing (Power and Whitty, 2008). This brings the everyday knowledge of the family context and pupil experience into the educational domain, but it does not hide the power relations between teacher and taught. However, it is also deeply problematic. The strong framing theoretically enables the everyday to be developed into the esoteric, the context-dependent into the abstract, the horizontal discourse into the vertical discourse. But there is no esoteric, abstract or vertical knowledge within it – or at least not as currently developed. It is empty of knowledge content – or at least the kind of knowledge that will enable disadvantaged pupils to have access to the forms of knowledge available to advantaged children. This is effectively the same critique that Bernstein makes of 'genericism' (Bernstein, 1990), an approach to regulating education which backgrounds content and foregrounds process. Bernstein applies the concept to vocational education and Young (2008a) to professional education, but it could also be applied to child-centred primary education and the recent curricular reforms in lower secondary education in England and Northern Ireland discussed earlier.

None of these approaches seems to offer the answer to working-class failure in English schools. It may though be that the answer to ensuring that disadvantaged pupils gain access to powerful knowledge is an approach that combines strong classification with weak framing. Bernstein's work argued that there are hierarchies of knowledge and discourse to which different classes have unequal access. While there were some ambiguities in his position, it was essentially that all children should have access to high status knowledge but might get there by different means. He would probably have supported the kind of approach recommended by Fantini and Weinstein in the 1960s, who argued that 'a curriculum for the disadvantaged must begin as closely as possible to the pupils' direct experience' because 'without such an approach, the abstract cannot be attained' (Fantini and Weinstein, 1968, p.347). But this is very different from the position of Nell Keddie and some other relativist sociologists of education at that time who derided the idea that home culture, while being seen as 'inadequate and of limited value', might be used to move children into the mainstream culture and 'bodies of knowledge' that need to be transmitted by the school.[8] They regarded this as unnecessary as 'all cultures – class and ethnic – [had] their own logics which [were] capable of grappling with ... abstract thought' (Keddie, 1971, p.18), a position that is echoed in some of today's postmodernist writings (Apple, 1993).

There was a time when Michael Young seemed nearer to Keddie than to Bernstein on this issue. That is clearly not the case now in his latest book, although he is clearer than Bernstein on whether it is classification or framing that needs to be weakened. In a recent seminar contribution he has clarified that his position is that, 'while pedagogy necessarily involves the teacher in taking account of the non-school knowledge that her/his pupils bring to school, the curriculum does not' (Young, 2008b). The use of non-school knowledge to lead pupils into the formal curriculum can also change over time. Indeed, Bernstein himself argued that the strength and nature of framing could change 'over the timespan of the transmission' (Bernstein, 1990, p.36).

Yet it is not clear that the distinction between curriculum and pedagogy entirely disposes of the issue, in that the difficulty of making meaningful pedagogic connections between disciplined knowledge and everyday knowledge partly lies in the nature of that knowledge. Making those connections has proved highly problematic for many pupils, and indeed their teachers, not least because using the different discourses entails acquiring what Bernstein called different recognition and realisation rules (Whitty *et al.*, 1994). His work on evoking contexts, recognition rules and realisation rules (Bernstein, 1981) helped us to understand the pedagogic difficulties in making connections between school and non-school knowledge. Different discursive contexts evoke different discourses, and one of the marks of competence is knowing the rules that enable the production of an appropriate response in a particular context. For Bernstein, 'recognition rules create the means of distinguishing between and so *recognising* the speciality that constitutes a context' (Bernstein, 1990, p.15). Recognition rules, therefore, are the clues which pupils need to determine what counts as a specialised discourse, in other words, a subject.

Realisation rules are the rules which pupils need if they are to produce appropriate practice in a lesson. Again, for Bernstein, 'Realisation rules regulate the creation and production of specialised relationships internal to the context' (ibid., p.15). They tell pupils what can and what cannot be done to demonstrate knowledge. They suggest acceptable forms in which subject principles may be demonstrated. So, realisation rules give the form that pupils' written work may take, acceptable methods of oral communication, types of movement in PE and forms of artifact which may be produced in technology and art. More sophisticated realisation rules may refer to the structure of arguments or the acceptable sequences of a process.

An example may be drawn from my own work with Peter Aggleton and Gabrielle Rowe in the early 1990s (Whitty *et al.*, 1994), which illustrates the problem. One of the schools we visited taught cross-curricular themes through conventional subjects and its own curriculum audit indicated that science was a major context for health education. During a science lesson about teeth and tooth decay, I asked a 14-year-old pupil whether he needed to write anything about the implications of the work they had done for the way in which people should brush their teeth. The exchange continued as follows:

Pupil: I don't think we're supposed to do that.
Researcher: Why?
Pupil: It's not what we're doing.
Researcher: Why are you doing this work then?
Pupil: Because it's in the National Curriculum, I suppose *(laughs)*.
Researcher: But the textbook has a picture of how you should brush your teeth.
Pupil: I don't think that's really science.

For this pupil, even the illustration in his science textbook was not enough to legitimate a connection between the National Curriculum subject 'science' and everyday life. To him the science lesson was self-contained and ultimately self-referential. To have produced work inconsistent with what he perceived as the subject code would have indicated that he had failed to achieve the required scientific competence. This was actually a middle-class pupil refusing to make the link between school knowledge and everyday life in the way that curricula that aim to produce 'successful learners, confident individuals and responsible citizens' seem to require. Possibly this was because his priority was learning science with a view to studying it at university.

Educationists seeking to challenge disadvantage have generally been concerned with 'bridging' in the other direction – that is, linking pupils' past experiences to new knowledge. Unfortunately, the experience over the years of 'compensatory education' in its various guises has hardly been encouraging in this respect (Power and Whitty, 2008). The work of Kris Gutiérrez and the University of California, Los Angeles (UCLA) Migrant Institute may, however, provide some pointers to what might be possible. She describes this programme as an example of a 'third space', a collective zone of proximal development whose object, in this case, is a socio-historical reconstruction of what it means to be a migrant student. While opportunities for learning are created in natural activity across the day, the emerging understandings and concepts are always elaborated in formal instructional activity. The programme offers students opportunities to extend social and cognitive development, whilst also preparing them for university and helping them to develop a 'sociocritical literacy' (Gutiérrez, 2008).

It is also important to keep in mind the importance of language and specifically the need to learn the rules that relate to the pedagogic use of talk in different contexts. The sort of talk that allows links to be made between subject discourses and everyday life challenges the strong conventional boundary between school talk and non-school talk. In the study cited previously (Whitty *et al.*, 1994), we found that the status of 'chat' and the extent of its permissibility was therefore ambiguous in the eyes of many pupils, as well as those of some teachers. Furthermore, those very types of talk that attempted to forge connections between school talk and the talk of 'everyday life', and which were therefore important to the effective teaching of themes, were valued differentially by different subject cultures. What counted as legitimate talk varied from subject to subject, making the cross-curricular treatment of the same issue extremely problematic in that what counted as appropriate talk about an issue in one subject differed from that in another. For some pupils, the consequent ambiguity led on occasions to the transgression of the rules applicable to particular subjects. This is a particular challenge for reforms like those discussed here that seek to combine subjects and themes or develop stronger cross-curricular and extra-curricular links.

Concluding comments

The justification for many recent curricular reforms, not only in the United Kingdom but elsewhere, has often been based on the notion that, in the context of globalisation, citizens need to learn skills rather than subject knowledge. In Bernstein's terms, such curricula may be associated with 'prospective' rather than 'retrospective' pedagogic identities, 'constructed *to deal with cultural, economic and technological change*' (Bernstein, 2000, p.67, italics in original).

In their most extreme form, these curricula may be devoid of any specified knowledge content. Young has now made a strong case that such curricula can further disadvantage the most socially disadvantaged pupils. This does not, however, imply that the curriculum needs to be organised into traditional subjects, although it may be, nor that making connections between 'powerful knowledge' and everyday life is either undesirable or impossible. It is, nevertheless, difficult. Indeed, the sort of analysis offered here suggests that the barriers to change may be rather more deep-rooted than the effects of the particular testing and inspection regimes or the specific subject traditions we currently have in place.

My argument here is that some of the key challenges in giving disadvantaged pupils access to powerful knowledge – and giving it meaningful and critical purchase on their everyday lives – are pedagogic ones. Bernstein's work gives us resources for thinking through why this might be and what we might do about it.

Of course education cannot, as Bernstein (1970) himself noted, compensate for society in any simple way. But that does not mean that educators should accept the continuing failure of the disadvantaged as an inevitability. If we are 'bringing knowledge back in' by insisting that all pupils have access to it and that they are not to be short-changed by different sorts of 'empty' curricula, then we have an obligation to explore ways of making connections between school and non-school knowledge that do not merely perpetuate middle-class success.

Clearly, this is only the beginning of an analysis using Bernstein's concepts of classification/framing and recognition/realisation rules.[9] However, it is one that has some considerable potential for clarifying the advantages and disadvantages of the new curricula currently being promulgated, as well as the pedagogic challenges involved in implementing them, particularly with socially disadvantaged pupils. While Bernstein's analysis shows us how class infuses the relationship between knowledge, schooling and social inequality, he also provides a way of thinking about what would need to be put in place if that relationship were to be interrupted.

Acknowledgements

I would like to thank Sally Power, Andrew Curtis, Emma Wisby, Sarah Tough, David Halpin and Michael Young for their assistance in developing this chapter. It draws on papers presented at the University of Bath, Cardiff University, the University of the West of England, and the University of Turku.

Notes

1 Similar developments in the primary curriculum are likely to emerge from the Rose Review (see: www.dcsf.gov.uk/primarycurriculumreview/). It has recommended a curriculum based on six 'areas of learning' which include subjects as well as cross-curricular studies (Rose, 2009). The revised curriculum is planned to be introduced in September 2011 (Rose, 2009).

2 The five outcomes are: be healthy, stay safe, enjoy and achieve, make a positive contribution and achieve economic well-being (see: www.dcsf.gov.uk/everychildmatt ers/about/aims/aims/ [accessed 19 May 2009]).

3 See: http://curriculum.qca.org.uk/ (accessed 19 May 2009).

4 The cross-curriculum dimensions are: identity and cultural diversity; healthy lifestyles; community participation; enterprise; global dimension and sustainable development: technology and the media; and creativity and critical thinking (see: http://curriculum.qca.org.uk/ [accessed 19 May 2009]).

5 New Basics (as opposed to the 'old basics' of the 3Rs) is an initiative by Education Queensland which sought to establish a curriculum formulated around four transdisciplinary areas: life pathways and social futures; multi-literacies and communication; active citizenship; and environments and technologies. An evaluation of the initiative notes teachers' difficulties in connecting subject principles and pupils' everyday lives and schools' need for support in implementing assessment in a way that develops pupils' higher-order thinking.

6 Physical; creative; communication; information management; learning and thinking; interpersonal; citizenship. See also Johnson (2007).

7 My usage of the terms here differs from that proposed by Young (2009), which seems to draw upon Bernstein's earlier definitions in which the distinction between classification and framing is less clear.
8 Keddie characterised this as a 'bridging' strategy.
9 Bernstein's writing on the relationship between the expressive and the instrumental orders of the school (Bernstein, 1977) may also be helpful in exploring how children from different social backgrounds relate to different styles of schooling (Power *et al.*, 1998, 2010).

References

Apple, M. (1993) 'What Post-modernists forget: Cultural capital and official knowledge', *Curriculum Studies*, 1: 301–316.
ATL (Association of Teachers and Lecturers) (2006) 'Subject to change: New thinking on the curriculum', Position statement, London: ATL.
Ball, S.J. (2003) *Class Strategies and the Education Market: The Middle Class and Social Advantage*, London: RoutledgeFalmer.
BBC Online (2003) 'Alternative curriculum "shows improvements"', Online at: http://news.bbc.co.uk/1/hi/education/2994966.stm (accessed 19 May 2009).
Bernstein, B. (1970) 'Education cannot compensate for society', *New Society*, 26 February: 344–347.
Bernstein, B. (1971) *Class, Codes and Control*, Volume 1, London: Routledge and Kegan Paul.
Bernstein, B. (1977) *Class, Codes and Control*, Volume 3, 2nd edition, London: Routledge and Kegan Paul.
Bernstein, B. (1981) 'Codes, modalities and the process of cultural reproduction: A model', *Language and Society*, 10: 327–363.
Bernstein, B. (1990) *The Structuring of Pedagogic Discourse*, London: Routledge.
Bernstein, B. (1996) *Pedagogy, Symbolic Control and Identity*, London: Taylor and Francis.
Bernstein, B. (1997) 'Official knowledge and pedagogic identities', in Nilsson, I. and Lundahl, L. (eds) *Teachers, Curriculum and Policy: Critical Perspectives in Educational Research*, Umeå: Umeå University.
Bernstein, B. (2000) *Pedagogy, Symbolic Control and Identity*, Revised edition, Lanham, MD: Rowman and Littlefield.
Cassen, R. and Kingdon, G. (2007) *Tackling Low Educational Achievement*, York: Joseph Rowntree Foundation.
CCEA (Council for Curriculum Examinations and Assessment) (2007) *The Statutory Curriculum at Key Stage 3: Rationale and Detail*, Belfast: CCEA Publications.
Craft, M. (1970) *Family, Class and Education: A Reader*, London: Longman.
Fantini, M. and Weinstein, G. (1968) *The Disadvantaged: Challenge to Education*, New York: Harper and Row.
Futurelab (2008) Memorandum on the National Curriculum – submitted to House of Commons Children, Schools and Family Select Committee, NC32.
Gleeson, D. and Whitty, G. (1976) *Developments in Social Studies Teaching*, London: Open Books.
Gove, M. (2008) 'Higher Standards, Freer Minds', Haberdashers' Aske's Education Lecture, Haberdashers Hall, London, 18 November.
Gutiérrez, K. (2008) 'Developing a sociocritical literacy in the third space', *Reading Research Quarterly*, 43(2): 148–164.
Hansen, K. and Vignoles, A. (2005) 'The United Kingdom education system in a comparative context', in Machin, S. and Vignoles, A. (eds) *What's the Good of*

Education? The Economics of Education in the UK, Princeton, NJ: Princeton University Press.

HM Government (2009) *New Opportunities: Fair Chances for the Future*, Norwich: The Stationary Office. Online at: www.cabinetoffice.gov.uk/media/119101/new-opportunities.pdf (accessed 21 October 2009).

Johnson, M. (2007) *Subject to Change: NewThinking on the Curriculum*, London: ATL.

Keddie, N. (1971) 'Classroom knowledge', in Young, M. (ed.) *Knowledge and Control*, London: Collier-Macmillan.

Keddie, N. (1973) *Tinker, Tailor ... the Myth of Compensatory Education*, Harmondsworth: Penguin.

NESTA (National Endowment for Science, Technology and the Arts) (2008) Memorandum on the National Curriculum – submitted to House of Commons Children, Schools and Family Committee, NC30.

Power, S. and Whitty, G. (2008) 'A Bernsteinian analysis of compensatory education'. Paper presented to the 5th Basil Bernstein Symposium, Cardiff University, 9–12 July. Online at: www.cardiff.ac.uk/socsi/newsandevents/events/Bernstein/papers/Cardifffinal.doc (accessed 30 October 2009).

Power, S, Edwards, T., Whitty, G. and Wigfall, V. (2003) *Education and the Middle Class*. Buckingham: Open University Press.

Power, S., Whitty, G., Edwards, T. and Wigfall, V. (1998) 'Schools, families and academically able students: Contrasting modes of involvement in secondary education', *British Journal of Sociology of Education*, 19, 157–175.

Power, S., Curtis, A., Whitty, G. and Edwards, T. (2010) 'Private education and disadvantage: The experiences of Assisted Place holders', *International Studies in Sociology of Education*, 20(1): 23–38.

QCA (Qualifications Curriculum Authority) (2009a) *A big picture of the curriculum*. Online at: http://curriculum.qca.org.uk/uploads/Big%20picture%20of%20the%20curriculum%20-%20Feb%2008%20working%20draft_tcm8-12685.pdf?return=/key-stages-3-and-4/organising-your-curriculum/principles_of_curriculum_design/index.aspx%23page2_p (accessed 19 May 2009).

QCA (2009b) *The aims of the curriculum*. Online at: http://curriculum.qca.org.uk/uploads/Aims_of_the_curriculum_tcm8-1812.pdf?return=/key-stages-3-and-4/aims/index.aspx (accessed 19 May 2009).

QCA (2009c) *Cross-curriculum dimensions*. Online at: http://curriculum.qca.org.uk/key-stages-3-and-4/cross-curriculum-dimensions/index.aspx (accessed 18 May 2009).

Reay, D. (2006) 'The zombie stalking English schools: Social class and educational inequality', *British Journal of Educational Studies*, 54, 288–307.

Reay, D. (2008) Tony Blair, the promotion of the 'active' educational citizen, and middle-class hegemony, *Oxford Review of Education*, 34, 639–650.

Rose, J. (2009) *Independent review of the primary curriculum: Final Report*, London: DCSF. Online at: http://publications.teachernet.gov.uk/eOrderingDownload/Primary_curriculum_Report.pdf (accessed 19 May 2009).

RSA (Royal Society for the Encouragement of Arts, Manufactures and Commerce) (2009) *Opening minds framework*. Online at: www.thersa.org/projects/education/opening-minds-old/opening-minds-framework (accessed 19 May 2009).

RSA Journal (2008) *Shopping for skills*. Online at: www.thersa.org/fellowship/journal/archive/spring-2008/may-2008/shopping-for-skills (accessed 19 May 2009).

White, J. (2005) *Towards an aims-led curriculum*. Online at: www.qca.org.uk/libraryAssets/media/11482_john_white_towards_an_aims_led_curr.pdf (accessed 19 May 2009).

White, J. (2006) 'The aims of school education', paper for IPPR seminar – Curriculum, Assessment and Pedagogy: Beyond the 'standards agenda', 3 April, London. Online at: www.ippr.org/uploadedFiles/research/projects/Education/The%20Aims%20of%20School%20Ed%20FINAL.pdf (accessed 19 May 2009).

Whitty, G. (1985) *Sociology and School Knowledge: Curriculum, Theory, Research and Politics*, London: Methuen.

Whitty, G. (2002) *Making Sense of Education Policy*, London: Paul Chapman Publishing.

Whitty, G. (2008) 'Twenty years of progress? English education policy 1988 to the present', *Educational Management Administration and Leadership*, 36: 165–184.

Whitty, G. (2009) 'Evaluating "Blair's educational legacy?": Some comments on the special issue of *Oxford Review of Education*', *Oxford Review of Education*, 35: 267–280.

Whitty, G. and Kirton, A. (1995) 'From learning reform to curriculum reform: Curriculum reform and integrated humanities in England', in *Issues in School Formation*, Tokyo, Japan.

Whitty, G., Power, S. and Halpin, D. (1998) *Devolution and Choice in Education: The School, the State and the Market*, Buckingham: Open University Press.

Whitty, G., Rowe, G. and Aggleton, P. (1994) 'Subjects and themes in the secondary-school curriculum, *Research Papers in Education*', 9: 159–181.

Young, M. (2008a) *Bringing Knowledge Back In: From Social Constructivism to Social Realism in the Sociology of Education*, London: Routledge.

Young, M. (2008b) 'Education, globalization and the "voice of knowledge"', paper presented to the ESRC Seminar Series Education and the Knowledge Economy, University of Bath, 26–27 June.

Young, M. (2009) 'What are schools for?', in Daniels, H., Lauder, H. and Porter, J. (eds) *Knowledge, Values and Educational Policy: A Critical Perspective*, London: Routledge.

Index

Note: Page numbers for figures and tables appear in **bold**.